I Will Not Be SILENCED

MEGAN BESLER

Follow Megan on
WWW.MEGANBESLER.COM

Dedicated to:
My beautiful cousin & friend.
Shelli Marie Gray 1980-2019
Thank you for allowing me to find
the courage to write this book.

I Will Not Be Silenced

©2020 Megan Besler

print ISBN: 978-1-09832-618-0

ebook ISBN: 978-1-09832-619-7

Contents

Introduction   1

Sometimes I Ask Myself...   4

Self-realization   5

Tattoo   6

#MeToo   7

Car Accident   9

Nerve Damage   11

Stay Weird   12

Freedom   13

Lori Petty   17

Kitty   19

Life Is Hard, But Happiness Shouldn't Have To Be   20

When You See Me Start To Get Emotionally Detached
And Start Pulling Away, Please Pull Harder   21

This Shouldn't Be Happening: Part 1   23

This Shouldn't Be Happening: Part 2   26

This Shouldn't Be Happening: Part 3   28

I Cleaned This Room Yesterday   30

The End Of An Era   33

Traveling   36

MIA   37

Happy Birthday!   39

I Want My Friend Back   40

Re-set, Re-adjust, Re-start, Re-focus As Many Times As You Have To.
Just Don't Quit.   42

"Vulnerability Is Not Weakness;
It's Our Greatest Measure Of Courage." —Brené Brown   45

Travel. Because Money Returns, Time Does Not.   48

"Those Who Teach Us The Most About Humanity
Aren't Always Human." —Donald L. Hicks   50

Skin Deep   53

"It's Kind Of Fun To Do The Impossible." —Walt Disney   56

Doors Will Open For Those Who Aren't Afraid To Knock   57

Depression   62

What Doesn't Kill Us Gives Us Something To Write About   65

Narcissistic Abuse   69

Shelli Marie Gray: Part 1   76

Shelli Marie Gray: Part 2   78

"You Deserved All Of The Abuse You Suffered"
—actual comment from cyber bully   81
Happy Birthday, Bo!   84
A Thumbprint On Thanksgiving   86
If All You Did This Year Was Survive, That's OK!   87
Shelli Marie Gray: Part 3   90
The Truth On Losing My Child.   94
Do What You Love, And You'll Never Work A Day In Your Life   103
A Letter To Him   107
A Christmas Without You   112
The Ornament I Didn't Think I'd Have To Hang   115
It's OK To Live A Life People Don't Understand   117
Another End Of An Era   120
Pleasing People   122
New Year's Eve   124
Anxiety   126
The Engagement Story   128
The Packer's Game   135
Advice From Friends   138
I'm Sorry I'm Never Good Enough, But I Really Do Try   141
Children   145
Girl 1   148
The Silence Of Spousal Abuse   152
The Wedding Night   155
Estate Planning, Life Insurance, And CPA Meetings   160
This Is C   165
G and S   167
"I Believe All Women Are Beautiful Without Makeup, But With The Right
Makeup, We Can Be Pretty Damn Powerful." —unknown   171
Direct Sales   173
Girl 2   175
Emotional Abuse vs. Physical Abuse   178
Gaslighting   182
My Coming Out Story   185
Letting Go Of Other People's Expectations   191
The Topics I Talk About   193
Finally Deciding To Leave   195
A   199
Intuition   203
Defending My Name   205
Selfies   207
What Is Your Level Of "Have To"?   209
Bullying   213

Abuse On Others   217
Wanderlust   220
Is It Over Yet?   222
Emotions Before Trial   224
My "Crazy"   226
I Will Not Be Silenced   229
Chakra Opening   231
Elective Surgery   233
COVID-19   237
The Narcissism Lives On(No, this is not an April Fool's joke)   241
I Am Strong, But I Am Tired   243
Happy Birthday, Shelli   245
Pressure Makes Diamonds   246
This Is What Anxiety Looks Like   249
Hi, I'm Crazy   251
The Wedding Ring   253
Let's Talk About Sex   257
I'm Sorry I Can't Hang Out. I'm Busy Doing Absolutely Nothing.   261
How I've Changed Since Her Death   263
Growth Is Uncomfortable   267
CHEERS!   270
"This is our Nashville"   273
A Letter To Him   275
The Final Chapter   279

Introduction

August 19th, 2019

Hey, friends! IT'S MEGAN!
  I know some of you know me from my social media accounts, and some have followed me for quite some time now. But if you don't know me, well, welcome to the dark side!

I've said this for a few years now: everything I've done leading up to now was truly a stepping-stone to what was going to happen in my future. I didn't know at the time what the outcome would be, but, man, it has been a whirlwind! Because of the company I work for I was able to pay off all my debt, and I was able to open my very own clothing line in 2017. And because of that clothing line, was I able to get to know all of you! Little did I know that starting up something so simple as a clothing line would lead me down a path I could only have dreamed of. I created a movement. A movement with power. A movement with force. It was something I had always wanted to do—to help people with struggles that I, too, have dealt with for a long time. Struggles that I wish somebody had helped me with back when I was younger.

Those of you who truly got to know me while watching my live Facebook shows know exactly what I am talking about, and I am just so dang thankful for the opportunities you have thrown my way!

The year 2018 was a hard one. Some of you already know the majority of what went on in my life, and those of you who don't will be seeing the majority of it here. I just want to tell you how much I have grown in just one year. It's a little incredible to me to consider where I was at in life then versus where I am now. I don't mean financially or career wise; I mean my emotional well-being. I had never been at a point in my life where I could say I was happy, but I can now! And I am in such

1

a better place emotionally, physically, and mentally. I want to allow you into my life for a few brief chapters so that maybe, just maybe, you too can experience this word we like to call "happy."

So here we go! I would like to introduce you to my blog. This is about a year's worth of blogs, showing what I went through, how I dealt with it, and just the pressures of life. As someone who has had multiple struggles in life, including a reading and learning disability, I can affirm that the majority of people who need "self-help" do not want to go to that section of a bookstore and grab a book just to see a step-by-step method on how to cure themselves. Please take no offense, but I don't understand how a "step 1, step 2, step 3" method can make me go from depressed to happy in a matter of 18.9 chapters. I'm here to show the real and honest truth of LIFE. Not something that a twenty-year psychologist thought up, and not something that a public speaker can talk about just because they are good at getting people to believe them, but something that is easy for people like myself to read, and something that shows the real and honest truth of these struggles.

My blog was meant to speak openly about topics that we don't necessarily like or want to talk about. Those hush-hush topics—you know, like rape, abuse, abortions, depression, anxiety, love, death, and so on. There's nothing you can really type into Google that gives you the EXACT mechanism on how to get through a divorce. You feel me? That's what I am here for. This book is a collection of the blogs that I have written over the past year or so. These blogs sometimes go out of order, depending what I felt like throwing in when I was looking for old writings of mine, so don't be alarmed and think it's a mistake! I assure you it is not. There's always a method to my madness! Also, full disclaimer, some of the topics discussed, once again, are topics we don't always openly talk about. Please keep judgment out of this. I will not tolerate harassment or bullying of any kind. My platform was built on love and support, and I will not allow anything less to be said about me or anything I say used against me. I assume that, if you have read any of my blogs, you have noticed, but if not—SPOILER ALERT!—this book contains a lot of f-bombs! Sorry if that's not your thing, but unfortunately for you, it's mine! This book also has never-before-read blogs that were not published during my weekly newsletter this year. So you are in for a treat! And by "treat," I mean... well, let's just see what you think of me after experiencing all of my baggage!

With all that said, I have also recently also started up a YouTube channel for this same reason, in hopes that I can reach an audience who truly just needs to physically HEAR that it's going to be OK and that they are not alone. Lord knows I have a lot to say, and even more people who want to hear it. You can head to my YouTube channel and Facebook page by using the URL inside the cover. There, you will find a safe haven to vent, feel safe in talking about certain situations, watch my self-help vlogs, and just have a reason to smile.

Thank you all for the support you have always given me! You all tell me time and time again that I have helped you in many ways, but you truly will never understand just how much you have helped ME! I hope you enjoy my craziness, and we will see each other soon!

Love, that crazy redhead with too much creativity in her brain,

Megan Besler

P.S. Please note that the names in this book have been changed out of respect for the parties involved. Thank you.

Sometimes I Ask Myself...

**November 30th, 2018
(See, told you I'd go out of order.)**

S ometimes I truly ask myself if I deserve to be where I'm at in life. Lord knows I've made my mistakes and learned from them. But also, I wake up some mornings and think, *Holy hell... I'm 100 percent in a better place.*

It's a back-and-forth battle, though. I'll never be where I want to be, but maybe that's not such a bad thing. Maybe I will always long for more and want to aim for more possibilities. Sometimes I ask myself why this was never in my "life plan"—to own my own successful business at age thirty, open a clothing line, have 60,000+ people know who I am, sing at multiple professional sporting events, and so on. But then I say to myself, *Was there ever a true life plan?* No, definitely not.

Moral of this blog. I'm not 100 percent where I want to be, but I know I'm 200 percent better than where I was at, and that speaks volumes to me.

Thank you to everyone who supports this crazy version of me, and I hope there's more to come.

Until next time...

Stay kind, folks,

Megan

P.S. I'm obviously in a "mood," so thanks for letting me ramble.

Self-realization

January 3rd, 2019

"Self-realization" is my motto for 2019.

I'm so ready for this year because I've finally gotten to a point in my life where I know that I am what I need.

I know I'm worth it.

I know I can do more.

I know I have dreams. I know I can achieve those dreams and do whatever it takes to get there. I know I have emotions, and that's OK. I know I can be ME for once.

I've honestly never been more ready for something, and although this is probably going to create a lot of sleepless nights, a lot of heartache, and a hell of a lot of tears until I get to the top of this stairway I'm climbing, it will be worth it. Why? Because it's for ME. And never once in my life have I been OK with that. Until now.

So now, my dear lovely universe, please be good to me, because I KNOW deep down I need this more than ever before.

Love, your friendly "doer,"

Megan

Tattoo

January 29th, 2019

My tattoos always have a deep meaning behind them, and this new one is no different.

I've wanted a floral piece to finish the majority of my sleeve for awhile now but never really knew what to do with it. Recently I've been going through some life changes and realizing some growth within myself. Without going into too much detail, I'll say it's just a time in my life where I'm realizing change isn't such a bad thing, and that focusing on myself for once isn't so bad either. 2019 is going to be the year of ME. The year of growth, acceptance, and bravery. The year of wanting and needing to do more and be more in life. This is a floral piece starting with the budding flower, and it shows the changes the changes it must go through to be something beautiful. Cheers to 2019. No matter what happens from here on out, at least I know what I'm doing is for me, and nobody else.

#MeToo

September 28th, 2018

I need to get this out. I don't post a lot of political stuff on Facebook anymore, simply because it's honestly not worth the energy to argue with anyone. But something I will always talk about is exactly what is going on with the world right now. I'm referring to the #MeToo movement.

Look, I get it. People come forward with false accusations all the time. But do not for one second use the excuse "she should have said something sooner" to deny what happened. That is a BULLSHIT excuse and a pathetic statement, especially coming from other women.

I'll be 100 percent real here. I was sexually assaulted when I was seventeen years old. Only three people knew about this until now. I was in high school. I didn't want to be made fun of. I didn't want to be known as a whore, because that wasn't who I was. I told THREE people. ONE, TWO, THREE... and you know what those three people told me? They told me I was lying. They told me I was exaggerating. They told me I was making up a story for attention. One even told me I probably was the one who brought it on myself, so she didn't blame the guy for what he did to me.

DO YOU REALIZE WHY IT'S HARD FOR WOMEN TO COME FORTH WITH STUFF LIKE THIS? I WAS SEXUALLY ASSAULTED AT SEVENTEEN AND NO ONE BELIEVED A DAMN WORD I SAID, SO I KEPT MY MOUTH SHUT FOR YEARS AFTER THE INCIDENT!

I can be open and honest now and talk about it, but why would a high school senior open up her mouth when people didn't believe her and even made fun of her?

I was involved in SO much in high school. Everything from band to choir, the arts, performing, cheerleading, you name it. This kind of

7

thing would have ruined me if I had come clean with it. But even the people I did tell didn't do a single thing for me. They treated it like it was not a big deal and even told me to stop running my mouth before I got in trouble. Ironic, right? The people who scream "they should have come clean earlier" are the same ones who tell people to shut their mouths.

So I'll tell you what happened. At school that year I became a totally different person. I skipped school on purpose. I failed multiple classes. I got kicked out of the performance groups that once made me so happy. Why? Because I was torn apart. I was broken. Something happened to me that changed me, and no one seemed to care.

So, let me ask you this. When your daughter comes to you at nine years old, fourteen years old, twenty years old, whatever the case may be, and tells you someone touched her. Are you going to believe her? Are you going to think it's OK? Are you going to say men are just men, and this is what they do? Are you going to tell her to keep her mouth shut? Or are you going to step up and be a fucking decent human being and make it known that these monsters need to come down?

Those of you who haven't experienced this, consider yourselves lucky. Consider yourselves damn lucky that you never had someone touch you where they weren't supposed to. Never had someone grope you in public. Never had someone literally have sex with you when you screamed "NO." Never had someone touch you while you were unconscious on pain medicine after you were hit by a drunk driver (yeah, that one was me). And until that day comes, you do NOT—I REPEAT, YOU DO NOT GET TO DECIDE WHEN IT'S OK FOR SOMEONE TO COME FORWARD.

THAT. IS. NOT. UP. TO. YOU.

Because #MeToo,

Megan

Car Accident

February 24th, 2019

In 2006, my high school had multiple guys going to the state wrestling tournament. I was a wrestling cheerleader, so I got to tag along. The night of February 24, 2006, in the middle of downtown Des Moines, Iowa, the cheerleaders climbed into our van like we did after every meet and headed back to the hotel, only this time we were suddenly hit by a drunk driver.

I thank my lucky stars every day that no one was seriously injured, although I know some of us have lasting effects from that night. I'm one of them. I suffer from back pain, both skeletal and muscular, along with nerve damage from scarring, which is now the start of fibromyalgia.

In recent years I have had numerous doctors try to put me on pain meds. One of them actually told me it was a safe bet that I would need to use Vicodin the rest of my life. Those of you who know me know that I rarely take medicine, even for headaches. So to be put on such an intense pain killer when I was only twenty-five? No, thank you. The last time I was on pain meds like that was actually the week of that very same accident. I was so drugged on the pain meds that I actually was sexually assaulted by someone, and I couldn't stop them. Never will I ever be forced to take such medication ever again, no matter how bad the pain is. The only thing that has helped me recently has been medicinal CBD oil. And I will tell you what a world of difference it makes! However, I cannot currently get the dosage I need here in Missouri. So, here I am thirteen years later, dealing with the pain day in and day out, and I cannot get a medical card because I don't have epilepsy. Sad, isn't it? That someone my age is forced to choose to be on hard-core pain meds for the rest of my life or live with the intense pain that nerve damage causes.

I'm hoping this new law for medical marijuana goes into effect sooner than later. This will truly be life changing—not only for me, but for SO many more.

Stay green,

Megan

Nerve Damage

February 20th, 2018

I suffer from intense back and shoulder pain, almost every hour of my life, from the auto accident in 2006. I've been to countless chiropractors, massage therapists, physical therapists, acupuncturists, and more. Certain techniques help take the edge off, but standing for a few hours doing these live shows almost has me in tears by the end of the night. Nerve damage is no joke, my friends!

So, after tonight's show, I am laying on something hard and flat to help realign my back for even just a few minutes before I have to sit in a chair for two hours getting invoices out. It's not an easy task for me, nor do I pretend that it is. It's hard. It takes a toll on me, not only physically but mentally as well. Every night I have to take a hot bath and lie on a heating pad. I literally have the body of a ninety-year-old. Even my chiropractor took one look at my X-rays the first day I met him then walked in the room and was shocked to see I was under thirty.

I'm not telling anyone this story for a pity party; I'm just screaming out a big THANK YOU to those who are patient with me in getting invoices out. Just please know I always try to put you guys first as customers, because I adore each and every one of you for allowing me the opportunity to have the career of my dreams. But sometimes (like tonight), I just have to take a break for awhile.

Love, your friendly thirty-, going on sixty-year-old,

Megan

Stay Weird

March 21st, 2019

"She was one of the rare ones, so effortlessly herself, and the world loved her for it." —*Atticus*

I've learned lately that loving yourself means finding those weird quirks just so awesome! Those quirks you used to be embarrassed about, those quirks that you would hide behind that made you *you*. Open your mind a bit to understand that being you is NEVER a bad thing. JUST BE YOU. EVERYONE ELSE IS TAKEN! I never have appreciated uniqueness until I started to love myself again. And it's just so mesmerizing when you open your life up to that kind of love.

Stay weird, my friends. It's a beautiful thing!

Megan

Freedom

"Watch carefully the magic that occurs when you give someone just enough comfort to be themselves."
—*unknown*

There is a pressing issue that's been on my mind a lot recently, and I want to get it into words because I feel it's important, if only, at the very least, for myself to hear.

I want to talk about women and how society views femininity. We all know I'm this huge advocate for feminism and for being yourself in a world where there's so many "norms." We all know I fight for equality, especially when it comes to women's body issues and what society considers "beautiful." But this goes a bit deeper than a size 0 versus a size 32. This deals with society viewing women as women, and men as men, and what "society" has labeled beautiful as far as femininity and masculinity.

Now, I HATE labels. This is why I've come out as pansexual. Because as Daniel Levy from the TV show *Schitt's Creek* said best when referring to his preference on which gender to date, "I like the wine and not the label."

So why am I bringing this up? Great question. As you all may have seen lately, I'm taking 2019 to truly FIND MYSELF. In just three months I've already seen so much self-growth that I'm starting to think I wasted thirty good years of my life not realizing any of this sooner. But within all of this growth that I'm trying to accomplish, I've also been doing a lot of psychoanalyzing on myself. I know that's a harsh term sometimes, but I'm reflecting on my life and trying to come to terms with WHY I feel the feelings I do, WHY I act the way I act, WHY I love who I love, WHY my personality is strong, WHY I feel people can't truly handle me, and so on.

So in doing a lot of self-research and self-reflecting, recently I was trying on dresses. (I hate dresses. I know many girls *say* that, but deep down they love them. I don't.) I have always felt very uncomfortable in dresses no matter how good they may look on me. The last time I wore a dress was at my company's convention a few months ago, and although the dress was stunning and truly did look great on me, I was so uncomfortable. I've never been the type to show off my features, 1) because I really don't have that many, and 2) because I just don't feel the need to have an ego like that.

Now—DISCLAIMER—if you got it, flaunt it! Fuck, yes! If you look good in something and you feel even better in something, GIRL, GO OUT AND ROCK IT! But I guess me, personally, I can't do that. I'll stand by you all day long while you rock a cute cocktail dress with heels! But I'll be rocking that suit and tie.

Back to my point. The time before that, me wearing a dress, was my wedding. I wore chucks underneath because that little bit of "me" made a dress more comfortable. If it had been up to me, I would have worn a pantsuit. But then that begs the question, "Why wasn't it up to you? It was YOUR wedding, after all!" And this is exactly what I'm talking about!! I have such a twisted look on society. It's like I don't give a shit what people think but I obviously do, otherwise I would just do what I wanted and not care what other people thought about it. "Freedom is being you without anyone else's permission." Write that down.

I guess I'm just at this point in my life where I'm truly realizing the majority of my life has been lived trying to prove something to someone and living according to other people's standards. And if you're like me, who the heck are you trying to prove something to? I mean, really? Your significant other? Your family? Your friends? Your job? Because I'm here to tell all of you out there right here and right now, DON'T BE LIKE THAT! Why do YOU have to impress someone when it's YOUR life? If someone cannot understand YOU and what you bring to the table, they do NOT deserve to be in your life. That's just a simple fact.

Now, I'm obviously not targeting anyone specific when I talk about this, so calm down before writing a bible to me saying I'm targeting you. Calm your nuts. I'm literally saying this has been my WHOLE life. From elementary school, to middle school, and especially the high school and adolescent years, I wore girly things because that's what everyone else wore. If I had showed up to school in a suit and tie, I would have instantly been made fun of. If I had come out as gay in high school, I would have been targeted for bullying. If I had worn a pantsuit to my wedding, people would have had shit to say. (And just to point this out, people DID have shit to say about it, because I told a few people I wanted to wear that, one being my [then] husband, and he told me I'd look like trash.) So why the hell was I being told it would look bad? When I decided to go out and buy a suit and tie for a convention last year, I was told it would look bad, and I'd better shop in the women's section! This is this shit I'm talking about. This is why people can't feel comfortable in their own skin. It's because of society's twisted views on beauty and what women should look like, what women should wear, and how women should act.

I recently tried on an outfit. I saw someone wear basically this exact same outfit in Vegas and I thought it was the cutest outfit on the planet. It leaned toward being a little more gothic-looking but having this beautiful sex appeal. So I went out and bought something similar. I hated it. I was not comfortable in it even though it was truly super cute. So I changed into a pantsuit. Once again, because that's just ME. And if I'm going to wear something out somewhere, I'll be damned anymore if I'm going to waste a good night feeling uncomfortable, because "uncomfortable" isn't sexy. Confidence is sexy. And I feel real fucking confident when I can be me!

I'm very androgynous. I guess, maybe, psychologically it stems from being raised on a farm and loving being outside in the dirt, helping my dad do chores and fixing tractors. I love to build things with my hands, be outside, get dirty—you know, all the things women aren't really supposed to do. Androgyny is the combination of masculine and feminine characteristics into an ambiguous form. Androgyny may be expressed with regard to biological sex, gender identity, gender expression, or sexual identity. Well, that's me. Take it or leave it. Who says women can't wear pantsuits? Who says women can't wear a tie? Who says women have to wear makeup to work as part of their contract? Who says women have to wear dresses at their wedding? Who says women aren't beautiful if they don't "look" feminine?

So what I've learned the last few months of my life is that you have to just be you. Because you're going to attract the people who love you as you are. And when you truly can be 100 percent yourself around someone, something absolutely magical happens. I will say I've never, EVER been comfortable enough around anyone to be this open and vulnerable. Not my family, not my friends, not in any relationship. But I'm so content right now, I feel the world is opening. And I feel like being myself is praised, finally.

Man, it's freeing...

Do you, boo,

Megan

Lori Petty

March 29th, 2019

Last night was one of the purest, most freeing moments of my life. I've never felt so empowered as a woman who has been a victim of sexual abuse than I did last night watching this play and seeing a room packed with people who were standing up for the exact same mission.

When this play opened last year, I wanted to make it to New York so bad because of the story behind it. Unfortunately, due to life, I couldn't make it happen. Those of you who know me also know my favorite actress is Lori Petty. She happened to be the director of this play. Now, as amazing as she is as an actress, I truly have always loved her for so much more. Her stance on equality. When she fought and stood for Black Lives Matter. Her constant joy of cats! And her love for the LGBT community. When she posted this play was coming back for one night only, and as a fundraiser to benefit a local shelter advocating to put a stop to sexual violence, I knew I had to go no matter what.

Last night was that play. I got so moved by these situations that by the end of the play I was in tears. Not because I'm a bawl baby, because it truly was SO heavy to hear. It touched me SO deeply, and the writer's speech afterward was what truly got me. When she spoke of using this as her platform to reach an audience—guys, this is exactly why I started my clothing line, and now my blog page! I've said this so many times, but holy hell, did it come full circle when she said that! It's like she was speaking right to me!

I was able to get the courage to thank the cast after the show, and although it was incredibly hard, I'm so proud of myself for doing it. This kind of thing isn't talked about much, and to have people who can

17

stand up for this, focus on this, and truly build a movement on this is so, SO empowering.

After the show, a lady came up to me to tell me she liked the floral tattoo on my arm. She also mentioned she's only liked two other tattoos in her life, so that says something! I told her thank you and that I had a very personal story behind it, so I appreciated her pointing it out. After my "thank you" to the cast, she came up to me and said, "You're not a survivor, you're a THRIVER," and she gave me a huge hug. I explained that my tattoo was a symbol of growth throughout the floral piece, and she asked me for my business card because she was truly touched.

It's a funny thing, the people you meet in this world. It's about timing. I needed this night more than I can ever explain. Thank you to the cast. Thank you to the writer. Thank you to the director. Thank you to this beautiful organization. I will never forget this.

Love always,

Megan

Kitty

May14th, 2019

How blessed it truly is to stumble upon a soul that wants nothing but smiles and sunshine for you for the rest of your life.

I think I've waited my whole life for this picture. And by "my whole life," I mean "her whole life."

Side note: she will be twelve this year, and I'm taking that rather hard. She's had some bad days recently and it's tearing me apart, and I'm kind of a wreck while writing this because this photo is just so fucking precious. I've said it before, and I'll say it again. This brat saved me so many times, and these last couple months were no exception. I'm going to go sob in the corner now and hug her until she yells at me to stop.

Peace, love, paw print,

Megan

Life Is Hard, But Happiness Shouldn't Have To Be

May 22nd, 2019

It's crazy that every single thing I've ever been through, even the things I might wish had never happened, the things I literally cried on the kitchen floor over—these are the things that have brought me to where I am and who I am today. Like every shitty, horrible thing that you've ever wished you could go back in time and undo is part of the reason for any good thing that has happened along the path your life is currently on. You can chalk it up to whatever you believe in—the butterfly effect, karma, fate, magic, coincidence, or God—but the fact remains that every bad thing that's happened to you is partially responsible for every good thing that's going to happen to you. And I, for one, really love all of the "good" that's come my way recently. Life is hard, but god damnit, happiness doesn't have to be. Make note of that, and write it on your mirror. Read it every morning, and live your life being happy!

Love,

Megan

When You See Me Start To Get Emotionally Detached And Start Pulling Away, Please Pull Harder

June 21st, 2019

Anxiety is such a complex thing. It affects everyone so differently. My anxiety the past week has gotten incredibly weird, and it's a very big struggle for me right now. People tell me to just sleep it off. People tell me I'm overreacting. People tell me to go take a bath. People tell me everything will be OK in the morning. But that's not how my anxiety works. I have a lot of triggers. Some are worse than others. And unfortunately when I get something in my head, my anxiety doesn't just allow me to "sleep it off." It sticks with me for days, sometimes weeks, and eventually sinks me into some bad depression.

I do truly think I have multiple levels of anxiety, though. Some simple anxiety issues I deal with are meeting new people, talking on the phone, driving with someone in the car with me, doctor appointments, and being late to a meeting—you know, "normal" stuff. But the anxiety I've been dealing with lately is rooted a lot deeper. Anxiety from my past is being brought up. Certain triggers have left me with no choice but to think and act on them. I believe we associate this as PTSD. It's incredibly hard for me to explain. And it's even harder for me to hold relationships because of this, whether that be a romantic relationship or a friendship. It's hard, man. Life's hard! But I'll be alright. I always am. Just know that when I say I'm taking a mental health day, I truly am. This isn't something that's made up in my head. This isn't a cop-out to avoid having to go out of my house or to work. I truly deal with a lot of mental health issues, and I appreciate those who truly understand.

Be you. Be beautiful.

Megan

This Shouldn't Be Happening. Part 1

July 2nd, 2019

Thank you for all of the prayers and good vibes last week. I apologize for being so vague about it in my recent posts. I just didn't know how to talk about it because it's something that has been tearing me apart for the last few months. Today I received the news though. And sadly, I wish I could say that everything is fine. My cat has cancer. And it's everywhere. In basically every organ of her body. Kitty just turned twelve yesterday

This shouldn't be happening yet. I had always thought with having an indoor cat, she was invincible. She would live forever. And because I've had her since she was four weeks old, I just could never imagine life without her. She was my first pet after I moved out and on my own. I didn't even have a pet carrier to bring her home in from the humane society; I lied and told them I did. She sat on my lap the whole way home, and I will never forget the way she kneaded my legs the entire trip. She felt safe for once. She was found in a box on the side of the road, brought in by someone, and she was the only kitten out of four who was alive. I knew I had to have her the second I saw her big bug eyes look at me, and that beautiful calico coat. (I've been mildly obsessed with calico cats ever since I was young.) I brought her home, and I wasn't even in a pet-friendly apartment. I lied and told them I didn't have a cat, which resulted in multiple fines.

She was there for me through my depression. She was there for me when I wanted my life to end. She was there for me through heartbreak with family, friends, relationships. She was there for me when I moved from state to state. She was there for me when I lost my child. She was there for me through abuse. She was my emotional support animal, that's all there is to it.. Anyone who ever met her can attest to the fact that she was the most downright temperamental bitch of a cat. But she always knew who her momma was, and she always knew when I was hurting.

People would look at me crazy when I used to tell them we would "spoon" overnight. She was clearly baby spoon! But this was a nightly occurrence. I think I even have some blackmail photos from old roommates as proof. I'll never forget the way she used to cuddle with me, and only me. It was unlike anything I've ever experienced with a pet. I'll never forget how catnip made her look and act like a crackhead, or how she used to climb my door frames in the middle of the night after running full blast from the opposite side of the house, just to hang there like a koala. Or how she used to sit on my shoulders like a parrot, every chance she got. Or on my lap for HOURS while I worked late at night. And I can't forget about her playing fetch! Ever since she was a baby, she had this HUGE fascination with hair ties! To the point where we would actually play fetch for hours some nights! She was something else. But within the last few months, all of that has gone away.

I just wish I had one last day with her, the way she used to be. That happy, fucking crazy, bundle of "kitten" that she was up until the last few months of her life. But I won't have a chance to ever have that back.

She is back home right now with me, eating some food, looking a little rough, but her attitude seems to be OK. But cats hide their pain quite well. I may only have weeks left with her, and I plan to just spoil the shit out of her with as many cuddles as she will let me do.

Please, hug your babies tightly for me. Please cuddle them as long as you can. Please feed them endless amounts of treats, and give them as much catnip as they want! I'm a complete wreck right now, so if I become very distant in the near future, you all will know why.

What's sad to me is that my whole life has been turned upside down these past few months, with a toxic relationship, walking out of a marriage, and going through a rough divorce. But THIS is what's tearing me completely apart right now. I haven't truly cried in a long time. I think this divorce has given me so much growth that I'm just not as emotional a person as I used to be (and Lord knows I would cry on the drop of a dime)... but this. This has me in so much pain.

Please keep us in your thoughts the next few weeks.

Megan

This Shouldn't Be Happening: Part 2

July 10th, 2019

In the mail today, I received a blown-up canvas print of my favorite photo of Kitty and me.

Update on Kitty: She's doing OK. She has an incredibly hard time walking around and doesn't venture around the house much lately. However, her eating has been really good considering how picky she's been the last few months. She still has blood in her urine, but my amazing vet has stated that it's not a UTI like we originally thought but the tumor in her bladder causing that. She doesn't seem to be in too much pain; however, walking for her is getting pretty hard as days go by. I'm trying to spoil the shit of her with as much human food as she wants, as many soft blankets as necessary, and cuddles when she'll let me. I know my time is very limited with her, so all we can do now is wait.

Update on how I'M doing with this: not good. Days for me are hard. Being alone by myself with only the pets here, I feel like my dog Bo knows something is wrong and tends to stay away from her, unlike usual, when she's always chasing her around the house while Kitty beats the hell out of her. I never thought I would miss the crazy fights they used to have. Or them playing tag with each other at 3 a.m. But I do. I find myself missing everything I once knew and loved about Kitty. Her waking me up at 5 a.m. for food even though she had food in her dish. Her cracking out on catnip. Her dashing around the house like a two-year-old kitten on a sugar high. Her climbing my door frame like a koala bear. Her sassing back to me every time I told her NO! And most of all, our cuddling sessions, because lord knows she didn't cuddle with anyone but me. I find myself crying randomly throughout the day because some days are more real than others. Some days I cherish what hours I may have left with her, while others just prove how truly hard this is going to be for me. And as I write this, I'm crying and she pops her head around the corner and meows at me because she never likes when I cry. I think over the past twelve years she's come to figure out that when I cry, something is very, very wrong. And Lord knows she's seen me cry more than a few hundred times. She really is my emotional support animal. She helped me so much in life. So much that I don't think words can ever explain.

Kind regards,

Megan

This Shouldn't Be Happening. Part 3

July 11th, 2019

It brings me so much pain to write this.

Kitty has crossed over the rainbow bridge.

I've never felt this much pain in my entire life. It's the hardest thing I've ever had to endure.

Last night, I got this weird feeling around 6:00 p.m. She wasn't acting funny or anything; I just got this weird feeling out of nowhere. I went back to my sun porch where she has spent the majority of her time the last few months. She was lying on the ground, basking in the sun like usual. I put her favorite blanket in a small bed for her and picked her up and placed her on it. I had the hardest conversation I've ever had at that point.

I told her I was so happy she came into my life twelve years ago, and how I know I saved her from the shelter but in reality she saved me. And I wanted her to know how important she was to me, and how thankful I was that she came into my life when she did. She came into my life when I was in a very dark place. She was my emotional support through some really dark depression. Some really bad family issues. Some terrible relationships. I told her thank you for being there for me when no one else was, but that now, I was OK. And because of that, I wanted her to know it was OK to let go. I told her I never wanted to have this "conversation" with her, but I need to know when she's ready, because I couldn't make this decision alone. I told her it was OK to let go if she needed to because her mom was OK for once in her life, and although it saddened me to the core and I knew she was just as scared to leave me and I was to let her go, I had come to peace with her illness. I just kept crying to her. Lying on the ground with her, petting her while she kneaded her favorite blanket just like she kneaded my legs the day I brought her home in my car, when I lied to the Humane Society in saying I had a cat carrier to bring her home in when I really didn't. She was at peace that day I brought her home; she felt safe. And in this moment last night, I felt she was at peace once again. I needed her to know it was OK. I was OK. And she didn't have to be scared. I kept telling her how much I loved her and how sorry I was that she couldn't have spent more of this fragile life with us.

I left to head to my boyfriend's house about an hour later. This morning I came home to her having passed away in her sleep peacefully. And to my surprise (this is the craziest thing), she had passed away directly in front of the photo I had hung up of the two of us just yesterday—the one I received in the mail and posted about. If that's not a sign of closure, I don't know what is. She hadn't been able to walk that far into the living room for a good few weeks, and now suddenly she made it out there.

I'm broken. Truly broken.

She was my best friend.

She was my protector.

She was my support. The support I needed at such a dark time in my life.

She made me laugh, and she was there when I cried.

And just like that, she's gone.

Her being diagnosed with cancer last week felt like end of the world. This, though, is taking a bit of me with her.

I'm incredibly thankful to have had the closure I needed with her, and I truly TRULY think because of this, she knew it was OK to go. I feel she knew her mama was safe now. Safe from abuse. Safe from pain. And now she, too, is free from pain.

I love you, Kitty. Fly high. I hope you were able to cross that rainbow bridge and see a beautiful side.

Until we meet again,

Megan

I Cleaned This Room Yesterday

July 14th, 2019

I cleaned her room yesterday. It was incredibly hard. This was kind of considered "Kitty's room" there for the last few months of her life. And during the final few weeks, it really became her hospice room in a sense. She loved this room from the moment I moved us into this house because of the large windows and all the sunlight that always came through. She would bask in the sun for hours in here, even before she started getting incredibly ill. I purchased a cat tower right when I moved in because she hadn't had one in a few years. In my old house, we had a large sliding glass door where she could lie in the sun all day long, but this house doesn't have that, and I knew she would miss being able to look out the windows. I moved into this house in January, and I purchased the cat tower before I even purchased myself a couch. She loved it. She would get up on it every day, and I would find her here every morning while I made my morning coffee. I would open the window when it was nice enough out, and she would just sit in the window for hours until I closed it.

Eventually, as the months went on, the room became a little more filled. I had to move her litter box from my basement to this room because she could no longer walk up and down the basement steps. I had to move her food dish from the kitchen counter (where it sat because otherwise the dog would eat it) to this room for easy access. I then had to purchase a baby gate so Bo couldn't access the room while she was eating. A little more time after that, her one food dish became three food dishes: one for her hard food, one for treats, and one for her soft food that I had to blend every morning because she couldn't eat much of anything. This became routine. Get out the ninja blender, put a can of wet food in it, add some water, put some joint and pain pills inside, along with some CBD oil, force feed her some more pain pills, and then give her this liquid mush that she seemed to love, while giving her a B12 shot in the back of her neck. Then eventually as days went by, I had to add a water dish. For the last six years she just drank water out of Bo's water dish, but it sat higher off the ground, and I started noticing she couldn't lift her head high enough to get it anymore. Then the most recent purchase was a new bed for her because she couldn't hop in my bed with me any longer. That bed was where I last touched her. That bed was where I last saw those beautiful green eyes and heard that purr that I hadn't heard in months.

Now, everything is gone. I didn't think I could move everything. I didn't think I could get myself to throw stuff away, put stuff in storage, or even move it from the place where I last saw her. Sadly, I'm going through some depression, and to keep my mind off of everything I've cleaned my house probably sixteen times in the last forty-eight hours, this room included. I've thrown all her medication away, put all her unused food and toys in a box, and moved the litter boxes to storage. This is really surreal.

I wake up every morning to feed Bo, and I find myself getting an extra bowl for her.

I go to bed every night and find myself peeking my head in the sun room to check on her.

I sometimes think I hear her meow or hear her eating, which makes my heart skip a beat because I know she's not there. This is truly one of the hardest things I've ever experienced. I cannot even begin to explain the pain I am feeling with this. I promise I'm OK, but holy hell, this is hard.

This room was where I laid her down and said my final words to her. Words I truly think put her at peace. I am eternally grateful that I had that closure with her, and I will never, ever, EVER forget those final hours I was able to spend with her right here, right on this floor.

As I sit in here and stare at the room while I drink my morning coffee, I find myself sad. I find myself missing her terribly. I find myself angry. I find myself depressed. I find myself crying randomly throughout the day, which is why I've been trying to get out of my house more to keep my mind off of everything.

Thank you to all of those who reached out to me recently. It really does mean a lot. I enjoy hearing your stories of your beloved fur babies and those who have also crossed over the rainbow bridge. It truly does bring me a lot of peace to hear these stories, so thank you.

Love,

Megan

The End Of An Era

July 15th, 2019

Well, it's an end of an era. I went and picked up Kitty's ashes today. I'm a blubbering hot mess. I think it's finally hitting me that she's gone... and not coming back.

After I posted the story of cleaning her room yesterday, I received so many messages from all of you, and I so very much appreciate it. It's hard. I can't lie. And today was no easier.

It's incredibly strange to me how all this has fallen into place. Obviously, it's not something I wanted to happen, nor would I wish this kind of pain on anyone. But the way it has happened has made me understand my belief in animal spirituality. I truly believe animals have some of the deepest souls, and I would go as far as saying I believe they run deeper than most humans. When I had that final "conversation" with her, the night before she passed away, I felt so much peace. I knew it was going to happen overnight after I had that hour-long talk with her on the floor in her room. I sat her down in her bed and just kept crying to her, telling her how sorry I was, and telling her how much I loved her. I told her how I was eternally grateful that she came into my life when she did twelve years ago, because even though I saved her from a shelter, she saved my life in more ways than she or anyone else will ever know. She was there for me through twelve years of depression. Twelve years of bad relationships. Twelve years of family issues. Some of those years were darker than others, but she was always there. I often used to think how I was going to feel once she was gone, and I never could come to terms with it. But I think that may be because I was never OK in life. Never emotionally stable, never physically capable of being on my own. Depression was still lingering, and Lord knows she witnessed some abuse.

But I told her that night that I was finally OK. I cried so hard, but I swear to you, she heard me. I told her I was finally at peace with my life. I no longer needed her, and if she needed to let go, she could. I've dreaded this conversation since I got her twelve years ago. I told her if she needed me to make the decision for her, I have come to peace with her illness, but I needed a sign—or if she needed to leave me, this was my blessing to her. I've had numerous people tell me they think she hung on until she heard me say I was OK for once. And I believe that she held on as long as she did for that exact reason. She wouldn't have left this earth knowing I was in a bad spot or in a bad relationship. I know this may sound incredibly silly, but I think she knew I was finally with someone who wasn't going to treat me badly anymore. No more tears were going to be shed. No more heartache. No more hiding in a room crying myself to sleep. No more abuse. No more toxicity. I told her I was OK. And I assured her she would be OK too if she needed to let go. And that very next morning, I found her. She had passed away in her sleep. And of all places I could have found her, she was right in front of the photo I had hung up of her and me, the one I had received in the mail just the day before. If that isn't closure, I don't know what is.

But it's crazy to think about, right? Such a terrible situation that ended as peacefully as it possibly could have. I will forever be grateful for that last night with her. That last hour where I could just pet her and tell her how much I loved her. That last look in her beautiful green eyes. That last purr that I will ever hear from her.

Today I picked up her ashes. The same day I received not only her beautiful urn in the mail, but also two packages. One was a letter from my mom and sisters that instantly made me cry, and the other was a beautiful gift from some of my closest friends. Thank you all for this, truly. It's ironic all of this came in the mail the day I received her ashes, but once again, that's how fitting this is. I do truly think she's watching over me at this point. I'm not at all religious, but I do believe in souls. And I know she will show up in weird forms for months to come. This may have been one of her signs. The universe is looking out for me right now, that is for sure. And although this is the hardest thing I've ever had to deal with, and this is the most pain I've probably every felt in my life, it happened exactly the way it was supposed to. And for that, I can be thankful. I can smile knowing she is at peace, because her mama is too. I will continue to look for signs from Kitty, as I'm pretty sure a few have already happened. And I will never forget that little four-week-old calico kitten who starred at me with those big bug eyes the day I brought her home, and how she truly saved my life.

Traveling

July 21st, 2019

I feel incredibly blessed to be able to have the flexibility to do one of my biggest passions in life: TRAVEL! Working a "normal" job never fit my lifestyle. I worked hard for a minimal paycheck. I worked hard to be treated poorly. I worked hard to have to ask for time off when I needed it. I worked hard but couldn't advance. I took a leap of faith two years ago to work from home and have never looked back.

Working from home is a lifestyle within itself. Do not underestimate how hard it is! It's not all fun and games! It's hard work. I've worked harder than I've ever worked before. But for once in my life there's no more living paycheck to paycheck. I can afford to travel and see the world. This is truly MY American Dream.

Wanderlust,

Megan

MIA

July 30th, 2019

I'm sorry I've been kind of MIA on here lately. I've been incredibly busy with work, traveling, and getting this YouTube channel up and running. Which, by the way, just got approved for monetization!! Book deal, here we come! But for real, I've been busy.

When my cat passed away, I think I went into a bit of depression, though I tried really hard not to show it. I chose to hide for awhile so I didn't have to face it. It's taken a lot out of me lately, and I know the majority of people just won't understand why or how, but it's true. I miss my friend. I miss her terribly. I still cry a lot over her, every single day. But I've done a lot of reminiscing over the past few weeks. I've said it before: she helped me through a lot of dark times in my life. And now that she's gone, I'm really focusing in on the fact that I've grown SO much in the last twelve years. But also just in the last twelve months. I walked away from a toxic marriage with nothing, and I told myself 2019 was going to be my year. And it sure has proven accurate. No matter what was right or wrong in our situation, the fact of the matter is that I needed time for myself, and that's what I did to get it. I've finally fallen in love. Fallen in love with ME. And that has opened a world of opportunity for me right now. I'm very thankful for all of you who have followed this journey of mine and traveled right along with me. I truly feel so amazing. My emotional well-being is so much better. My physical well-being is amazing. My mental health is better than it's ever been. And I can just truly say I'm happy. And that in itself is such a milestone for me.

So here I am, take me or leave me—but just know that I'm not stopping! There is so much more to come, ladies and gents! SO much more!

Stay humble,

Megan

Happy Birthday!

August 14th, 2019

My birthdays, as of recent, haven't been all that great. I have a history of something always going bad on my birthday. Sad, but true. This year has been a little different.

Ever since moving to St. Louis, I haven't grown close to many people. Only a select few have I let into my life, and even with those few, I don't get to see them often. (Shout out to those few—you know who you are! Thanks for not abandoning me even though we hardly hang out!) But my point is that I don't love hanging out with people generally. And I've grown to love the few who I've grown super close with.

Cheers to bringing in my thirty-first with these incredible people I'm fortunate to call my friends. Who don't judge me, who love me for who I am, and who travel with me and don't get sick of me!

Can I also just say how fortunate I am to find someone who allows me to remember what butterflies feel like? Who allows me to be me and not feel judged. Who teaches me yet learns from me. Who can have a raw and real conversation with me for eight to ten hours on end. Who can handle me at my worst and certainly loves me at my best. You treat me the way I deserve to be treated, and I will be forever grateful for that. Happy thirty-one years around the sun!

Respect! Coming to you live from Jamaica!

Megan

I Want My Friend Back

August 17th, 2019

Whenever I used to go on a trip, whether it be for one day, or one week, coming home was always fun for me because I was always greeted at my door by a meowing cat who thought I had been gone forever. But yesterday was different. No cat. No meowing. Nobody here to greet me. You don't realize how lonely it is at home when your cat is gone and your dog is at grandma's house for the month.

I miss Kitty. Terribly.

I broke into tears yesterday because she didn't meet me at the door when I came home from vacation. I even woke up this morning ready to call for her because she wasn't in my bed with me. A little over a month has gone by and the pain hasn't gotten any better. There are some days when I can talk about it without crying, and some days when I don't even have to mention her name and it's instantaneous tears. Today is one of those teary-eyed days.

I've said this so many times, but I know a lot of you can relate when I say this pain is unbearable. I've never witnessed such pain in my life.

I miss my friend. I miss my rock. She was a part of me that I'll never get back.

No one ever prepares you for the death of a pet. You can pretend you understand, and you can pretend it'll be OK when that day comes, but truth is, nothing prepares you for it.

I think back to just a few months ago when she was still here, and I never thought this day would come even though I knew deep down it was closer than I had hoped. I know why she was put into my life. I know why I was put into hers. But what I'll never understand is why she had to go so soon.

So as I type this, I'm once again crying my eyes out because I'll never get to hug her again. I'll never get to see those beautiful green eyes again. I'll never get the joy of yelling at her to stop being crazy. I'll never get to be annoyed by her insane temperament. I'll never get to play fetch with her like we used to for hours. And I'll never get to sleep with her at night again, one of my favorite things to do.

I miss her, you guys, there's no other way to explain it. I miss her so, so much. :(

Lost,

Megan

Re-set, Re-adjust, Re-start, Re-focus As Many Times As You Have To. Just Don't Quit.

August 25th, 2019

The balance of life recently knocked me down. And it knocked me down HARD.

I believe life is a repetitive cycle of getting lost and finding yourself again. Sometimes I have to remind myself it's normal to have these intense, emotional days. I have to take a step back and just do me for a minute. And because my mental health is very important to me, when times get extremely busy, incredibly frustrating, or just downright stressful, I forget to take a breather. Instead I allow it to get worse and worse until I'm at my wits end. I need to remember mental health days are OK.

I can't tell you how many people write to me asking for advice on how to pick yourself back up after a bad situation occurs. Fact is, bad situations are GOING to happen. It's an inevitable part of life we cannot control. But what you choose to focus on, you CAN control. And how you choose your focus is key.

Look, I get it. Bad days suck. I, for one, know this firsthand all too well. As I am sitting here writing this, I literally have had a week from hell, and it just keeps getting worse. "When it rains, it pours" could never have been a truer statement. But I also know that with every storm comes a rainbow, and I keep telling myself deep down that this will all go away in time. I focus on the positives in life, even when everything around me is negative. Because we all know how manifesting negative energy only leads to more negative energy. So in times like these where it seems like nothing is going my way, everything seems to be against me, and the universe seems to be driving a sword right through every good part of my body, I just remember I am lucky enough and blessed to work from home. I have a dog who loves me more than anything on the planet. And I am in a relationship where I find myself asking every day, "What did I ever do to deserve this? How did I get this lucky?" I pay for my own roof over my head, my car is completely paid off, I have hardly any debt to my name, and I have been more successful in the past two years than I have been in my ENTIRE life.

Everyone's life is subjective, right? What is a blessing for me might be something minuscule to you, but we all bleed red at the end of the day. We all make a living somehow, we all breath oxygen, we all wake up every morning with a breath of air signifying life, and we all die the same way. Life is the same for everyone. We, as people, just make things overly complicated. Monkeys in the wild don't fight over who gets what tree for the day; they just know that's "home." We all seem to think our life sucks in some way, but we have to remember there are people out there who are far worse off than we are, yet they seem to be the happiest of people. So with this analogy, those of us struggling have to remember there are bigger issues in life than that bill that has to be paid, that flat tire your car just got, the relationship that just ended for good reason, that roof that needs repairing, or that child who drives you crazy. Because in the bigger picture, we are just but a TINY, TINY speck in the universe. Those issues won't matter a month from now, a year from now, and sure as heck not when you're eighty.

So if you need to re-set, re-adjust, re-start, or re-focus, THAT IS OK! Crying is OK. Staying inside for a day is OK. Taking a day off work to de-stress is OK! Because what do I always say? Life is hard, but your happiness shouldn't have to be!

To be honest with you, I truly tend to forget to give myself the attention and care that I allow myself to give others, and being an empath, that gets very heavy sometimes. It's hard. It's very hard. There are days where I sit and cry because I feel such an amount of heavy energy weighing on me that I don't know how to allow myself a breath of fresh air. And when times like this happen, this is where I find myself having to take two steps back for a minute. BUT AGAIN, THAT'S OK!

Don't let anyone ever tell you it's not! Because those of you who deal with issues similar to mine, we NEED that day to ourselves, we need that mental health day called off from work, we need that hot bath some nights, and we need to remember to value OURSELVES.

So, with this, I'd love to know: what do you do for your own mental health days? What helps you de-stress? After all, mental health is not a destination but a process. You never have to be perfect. Having those bad days is OK! You WILL do great things, and taking a day off won't stop that.

Love, your friend who clearly thinks far too deeply than anyone else,

Megan

"Vulnerability Is Not Weakness, It's Our Greatest Measure Of Courage."
—Brené Brown

September 5th, 2019

Writing.

It's been on my mind a lot lately. I never considered myself to be a good writer. I always liked to write, but it wasn't something I ever considered myself good at. In more recent times, the last few months more than ever, I have gotten numerous messages and emails saying how good I am with words, and I just couldn't seem to figure out why these people thought my writing was good! But I think I've finally figured it out. Someone told me once, "You're good with words because you write how you talk, and that conveys great emotion," and that really stuck with me.

That was something else I always struggled with. Emotion. Now, don't get me wrong, I have a LOT of emotion! But when it comes to actually speaking with emotion, singing with emotion, acting with emotion, I always found myself having a hard time with it, and I think it's because whatever I was talking about, singing about, or acting out, I never felt passion behind the subject line. Now, all of a sudden, I do. And I have this weird "need" for blogging all the time. And the more that I do it, the more people seem to respond. Then it got me wondering why. Why do people want to know about little old me? Why do people care about my day? Why do people have such a "want" to see this real, raw, open Megan? Then it occurred to me that it's because I do write like I speak, and when I speak, it's real. It's raw. It's honest. I speak about things that aren't usually talked about. I speak about things that people have a hard time understanding unless they, too, suffer from it. My blogs aren't just what I ate for breakfast, or what I wore to the grocery store today. They are about deep topics that can be somewhat taboo to most of society.

Someone recently wrote to me and told me, "It's outstanding that you can open yourself up like you do, and have that vulnerability that everyone craves." It took me awhile to respond to her statement because I wasn't really sure how. But in truth, that's reality. I don't know how to be anything but real. I don't know how NOT to be honest. I don't know how to not speak on issues like this when I know people need to hear it. That's my saving grace. And that's where suddenly it all came full circle, where I now know my purpose in writing and vlogging. I now understand why people think I'm good at writing, and I now understand why they feel such emotion behind my words, because there is a lot of truth behind it all. Sometimes the words I say are words people wish they could have heard decades ago. But let's be honest, even ten years ago you couldn't really go to YouTube and search "how to move on from a divorce" or "how to find happiness." I think in this day and age, we are at the peak of the digital world. People are making an income from social media marketing, influencers via Instagram, vlogging on YouTube about what diets they are on, and so on. I, for one, have never been out to make millions on this platform. I just want to get my content to the people who need it. I think being vulnerable is a big part of that. You have to be open enough to let people in. You have to be open enough to let people know they are not alone. And you have to be open-minded enough to hear the criticism that follows—and let me tell you, that's a hard one to combat!

If there is one thing I appreciate in someone, it's rawness. Being raw and true to themselves is something not a lot of people can say they do. The world is guarded with so many walls, so many past wounds that do not want to be re-opened. I am here to show you that being true to yourself is OK, and I truly think that is why people have latched on to me and this movement I've started. Even if it's for no other reason than just to feel safe in a safe platform where they, can be vulnerable with me. They can open up to people, and they can open up and be true to themselves.

I think a big turning point for me was to open up and be true to MYSELF, because I had never been able to face my demons. I always hid them, I always hid from them, and I always sheltered them far, far deeper than most so I wouldn't have to face them. But when I started being true to myself, everyone noticed. People respond to authenticity, and that's exactly what I bring to the table.

I'm not out to change anyone's mind. I'm not out to give you some psychoanalytical bullshit that your doctor probably talked to you about years ago. I'm not here to judge, and I'm not here to complain. I'm here to tell you what happened to me. I'm here to share my story. I'm here to share the tears I shed the last decade or more of my life, in hopes that it helps just one person out there, and if it does, then I'll know I've fulfilled my life's purpose.

People tend to get on social media and advertise brands they know nothing about, making money off of something just to pay their bills, and post their fabulous photos of their not-so-fabulous life. But in my mind, they're doing it all wrong. You create a credible brand by staying true to yourself. And that's exactly what I am doing! So cheers to us individuals who know they're messed up! Ha ha! Cheers to that baggage! Because that got you to where you are today, believe it or not! And here I am, able to help all of you, just by posting a few paragraphs in a social media blog. Thank you for allowing me to be real. Thank you for allowing me to be me. Thank you for giving me a safe haven to feel welcome amongst all of you!

Be real, be you,

Megan

Travel. Because Money Returns, Time Does Not.

September 17th, 2019

So here I am somewhere over Germany, flying toward Greece, and I cannot help but think how lucky a human I am. I feel incredibly blessed recently, and I'm not sure what I ever did to deserve any of this.

Just a mere two years ago I started with a company on a whim. I didn't think it would amount to much, but hey, if it paid my car payment, I was cool with it. I'd never had a passport, I'd never been out of the United States, and I'd barely traveled within the States. Now, two years later, this company has brought me to two islands in the Bahamas, Mexico, Key West, Punta Cana, and now Greece! Not to mention the financial stability to go to Barbados for two weeks, Jamaica for my birthday, Mexico again, and more. It's truly MIND BLOWING to look back to just two years ago, when I had –$462 to my name, eleven credit cards maxed out, was unhappy as fuck, and just trying to figure out who the hell this Megan girl even was. I was in a toxic relationship, I was dying inside even though I hated to admit it, I was stuck financially, and I hated my life. Now, it's like the world has completely changed.

When I walked out of my ex-husband's house last year, I literally told myself at the door that if I'm going to do this, I'm going to REALLY do this. I'm going to seriously change my life. It wasn't a want, it was a NEED. I NEEDED to make it on my own, I NEEDED to find love for myself that I never had, I NEEDED to take hold of this depression and this anxiety, I NEEDED to find myself, and I NEEDED to take time for ME.

One of my biggest passions in life has always been traveling. I think it stems from growing up in small-town Iowa. I always felt like I didn't belong. I always felt I was too open-minded for that small, closed-minded town. And I always joked about how my dreams in life were far bigger than the town itself. Traveling was something I had only dreamed of, and when I walked out that door last year telling myself I needed time for myself, I knew exactly what I was going to do. I was going to travel. Since then, for a year straight, I have gone somewhere once a month. Now, before I go any further, and before y'all start judging my spending habits, just know this wasn't cheap, and I'm no millionaire. I worked hard to make this happen for me, but I knew it was what I needed to be able to find myself and allow myself to travel and explore the world. So that's exactly what I did.

January—Nashville, TN

February—Las Vegas, NV

March—New York, NY

April—Cedar Rapids, IA

May—Cancun, Mexico

June—Cedar Rapids, IA

July—Seattle, WA

August—Jamaica

September—Greece

October—Disney World

November—Las Vegas, NV

December—home for the holidays

I'm not telling you any of this to brag; I'm telling you this to show that if you want something badly enough, you can make it happen. In my case, I needed it to happen. I needed to travel for a year to experience a "me" I had always dreamed of. Here I am, living MY best life. My bank account may hate me, but I have experiences that will last my entire lifetime. Do what you can, when you can. Because money returns. Time does not.

Wanderlust,

Megan

"Those Who Teach Us The Most About Humanity Aren't Always Human." —Donald L. Hicks

September 23rd, 2019

Everyone, I'd like you to meet Ivy, the newest member of my little family!

I told myself I wouldn't get another cat until I had some kind of sign that it was right. I'm still incredibly heartbroken over Kitty, and I cry for her on a daily basis. I never imagined losing her would be this hard. I thought about it periodically as years went by but always blocked the image out of my head because I honestly just thought she was invincible. Clearly that's not reality, but no one ever thinks their pet is going to suddenly get diagnosed with terminal cancer and only have weeks to live, then to pass away a week and a half later. It happened so fast. It happened so suddenly. Not a single part of me isn't still hurting over this, and it's still so hard for me to even type this, let alone think about it. After EVERYTHING that's happened with me in the past twelve months—leaving a very toxic relationship, a career change, a divorce, moving into a new house—THIS is what completely broke me. Nothing else.

I told myself I wouldn't get another cat for a very long time because it just would be too hard. It's hard to even look at cats right now, let alone get another one.

The night before kitty passed, I had a long talk with her, letting her know it was OK to let go if she needed to. Letting her know I was finally OK and I no longer needed her as my emotional rock. She helped me so much in the past twelve years, and I know with 100 percent certainty that I wouldn't be here if it weren't for her. I laid with her for two hours that night crying to her, letting her know it was OK if she needed to let go. She hadn't purred in months, but she sure was purring then. She kept looking at me, right in my eyes, slowly blinking as if she understood everything I was saying. I told her there would never be another animal that would replace her, because she truly was a part of my soul. I told her I promised her I was OK now, and I thanked her for saving my life. That next morning she was gone. I found her lying under a photo of her and me. If that's not fate, I don't know what is.

Fast-forward three months. I took a trip with my boyfriend and my very best friend and her husband to Jamaica for my birthday. The day before my birthday I got a call from my dad. Numerous calls, to be exact. I thought something was wrong, so I called him back. He called to tell me there was a litter of kittens born on his farm. Let me preface the rest of this story quick: My dad lives on a farm. There are lots of farm cats. Lots of strays. Lots of litters of kittens each year. He calls me whenever he finds babies, but they're always black, white, or gray because our original cat when we moved there twenty years ago was all black. So as many times as he's called and told me there's new baby kitties out there, I've learned to stop asking if there are any calicos, because there just never are. So I called him back that day in Jamaica, and his first words were, "Guess what I got?" I said, "What?" and he said, "Baby kitties." Then he paused for awhile and slowly said, "Guess what color one is." He knows my love for calicos is hard-core because I've ALWAYS had an obsession with calicos since I was young, and he knew the loss I had just encountered, which was obviously for a calico cat. I instantly started crying, there in Jamaica. He didn't even have to tell me it was a calico; I just knew it was. Legit INSTANT tears. A calico born the day before my birthday? No way! I told him I may want her, but I just wasn't sure yet. Was this the sign I was looking for? I wasn't sure yet. When I woke up the next morning, on my birthday, I received a notification on my phone saying there was motion at my front door on my doorbell camera. I clicked it, and there was a cat on my front porch. I've only ever seen ONE stray cat in my neighborhood, and never has it ever came on to my porch. Instantly I knew that was my sign, because guess what. It was a calico. I can't make this shit up, folks!

Signs come in weird forms if you're looking for them. My dad has told me this since I was very young. He consistently reminded me of this when my cat was sick and had passed. He said, "if you're open to seeing the signs from her, you'll know she's with you."

Ivy is an evergreen. It represents dependency and attachment, which can be seen in the way it climbs trees and buildings. Ivy symbolizes eternity, and for anyone who has ever had the plant climbing a wall of their home, the notion of "forever" seems accurate. Ironically, after Kitty had passed, this beautiful ivy plant completely took over the back of my house at the area where Kitty's room overlooked. It's obvious this had to be my new friend's name. Kitty is a soul that will never go away, and not to get too deep into my own personal beliefs, but I truly think this was Kitty reincarnated. All signs point to yes. The test will be if she plays fetch as good as Kitty used to!

So please remember to hug your babies a little tighter each and every day, and know that when their time comes to leave us, they will never actually leave our side. They show up in many ways. Some might be forms of animal symbolism, some might be in forms of plants growing. Some may come in dreams, and some may show up as a cat randomly on your front porch. Always keep your eyes and your mind open. I'm sure glad I did.

I may never replace that part of me, but I know she's out there watching over me forever. And until we meet across that rainbow bridge someday, I'll continue to hold on to the memories I had with her, and create new ones with little miss Ivy here as she drives me crazy just like Kitty always did.

Sincerely, your friendly animal whisperer,

Megan

Skin Deep

September 27th, 2019

Sometimes I think we get so lost in an image that we, for some reason, think we need to portray on social media. The need and the want to fit in. The need and the want to stand out. We somehow forget there are real faces behind the filters, and real struggles behind the smiles.

I know I, for one, get sucked into the social media life. My entire business is run via social media platforms, and it's entirely too easy to forget what real life is sometimes. You portray this image of yourself where sometimes people never get to see the REAL you. I've marketed my platform, however, on being completely open and honest, 100 percent transparent, and I know for a fact that's why it's been successful. But yet I'm scared to go out in public without makeup some days. Why is that? Why is someone who is SO passionate about proving society wrong on women's body issues, sexism, views on what "beauty" is, etc.—why is it that some days I find it hard to practice what I preach?

I've gotten better over the years, I will say. There was a big point in my life where I was bullied nonstop from people who could not bear the thought of not saying hurtful things to a teen suffering from acne. I never felt comfortable in my own skin from then on. I grew up feeling the need to wear makeup to hide the scars and the pain that bullying left me with. But recently, it's been different. And it's been amazing. I still feel the need to put a filter on my photos every now and then, or hyper focus on removing those pesky blemishes. But for me to feel finally content with the skin issues that I know aren't going anywhere, to me, is priceless.

I guess over the last few years of my life I've truly grown to love the woman underneath the skin. I was always trying to hide her and put on this facade so that people paid attention to my humor or my hair rather than my horrible skin. And that's not a healthy way to live. I find myself, now, not really caring what people think and being able to just go out in public and not spend forty-five minutes a day putting on my war paint for the world to see. Why? Because 1) if those people are judging me based on my skin, then that's completely their problem; 2) I won't see 99 percent of those people ever again anyway; and 3) SKIN ISSUES LIKE MINE ARE NORMAL! EVERY SINGLE PERSON ON THIS PLANET HAS DEALT WITH SOME FORM OF A SKIN ISSUE! There is literally no reason for me to hide something that everyone else out there has. And I think that's where social media has us so tainted. We, as humans, see this perfect person on Instagram and want to be like that. We see a Snapchat filter that we clearly know is fake, yet we get embarrassed when we can't amount to that. It's a bit ridiculous when you say it out loud, isn't it?

Now, do I still love makeup? Heck, yes, I do! It's what I went to school for! Skincare and makeup! The whole skincare realm is a huge passion of mine. But it's because I want to help people who deal with similar issues as I do. Makeup is an art to me—an art that can be absolutely beautiful. I love getting ready for a nice date night with my boyfriend, and taking the time to do my hair and makeup is rather calming for me. And heck, ladies, we can all agree, it's nice to get dolled up every once in awhile! It feels good! But you don't NEED it.

To all the women out there: just do you! You are you for a reason. And people love you for you! Don't compare yourself to others. Don't look at the fake world of social media with filters and photoshopping. Another woman's beauty is not the absence of your own. Find what stands out for you! For me, it's my comedic humor and public speaking. THAT is what I am good at. THAT is what people look at my social media pages for. Not to see my not-so-perfect skin, not to see what makeup I'm wearing for the day. Accept who you are, find your purpose.

I promise when you stop living for other people, you will finally live a life for yourself you never thought was possible.

Love, your acne-ridden friend,

Megan

"It's Kind Of Fun To Do The Impossible." —Walt Disney

October 13th, 2019

That's exactly how I feel this past year of my life. "Impossible" is a word I used to live by. It was impossible for me to be happy. It was impossible for me to leave. It was impossible for me to smile. It was impossible for me to breathe.

In 2019 I walked out of a toxic relationship, telling myself ENOUGH IS ENOUGH! And I left without looking back. I told myself it IS possible to be happy. It IS possible to leave. It IS possible to smile for once. It IS possible to breathe and have a life outside of working 24/7 just to make someone else happy. I told myself 2019 was going to be MY year, and I wasn't lying.

Here I am coming to the final "quarter." The final countdown of the year. And I have NO regrets! I've never been this happy with myself, with my life, with anything.

When you finally allow yourself to realize you deserve better, you will never look back! Take it from me!

When you wish upon a star,

°o°

Megan

Doors Will Open For Those Who Arent Afraid To Knock

October 15th, 2019

Two years ago today, I, on a complete whim, opened up a business. Not knowing if it would succeed or fail, desperately needing to find a purpose in life. I was in a financial rut for awhile, and my depression had come back for various reasons. I started to come out of it all when I joined an online company and suddenly felt I had a purpose. I felt something bigger was calling me, but I just didn't know what it was. I didn't know it at the time, but this online business was such a stepping-stone to my own start up company, and eventually this blog/book, and I think if you read further you'll understand why.

I went to my husband at the time with the idea of opening up something I could call my own. I had the ideas all drawn out in my head, and I'm pretty sure he thought I was crazy. Which, all things considered, I was. I wanted to be a small business owner, so I chose to build something from the ground up instead of joining another company as a consultant. I spent $15,000+ of my own money (not a loan) as the initial investment. I spent countless hours researching clothing brands, designers, laws of owning a business, costs of advertising and marketing, creating a logo, and so on. I kept this a secret from everyone until the day I officially launched the Facebook page. I had NO idea if it was going to succeed or fail. I had no idea if my $15,000 would be a complete waste, if I'd get any customers, or if people would even understand what I was doing. Little did I know what the future held for me.

I gained the majority of this blog following specifically from this company I had started, so many of my readers already know the backstory on all of this. But for those of you who don't, I'll go into more detail so you can understand just why I am here today.

When I first started the clothing line, I had a goal to offer clothing that fit EVERY body shape. A huge passion of mine is helping women with sexism, society's view on beauty, and body issues. I constantly was striving to prove society wrong, and people followed in my footsteps and caught on very fast to my mission. Suddenly things exploded— faster than I ever in a million years could have anticipated. My goal when I opened the company was to get 10,000 followers in one year and to have $50,000 in sales. Well, to put this into perspective, I ended one full year with 50,000 followers and almost half a million in sales. I say these numbers because this wasn't something I paid for in marketing and promoting. This was all done ORGANICALLY! And in a social media world full of influencers, YouTubers, bloggers, Facebook celebrities, and viral videos, the majority of success is built from paid promotions to gain a following. Mine wasn't.

I'll never forget the moment I realized something unique was happening. I received a few messages here and there from people telling me how my clothing line made them feel finally comfortable in their own skin, but when I received a message from a cancer patient telling me my clothing not only kept her comfortable while going through her chemo treatments but comfortable in her own skin, I lost it. The very next day I received a message from a gentleman telling me he had been ordering from me under a fake profile so people didn't know he was a male ordering women's clothing. He then told me that, at fifty years old, he finally felt comfortable to come out to his wife and kids as a gay man, and never had anyone in his life made him feel as comfortable as someone he watches on the internet whom he'd never met. Suddenly more messages came through on a daily, sometimes hourly basis. This is where a pivotal moment in my business happened, just two months in. At this point it occurred to me this was no longer just a retail clothing store. This was so much more than that. What I was leading was a movement. A movement with power. A movement with force! Everyone is unique in their own way, and I was here to prove the beauty in that! So I put in thousands more dollars to rebrand myself and focus on what I was preaching, and suddenly my business went viral. I was able to make enough of an income where I could keep my husband at home so he didn't have to work, I could provide for my family like I had never been able to before, and I could show the world what I truly believed in. But as with almost anything, most good things eventually have to end. At the end of 2018 I left my husband and our very toxic, unhealthy relationship. I left with a mindset that I was finally going to do ME for once in my life, and this business had opened my eyes and my self-confidence to do just that.

You see, believe it or not, I was always a very standoffish, guarded individual. I was a happy-go-lucky person with a bubbly personality, but had a lot of walls and a ton of baggage. I never had self-confidence. I never knew what the simple word "happy" meant. I was living for someone else, and I couldn't bear that anymore. A few months after I left my ex-husband, the business went with it. In April of 2019, I decided to officially close this chapter of my life, and in May it was over. It was one of the most trying times of my life. I was not only walking away from a huge income but walking away from something that so many people latched onto for help. That was heavy for me, and it was truly hard to see people so devastated that something so simple was closing. I cannot even begin to explain the amount of tears I cried over this and the arguments I had in my own head about whether to keep trying or to grow into a different phase of my life. I then made the decision to close the clothing business and focus on the direct sales company and my huge team, but more importantly I chose to switch directions with my clothing business and turn the page into a self-help channel.

All the months of people messaging me, all the endless nights of late-night packaging and discussing life with my customers, all of the posts, the photos, the self-confidence my customer base was growing was because of me—and that was all very heavy! But suddenly it was all gone. Or was it? I may have lost a lot of my following due to the closing of the business, and I know that. But I gained more confidence in myself. I could now suddenly see in myself what all of you guys saw in me, and that, my friends, had never happened in my life.

The closing of this business was a blessing in disguise. It happened right in the middle of my divorce, which should tear a person down, but it didn't. It grew me. As many times as you all have told me day in and day out that I've helped you somehow or another, you all helped me more than you will ever know. I suddenly have a platform, a safe haven, to feel comfortable. To talk about life's struggles. To discuss hardships. I even got the courage to come out as a bisexual woman to the world and to my family, and I cannot thank everyone enough for allowing me this comfort in life, because it was truly what I was missing.

The countless nights of working. The countless hours of packaging orders. The fifty-two-hour runs of no sleep just to nap and do it all over again night after night after night. The endless customer service emails, while still doing a show every evening. The constant inventory orders and moving 10 ninety-pound boxes at a time up and down a staircase by myself. The endless messages I'd be answering through Facebook providing tracking numbers. The six-hour show runs, dealing with my terrible nerve damage on top of it all. Y'all didn't see the tears shed after most shows because of the physical pain! Worth it? 1,000 percent! But I was killing myself to make this work. And this was on top of having my online direct sales business with a thousand-person team, and having a life, while being married. It was hard, you guys! I had never worked this hard in my entire life. And now suddenly I can breathe.

This clothing business was a stepping-stone to finding my true purpose in life, which was helping all of you. I truly believe I was placed on this earth for a reason, and that reason was to help people—to lead and to coach. I cannot even begin to explain to you what it means to me to finally know why I'm here. As someone who struggled for so long— SO LONG—to figure out who I was, I can finally say I'm in such a better place in life now, finding this. Emotionally, mentally, physically. And that is why I knew leaving a very toxic relationship was good for me. I told myself it was a good thing, and no one (no matter how many opinions people had) was going to tell me otherwise. And here I am eleven months later, the happiest I've EVER been.

So thank you all who are reading this who allowed me a platform to speak the truth. Thank you all for allowing me to be me. Thank you all for never judging. Thank you all for helping me spread this mission of kindness and love.

Please share this with someone you know who may be struggling.

Doors will open for those who are not afraid to knock. I love you all. Thank you. And cheers for more good days to come!

Love, your friendly entrepreneur,

Megan

Depression

October 28th, 2019

I've been sitting in front of my computer for thirty minutes trying to figure out how to start this blog, and I've come to realize there's no simple way to go about it. As I sit here, my desk is a mess, laundry needs to be done, the dogs need to be walked, my house needs to be cleaned, and all I want to do is go back to bed. My depression is coming back. I'm completely OK, I promise, but it's showing its ugly face once again. I don't know if it's the changing of the seasons, the amount of stress I'm under with work and life, or my divorce, but it's back, and it's hitting me hard.

I find myself wanting to sleep all day. I find myself completely unmotivated. I find myself in a significant funk that I cannot seem to break. I have been MIA lately on my blog, on my YouTube channel, and in life in general. I'm really just trying to get everything sorted out in my life recently, and I think for someone who deals with a mental illness, that can be hard and even overwhelming.

As I said, I'm completely OK. No need to worry. I just want to make it known that, as happy as I have been lately and how empowering I feel when I help all of you, that in itself can weigh very heavy on a person. I felt like I was doing a really good job at separating work life from personal life there for awhile, but maybe I need to do more of that. Or maybe I just need to wait out this rough patch of life and hope for the best. Or, heck, I don't know, maybe this gloomy weather really just sucks. Whatever it is, know that I'm still here hustling; it's just taking more out of me than normal to do it.

I don't write these blogs for pity, and I don't write them for advice. I write these blogs to make it known that mental illnesses are real and more common than people think. And the stigma of mental illnesses being a bad thing and not being talked about simply needs to go away. I have a platform here, and I've built it on being completely open and transparent, and that's why it's become as successful as it has. I talk about topics that normally go undiscussed. I talk about things that both men and women suffer from immensely. Depression is one of them.

I have suffered from depression since I was pretty young, and as I was growing up it was not OK to talk about it. It was not OK to get help, because then you were made fun of. It was not OK to talk openly about it because then you were considered crazy. I am going to end that stigma right here and right now. Although depression can be completely debilitating and incredibly hard to deal with on a daily basis, I am here to tell you it's OK. Take those mental health days when needed. Your body will let you know when you've just had "too much" and need a break. Listen to your body. Listen to your mind. If you feel like you need a break, TAKE THAT BREAK. I don't care if it's for an hour at night taking a hot bath, or for a week off work. I'm going on about a month now with the depression setting back in, and I'm not ashamed of it. Do I wish it would go away? Yes.. But the reality is it just won't. So I continue to just take some time off and give my mind a mental reset. I encourage you who deal with similar issues to do the same.

I have been through different stages of depression. Some are more severe than others. But the bravest thing I ever did was continue my life when all I wanted to do was die. I remember very vividly feeling these dark feelings twenty years ago. And if you don't take care of yourself, you will eventually spiral down a deep, dark hole that you truly will struggle to get out of. I am very proud to say I have a pretty good grasp on my depression in recent years. It's still EXTREMELY hard to deal with, but I know my signs, and I know what triggers me enough to sit myself down and have a talk with myself before it's too late. If there's anything I can do to help all of you get to this point, DO NOT BE AFRAID TO REACH OUT. I AM SERIOUS.

Do not be ashamed of what you suffer from. Those who belittle you for it will never understand what you go through on a daily, sometimes hourly basis. But I do. <3

Love, a basket-case just like you,

Megan

What Doesn't Kill Us Gives Us Something To Write About

November 4th, 2019

I'm having a bit of writer's block lately. I can't seem to come up with any pertinent quotes, valuable help tools, or vlogs people would want to watch. Then it occurred to me this morning to just tell a story. A story on my anxiety. A raw story that could help people relate to my day-to-day activity, from someone who suffers from a high-functioning anxiety disorder.

Recently I have seen my depression slowly sneaking its way back in my life. (I wrote about this in my most previous blog, and I did a recent YouTube video on it.) With my depression always comes my anxiety. My anxiety is different from most. It's incredibly hard to explain what "high-functioning anxiety" is to someone who just doesn't understand. It's like explaining that depression doesn't always mean you're sad to someone who just doesn't quite get it. Little triggers can set me into a whirlwind of emotions. It deals with my past of abuse and the PTSD I now suffer from because of it.

A few nights ago I was having a normal day. Nothing crazy happened, but it was the day after I realized my depression was starting to come back. I was watching a movie, my boyfriend came home from work and we continued watching the movie, then he left to run an errand, and BAM—anxiety came out of nowhere. I reached out to a girlfriend of mine on Facebook just to chat and help get my mind off of the overwhelming anxiety that had struck me. She didn't answer. She read my message but didn't answer. Now, the common sense in me tells me she was busy. She has three kids, she works two jobs, and she's busy—probably making dinner, whatever. But the anxiety in me tells me she's sick of me. She doesn't want to help me, doesn't want to encourage me to think other thoughts, doesn't want to listen to me vent because she's heard this same story nine hundred other times. Just then, my phone rang. I couldn't answer it. I had no idea whose number it was, but I couldn't answer it. My anxiety wouldn't allow me to answer it. I hate answering the phone. It's a big part of my anxiety to begin with, let alone during an episode where I'm having a hard time.

I decided to order some food since I was not in the mood to fix a meal. I ordered some food from Grubhub and started the waiting game for it to arrive. I couldn't even place the order without feeling anxious. I didn't want someone to come to my house to drop off food, didn't want someone to ring my doorbell, didn't want to open the door just to grab food and say thank you. So I literally wrote in the order description, "Please do not knock or ring doorbell. Kids are sleeping. Please leave food on chair on front porch, someone will grab it." Spoiler alert - I don't have kids. This is how bad it is, you guys! I then waited for my ring doorbell app to alert me that motion was detected and that the food was indeed left where I had asked it to be left. I grabbed the food, ate some, and then decided to take a bath.

With my depression recently, I haven't been in the mood to clean the house, work on projects, work, write my vlogs, do my YouTube videos, even shower on a daily basis. I just really want to sleep for five days and not worry about life for a hot minute. You feel me? I finally decided to take a bath and wash my hair. I normally let my hair go for about three days without washing it because it's great for your hair and scalp, but I was on day seven, and I'll tell you... it wasn't because it was healthy! It's because I was lazy and depressed. In washing my hair, I realized I had to do a double cleanse because it was pretty nasty for not washing it for that long. But hey, the joys of messy buns, right? I got out of the bath about an hour later, not feeling at all better about myself. In fact, I kind of felt worse. Now I was staring in the mirror at a very vulnerable naked human, who now I just wanted to pick apart and tell her how ugly she is, and how stupid it is that she deals with such mental illnesses. I put on my pajamas and headed back to the living room. My boyfriend still wasn't home, which then brought on even more anxiety and just simply put me in one awful mood. When he did get home, I felt terrible. I wasn't mad or anything; I just felt like I was overwhelmed with emotion, and the amount of energy it took for me to feel all of those emotions over the past two hours had clearly drained me. I was exhausted. He sat down, and I acted like nothing was wrong, but deep down I just wanted to cry. I eventually asked him if I could lie on him while he rubbed my head (I'm obsessed with scalp massages; don't judge), and he of course said he would. The instant I felt him touch my head, a lot of stress was gone. The power of touch is a wonderful thing, really. And in about ten minutes I felt the majority of my anxiety dissipate. I had never had that happen before. Normally when I'm this stressed, depressed, or feeling that much anxiousness, I hide in a corner and don't speak for fear that I will say something dumb, get mad for no reason, cause a huge emotional scene, or just say something I don't mean. This time was different. This time I told myself maybe this is what you need to feel a sense of calm, and it truly worked. I woke up the next morning feeling better than I had in the days before this, and all it took was someone to show me just a tiny ounce of love and comfort.

So obviously this is just one tiny story in my huge world of dealing with anxiety. This is one tiny story amongst the thousands I've had that are much more severe. But this is still a tiny story of truth—the truth of anxiety and what it does to a person in small doses or larger, more serious ones.

To those who suffer from anxiety, I know every anxiety attack is different. I know certain people have certain triggers, and triggers are different from person to person, situation to situation. I do not have the answers when it comes to anxiety. I can't even help myself most days when anxiety decides to show its ugly face in my life. But what I can do is accept being different. I can accept myself for holding different traits from most, and for not letting anxiety or depression ruin me. Like I said in my last blog, the best thing I ever did in my life was continue to live when all I wanted to do was die. And that holds true for anyone dealing with depression or anxiety, or whatever else everyone holds.

Every day I'm understanding more and more about what I go through. And every day I start to understand more about my anxiety and depression. I'll more than likely never be "cured" of these mental illnesses, but understanding them helps heal me in a different way. I hope all of you reading this can begin to understand yours too. So, coming from someone who deals with this on a daily basis, I understand. Please know you guys are not alone.

Love, your anxious friend,

Megan

Narcissistic Abuse

November 5th, 2019

Recently I have been wanting to talk about something that multiple people have brought up to me. This is a very hard topic for me to come clean on, and I have to say I am a bit nervous to write about it. Nonetheless, when I decided to write this book, I knew eventually I would have to come clean.

I had recently had some conversations with some friends of mine regarding my past relationship with my ex-husband. It's a hard thing to discuss for two reasons: first, because I suffer from some pretty bad PTSD as a result of it, and second, because this involves another person, and I don't think it's fair to discuss such events on a public platform like this. But, with that said, many women have reached out to me asking to hear this. Why? Not because they are nosy, but because they know they are going through similar issues, and they are grasping at anything they can to try to help them better understand that reality.

I want to make a disclaimer first before I go into this.

This is not meant to be a "he said/she said" cry for attention.

This is not meant to call someone out to make them sound like an asshole.

This is not a cry for help.

This is not to throw somebody under the bus for the terrible shit they did.

Hell, this isn't even to help people better understand the story.

This IS, however, to show people the reality of toxic relationships.

This IS to show what truly can happen to a person when there are clear red flags being thrown up and they are ignoring them. And although this isn't me going into details on everything that ever happened with me, these are some situations that are very clear warning signs of abuse, and I truly hope that someone out there can read this and take something away from it. Emotional and mental abuse are just as bad as the actual physical abuse, and sometimes worse. And I would never wish this upon any man or woman out there. So if you think this blog isn't for you, or if you are simply reading this to bitch and moan to my ex or to one of his friends or family, or just to see how "shitty of a life I am living," then I would respectfully ask you to read no further. If you are a man or woman who thinks they might be being abused, and you want to know what I suffered through, the warning signs I ignored, or the red flags my friends pointed out that I never wanted to believe, then please, I beg you to keep reading.

Last year, a very close friend told me that my relationship with my husband was very interesting because he and I were polar opposites. I didn't think too much into it because that was the truth—we were polar opposites. In fact, I always made light of that fact. He was all logic; I was all creative. But in my head I felt like we balanced each other out, and it was kind of a running joke for awhile. Little did I know, she was trying to show me that she was concerned. Not concerned because we were both very different but because she saw the warning signs before I did. These were little things like the way he spoke to me in public, the way he talked down to me, the way he would make rude comments that were funny to him but not funny to anyone else who could read between the lines. For example, one time very shortly after we were married, someone asked me how it felt to be Mrs. _____. He looked at this person and at me and jokingly said, "That's right, I OWN you!" I didn't think too much into it. I actually remember laughing at the time. But although he claimed to have been joking, he obviously wasn't; that's not just something you say to someone. Snide remarks like this were an everyday occurrence for him. He would say things to rile me up. He would say something that clearly targeted my past, my sexual abuse, being bisexual, and similar things. He would make jabs at me time after time. When it hurt me, I would say, "That's not funny. You should never joke around about stuff like that, especially to a person it's happened to!" and at that point he would say, "Oh, my God, take a joke, why don't you? I was kidding!" But "joking" and "joking about sensitive topics" are two completely different things. He never could understand the difference, and when I would get upset and emotional over it, he would then get in my face, calling me "overly sensitive," which would eventually lead into "you're crazy."

The "you're crazy" thing was his favorite. I was "crazy" for catching him cheating on me. I was "crazy" for catching him with five other women. I was "crazy" for not having trust in him after all this went down. I was "crazy" when he was talking to his ex on our honeymoon. I was "crazy" when I still grieved the loss of my child. I was "crazy" because I felt he was making fun of me a lot of times. And the best one: I was "crazy" for walking out on him after I had had enough, to where he told his parents and mine that he was convinced I deserved to be in a mental facility.

The emotional trauma this man put me through is something I didn't even know was happening until it was FAR too late, and that's the terribly sad part. Had I known these warning signs, had I paid attention to the red flags, had I not been so insecure, and had I known my own worth, this would have never happened.

Now, after all this is all over with, I have had numerous people tell me recently how scary it was for them to watch it happen to me. I have had his family reach out to me. I have had multiple friends of his reach out to me. I have had his past relationship partners reach out to me. And I have had MANY of my own friends and family tell me they saw the signs, but it wasn't their place to try to convince me otherwise. It's one thing when one person brings it to your attention, but when twenty or more people tell you the same scenarios, you begin to question why you ever allowed yourself to go through such trauma to begin with. But I've said it once, and I will say it again: no matter how many people tell you THIS IS A BAD IDEA, you will never do anything about it until YOU see the reality of it. And unfortunately for me, I wasn't in that position until the past few years of my life. And even after I finally started realizing it, I remained in denial, thinking it would get better, he will get better, he will change once we are married, I will fight for him, it'll change, just give it time. Well, newsflash—nothing changed.

Look, I know I'm hard to handle sometimes, and I will be the first to admit that I have some serious baggage. But never have I ever been a bad person. Never! I am one of the most loyal, loving humans on this entire planet, and I don't have an ego by any means, but I know for a fact I have a damn good heart. And when I fall in love, I give everything I have to make it work. But he didn't see that. He used and abused me like any other narcissist would. His narcissistic behavior turned into a power trip, and his ego never went away. A friend of his, who will remain completely nameless, reached out to me and wrote this message: "He couldn't handle you succeeding. He needed to be on top, and the fact that you were doing better than him was terrible for someone with his type of ego. The fact that you were doing better than him, hurt his ego so bad, where every time you did something good for this world, for your business, or for yourself, he put you two steps back because he always knew how to put you in your place and make you feel guilty for it. And we all saw this happening in front of you."

Most narcissists see their victim as prey. They prey on them much as animals would their kill. They often see their prey as crazy, overly sensitive, or too dramatic. They deflect any and all responsibility from themselves and shift the blame to us as the victims so we end up always apologizing. They are so "in control" that you'd think you were connected to a video game controller. They control you. And they will never stop. When they start losing that control, that's when shit hits the fan. They make you feel that your emotions are wrong, which then makes you doubt yourself in every scenario. That in turn affects your self-esteem and your self-worth. Suddenly, in a sense, you are their slave. They have control over you to the point where you literally have no control over your own emotions, your own thoughts, your own actions. This is a true form of narcissistic abuse and manipulation, which is essentially emotional and mental abuse.

Narcissists are truly some of the worst people to deal with. Why? Because they take away everything that makes you YOU.

You're beautiful? Well, they're going to point out your flaws.

You light up a room when you walk in? Well, they're going to keep you at home.

You have an amazing smile? That's why they wiped it off your face.

Your personality is contagious? Well, they wanted that too.

You're smarter than they are? Well, they can't have that, so they make you feel stupid.

Any man would be lucky to have you? They will need you to believe that nobody else wants such a crazy person in their life. See where I'm going with this? This is EXACTLY what I lived with for almost ten years.

Now, some people have considered me crazy when I tried to explain these scenarios, and in truth, they have every right to think it's nuts to know all the behind-the-scenes stuff but without doing anything to stop it. And I wholeheartedly agree - it is nuts! Why, even when I knew it was happening, did I continue to stick around? How did I somehow think I would change him for the better? Why did I stick around hoping and praying that every day would be a little better than the last? I cannot answer those questions, but what I can tell you is THEY WILL NOT CHANGE. IT WILL NOT GET BETTER. And that is me saying this with 100 percent certainty! YOU CANNOT CHANGE A NARCISSIST BECAUSE THEY DO NOT THINK ANYTHING IS WRONG, AND THEY DO NOT WANT TO BE CHANGED! Read that again. Now read it again out loud. Now say it louder for the people in the back!

I encourage all of you who think you are dealing with this to ask yourself honestly, deep down, "Is this worth it?" Because I can assure you, it's not. It's not worth losing your identity! It's not worth never trusting a person! It's not worth the pain and suffering! It's not worth being called names! And in the end, when you do leave, you start to realize the PTSD it's left you with because now suddenly you see the effects it had on you. You start seeing new relationships form, and you notice that you won't allow the "good ones" in. You will continuously apologize for everything to everyone. You will have such low self-esteem that you find yourself almost wanting that mental abuse back in your life so you have something to latch on to. You see how traumatic this can truly be on a person? As I stated before, sometimes I honestly think this particular kind of abuse is worse than physical abuse because it lingers. It never goes away. They have your brain so trained to think a certain way that it becomes second nature. I am currently still battling these demons and almost having to retrain my brain to think correctly, and, I'll be honest here: fuck, it's hard.

So I want to leave you with some facts about narcissists in hopes that it will eventually help someone open their eyes faster than I could. If anyone reading this EVER needs someone to talk to, I'm here. Let me be your outlet. Let me show you the facts. Let me prove to you that you are worth more than this asshole is putting you through, because

NO ONE—NOT A SINGLE PERSON ON THIS PLANET—DESERVES TO BE TREATED THIS WAY!

Here are some facts about narcissists (which I will call narcs) and narcissistic behavior:

- Narcs will frequently interrupt or talk over someone. They will pretend people are talking over them and then scold them for it, just so they can have the final word.

- Narcs are charming, skilled con artists who are INCREDIBLY smart and oh-so-good at manipulating thoughts of others.

- Narcs are very skilled at identifying weaknesses within their victims, and they use that to play up their game.

- Narcs have a huge problem with jealously, even though they'll never admit it. They resent other people's success and somehow feel entitled to it themselves.

- Narcs most definitely can be both men and women.

- Narcs slowly groom their victims to accept the abuse. It's done very slowly over years, and they've mastered this craft. That's exactly why it's manipulation. Most people will not accept outright abuse, but when it slowly grows over time, they become conditioned to accept it as normal.

- Narcs have a love for "gaslighting." Gaslighting is a psychological term that means to manipulate someone into doubting their own sanity.

- Narcs will never take responsibility for their actions.

- Narcs will always put down others to feel good about themselves.

- Narcs "attack" when confronted or questioned. They cannot have anyone in authority over themselves.

- Narcs will use insults to make others feel insecure.

- Narcs believe nothing is ever their fault.

- Narcs will ALWAYS play the victim.

- Narcs will always be "my way or the highway." They never give an inch but demand a mile.

- When you finally leave, narcs will spread lies and rumors about you, grasping at anything they can to take the blame off themselves.

- Narcs have an exaggerated sense of self-importance, or what I like to call a rather large ego.

- Narcs have a large sense of entitlement and require constant admiration.

- Narcs will exploit others without greed or shame.

- Narcs will frequently demean, intimidate, bully, or belittle people. It's a way of coping for them.

- Narcs will monopolize conversations and belittle or look down on people they perceive as inferior.

- Narcs will take advantage of others to get what they want, even if it means hurting them.

- Narcs insist on having the best of everything.

- Narcs become impatient or angry when they don't receive special treatment.

- Narcs will play games with your head, making life hard one moment but then warming up to you the next, making it very hard for the victim to distinguish between right and wrong. This is a game they will constantly play with you to make sure you stay around. Often, the victim will think the narc is changing for the better, so they stick around from hope.

Shelli Marie Gray: Part 1

November 7th, 2019

I don't really know how to write this.

I'm at a complete loss of words.

I'm numb.

I'm heartbroken.

I'm angry.

Last night my family lost someone. Someone who I was very close with. I can't even begin to process my thoughts or put them in any sort of words of empathy for her family, her kids, her husband... I just don't know how.

Shelli was a rare breed. She was ALWAYS smiling. She was ALWAYS laughing. I grew up very close to her because she never once judged me for anything, and this was back when there was a lot of judgment being cast on me. She was the only person I talked to about my current relationship after my ex-husband. She always told me how proud she was of me. She gave the community the kind of light that not many people have to offer. And just like that, she's gone.

Shelli meant a great deal to me, more than anyone will ever know, and I'm having a hard time processing the fact that now I'll never get the chance to tell her how much she helped me through life. The last time I saw her was in June for my cousin's wedding. She and I danced the night away! In fact, I have some pretty great videos of us from that night! She loved to laugh. She loved to smile. And she and I hadn't hung out in a LONG time, so this was very much needed. After the wedding she invited me out to go dancing at a bar with her, her husband, and my aunt. And man, I couldn't have been more thankful. I was having a hard time with my divorce, and this was the first time I had seen my family since walking out on my ex-husband. This was also the first wedding I had gone to since then. So, as you probably know, I was struggling emotionally. At the wedding, we talked about it. We talked about life, we talked about divorce, we talked about the abuse I went through, and we talked about my current relationship. She was the only one I'd told yet. In fact, she knew before my own mother even knew. Once again, this amazing human never cast any judgment on me. She just kept telling me how proud she was of me, and how motivating I am to so many women out there. That night on the way home from the bar we had an even more in-depth conversation, and I will never forget it. And on the way home from her hotel, I got one last text from her that I will forever save and cherish.

I like to think I'm very fortunate to not have had to deal with death much in my life, but we all know it's inevitable. What I don't understand is why. WHY HER? Someone so good, someone so beautiful, someone who held no hatred. There's a lot of things in life where I can look at the situation and say, "Everything happens for a reason," but I just cannot seem to process this.

My heart is just completely broken.

I cannot sleep.

I cannot stop crying.

I cannot begin to understand life's reasoning.

Please hug your children a little tighter today. Please call up your mom and dad and tell them you love them. Please never go a day without letting your loved ones know how you feel.

Love hard, love always, love NOW,

Megan

Shelli Marie Gray: Part 2

November 13th, 2019

As I reflect back on this weekend, it's hard to put all the thoughts from my head on paper. When you experience a death in your family, you often go through a mix of emotions. A whirlwind of grieving. And what I've learned after losing my pet and now a family member within six months of each other is that there's no right or wrong way to grieve. There's no set of rules when it comes to grieving. And there's no "one size fits all" when it comes to how you're supposed to feel or act. My emotions are high. My thoughts are scattered. I go from sad to angry in a matter of minutes. I go from reflecting on happy memories to the point of massive anger spread through anything I can lash out on. To say I'm OK isn't accurate. I'll be OK, yes, but I'm sad now. I'm emotional. I'm scared. I'm angry. I'm depressed. I'm pissed. I'm heartbroken. There's no other real way to describe this. Every emotion I know of, I've felt in a forty-eight-hour time frame, which I understand is normal, but it's very hard to cope with.

What I've also realized is that life is scary. My sister wrote to me late the night it all happened and told me, "I don't understand. I'm scared. This could happen to anyone at anytime, and that scares me so much, Megan," and my heart just broke even more. She's not wrong. We like to think we know how life is supposed to work. You live, you get old, you die. We all know death is inevitable, but we never expect someone to be stripped from our life like this in a matter of one split second. She's right. It's so scary. It's something I'll never be able to explain. Not to her, nor to my cousin's children, nor to her husband and family, nor to myself.

I've learned a lot this year. Life doesn't always go as planned. Someone you thought you'd be with for the rest of your life can hurt you. You can walk away from things you'd never thought you'd have to walk away from. You can climb mountains and leap over so many boundaries, only to have everything fall flat. You can lose, and you can gain. You can have your heart ripped out, stomped on, and put back in and hope it continues to beat properly. All in all, that's life, right? A whirlwind of not only emotions but obstacles. This just adds to the emotional roller-coaster of a year. But I do have to say, after everything this year has handed me, I'm incredibly thankful. You may ask how, considering I just spewed off every reason to be angry at the world right now. I'm thankful to have a family in which, even though we have our differences, in times of need we have ALWAYS had each other's backs because we know what's truly important. My family is everything to me; they always have been. That will never, ever change. And it's unfortunate that something like this has to happen to bring us together but I'm thankful for a deeply connected family whom I can always count on. I'm also incredibly thankful for the love everyone has sent myself and my family this past week. It's so encouraging to see the messages everyone has been posting, not just to me but to everyone involved. It reminds me that humanity isn't so lost. And that's a lot of what Shelli stood for. I'm thankful to have found someone to come home to when times like this arise, someone who can offer me their shoulder to cry on, to vent to, to be angry with, and to offer a loving hand. He's my rock right now through life. Not just through a divorce, not just through the death of a pet or a relative, not just to vent to on daily bitch fests, but he's my rock and my biggest support system right now. I guess this is the time of year to be thankful right? All of this is really making me count my blessings.

Shelli, this past weekend I showed up to the funeral home to see my family, but you weren't there. Normally I'd have seen your beautiful smiling face and your arms reaching out for a hug in situations like this, but this time our hugs were about you.

If only we had warning. If only we had time to prepare. If only I had known, I'd have held you a little closer that night after the wedding in June. If only I had known, I'd have bought you one more beer just so we could dance a little longer. If only I had known, I would have sat and laughed with you for one more joke just to hear your infectious laugh.

If only I had known, I would have told the cab driver to circle the block about twenty more times just to continue our conversation. If only, if only. But when I arrived at the funeral home this weekend, you weren't there. And that's what saddened me the most.

Thank you for saving my life numerous times. Thank you for being someone who never judged me. Thank you for being proud of me when it seemed like no one else was. Thank you for making me prom flowers every year and giving me the "family discount" of "free"! Thank you for being so good for my cousin, Jamie. Thank you for being you and never straying from that.

As I hugged you with one final goodbye this weekend, I told you how much I'm going to miss you, and I meant that. To say I'm going to miss you terribly is such an understatement. I really don't know life without you. But all in all, thank you for touching so many lives. The beauty in this terrible situation is that three thousand people showed up to say their goodbyes to you. It was one of the most incredible things I've ever witnessed.

Please count your blessings, and never EVER take ANYTHING for granted, I beg you. You just never know when it'll be the last time you say goodbye to someone. The last time you hug someone. The last time you say "I love you" to someone. The last text you send to someone.

Fly high, Shelli. I'll forever miss you. Hug Kitty up there for me, would you? She'd like that.

Megan

"You Deserved All Of The Abuse You Suffered" —actual comment from cyber bully

November 20th, 2019

Yes, this is something someone ACTUALLY said to me, and it's been something that always seems to be on my mind lately. BULLYING. Whether it be making fun of someone in person, bullying someone behind their back, cyber bullying, whatever the case may be, it's not OK.

I've talked many times on my shows regarding the bullying of my past and how the pain and scars are still present. They, truthfully, will probably never go away, but what doesn't kill you makes you stronger, right?

My immediate response to bullying when I was younger was to ignore it and hope it would go away. Unfortunately, that doesn't always work. Then it turned into becoming defensive, because I thought if ignoring it didn't work, the only other option was proving your point, right? So I became extremely defensive for a lot of years. I would get so defensive that people would come to me and tell me I'm better than that, and that my actions were just as bad as the bullying. The words I would use as defense mechanisms were no better than the words they were using on me. In the last two or three years of my life I've realized that ignoring bullies in a different way completely makes them stop. Why? Because they get bored. And when they get bored, they stop because it's no fun for them anymore. But over time, the bullying has gone from "the acne on your face looks like you don't shower" to "the stuff you preach on your page is stupid and won't help anyone—you're no one special, stop acting like it." Or some of the more recent occurrences:

"You sick fuck, you cannot be a child of God if you like both men and women."

"Die Bitch."

"You are incredibly narcissistic to be wanting to write a book about YOU."

"Are you a he/she? Your face looks like you're trying too hard to be a woman."

"Your business will go nowhere."

"You can't possibly think you're helping anyone like you think you are."

"You are crazy."

"You deserved all the abuse you suffered."

Before you think these messages aren't real, I've saved screenshots of these words from the exact people who said them. These words have literally been thought out and written to me. And before you say anything—yes, I know I own a public platform via social media, and this shit happens all the time when you own a platform as big as mine. I KNOW THAT. BUT IT DOESN'T MAKE IT OK!

So ignoring them really is fun. Why? Because these people leave you alone real fast when you don't waste your time and energy on them. Honestly, let's take a step back and ask ourselves, is writing back to these people even worth it? Am I even going to change their mind? Or is it just going to fuel the fire if I continue defending myself here? Because here's the honest truth. NOTHING YOU DO OR SAY IS GOING TO MAKE THEM THINK ANY DIFFERENT! SO WHY ARE YOU WASTING YOUR PRECIOUS TIME AND ENERGY ON SOMETHING LIKE THIS?

People (especially those who do this all online) half the time don't even mean what they say. They are just THAT unhappy with their life, so they take it out on someone they know is vulnerable. SO DO NOT BE VULNERABLE! I used to go down the route of trying to get them to understand their own mental illnesses, and sometimes that eventually worked, but is it really worth your time and energy to fix every person out there who has that much hate in their heart? Now, disclaimer, I am always willing to help someone who wants the help! But when someone is literally writing to me to tell me to "die, bitch!" I don't think they're worth saving at this point. My point of this is truly to ignore, and go all Disney on them and "LET IT GO!" because, once again, it's not worth your time or your energy. SAY IT LOUDER FOR THE PEOPLE IN THE BACK!

IT. IS. NOT. WORTH. YOUR. TIME. OR. ENERGY!

You are a kickass human who has better things to worry about! So BE THAT KICKASS HUMAN and go on with your daily life, because proving to them that this kind of stuff doesn't bother you is truly what will get them to stop! The platform I have created, where we have this safe haven for people to talk openly about their issues without anyone judging, is a rare thing to see these days. I'll be damned if I'm going to let someone come in and ruin that for all of us here! And it's mind-blowing when people follow my page for that reason but then have something rude to say to someone. But, as I always say, haters will always make you famous, and honestly, I'm slightly flattered that I seem to always be someone's trending topic for the day!

So let's just all take a deep breath. Remember who YOU are. Because YOU aren't at their level. YOU are the bigger person. If people are trying to bring you down, it only means that YOU are already above them! And if you are one of those people who have had something to say to me, about me, behind my back, or about anyone else for that matter, just remember: You never look good trying to make someone else look bad. I am a firm believer in karma. So I just take a seat in the back, grab some popcorn, and watch the shit show about to happen. And as long as I know I can sleep well at night and am at peace with my life, that's ALL that matters!

Go kick ass,

Megan

Happy Birthday, Bo!

November 23rd, 2019

If you had told me six years ago that this dog would be my world, I'd have laughed at you! I've always been an animal person, but deep down, I'm a crazy cat lady. I never knew a dog could give this much love, be this loyal, be this smart, be this much of rock for me, and feel so much empathy that I cannot even begin to understand it most days. Today, Ms. Bo turns six years old, and I'm not sure how! Where did the time go?

This dog is the canine version of me. She shows love so differently from what I've witnessed in any animal, and you can just tell her soul goes so much deeper than most. I can literally feel her feeling when I'm sad, happy, upset, whatever. She has the biggest heart I've ever seen in an animal and truly is a healer. I can look her in the eyes and typically feel her feelings then step back and feel her feeling mine. I've never realized until recent years with her that animals could be empaths, and I truly feel like Bo is one.

This dog, ladies and gentlemen, is a crazy border collie with SO much energy! Some days you just have to let her do her thing until she figures herself out! Even if it means letting her run in circles at full speed for twenty minutes. She's the best dog I've ever owned. She's INCREDIBLY smart. So loyal. So perfect. I couldn't have asked for a better companion.

When my ex-husband and I picked her out six years ago today, he didn't want her. But I sure did! Something about her was calling me, and we took her home six weeks later. What a whirlwind six years! This dog has witnessed me break down and cry more times than I'd like to admit, but amidst the sadness, she's always been there to lick my tears. I never imagined loving a dog like this until we got Bo.

Happy birthday, precious pup. You are everything to me and more. You've been there through the loss of a child, a divorce, depression, loss of a pet, and loss of a family member. Please stick around forever, OK? I love you far too much to ever think about you gone. Happy six years young, pup! Keep running in circles! Keep playing with your frisbee! Keep being the only dog my mom allows at her house! Keep cuddling! And keep being annoying! Because I wouldn't change you for the world.

Cheers to the rest of the animal world out there!

Megan

A Thumbprint On Thanksgiving

November 28th, 2019

I received a beautiful necklace in the mail yesterday. My cousin Shelli's thumbprint on a compass. We both shared a love for traveling. Ironically, yesterday was also her and my cousin's twentieth wedding anniversary. So it was strange that yesterday was when it decided to show up in the mail.

I cried when I opened it, much like I'm crying while typing this. And to make my tears fall harder, as of yesterday, we also lost my Great Aunt Helen. This has not been a good end to 2019 for my family.

I just sit here thinking Thanksgiving should be your family and friends around a table, stuffing their faces full of food, playing board games, having conversations about life, laughing about stupid inside jokes, and telling each other what we're thankful for. This year it seems very hard for me to do that.

I'm struggling through this a lot recently. I find myself crying randomly throughout the day when a chance memory pops into my head. I cry at night when I'm trying to sleep. I cry when I think about Shelli's beautiful kids and husband. Life is seriously so unfair.

Hug your friends & family oh so tightly today you guys. Please. Happy Thanksgiving.

Megan

If All You Did This Year Was Survive, That's OK!

December 4th, 2019

This year has truly been *interesting*, to say the least. I had the highest highs and the lowest lows happen. I took 2019 to find myself, and I definitely succeeded, but the last few months have been the worst I've experienced in a very long time.

Picture this. Abusive relationship, very toxic marriage. You decide for ONCE in your life you are going to do something for YOU, despite what anyone else out there thinks. You walk out on your husband because you are sick of the abuse, you are sick of being mistreated, you are sick of being disgusted in yourself when you know you were meant for so much more. You make the decision to leave your husband, move out on your own, fund an entire new house by yourself, and take the year to do what you love—travel. You go to places you've always dreamed of. You have some of the best experiences with the best people. You literally travel somewhere new once a month for twelve months straight. You finally find yourself. You finally find love for yourself you didn't even know existed—and in the midst of all that, you allow love into your life that you also never knew existed, and suddenly you've found your soul mate. Everything is going amazing, and then your cat, your rock, your emotional support animal, unexpectedly gets diagnosed with cancer and passes away a week later. Your life is now turned upside down. You battle the onset of depression but fight back because you know deep down you do not want to spiral down that hole again. You keep busy, keep traveling, keep up with friends, and are still building this new, strong, relationship, with the man of your dreams. Then your ex-husband decides he wants more out of you even though you left him EVERYTHING. (And when I say everything, I mean everything. That's a whole separate story.) You're drained. You're stressed. You haven't been this stressed in months. Your finances suddenly are going downhill fast because of this $22,000 divorce that isn't ending any time soon. You do more traveling, you realize life is life, life is hard, but you'll get through it, you always do. Eyes on the prize. You needed this year and no matter what happens, you know you'll make it through. But then suddenly your life is turned COMPLETELY upside down. You get a phone call that you never imagined. Your cousin, one of your best friends, gets tragically killed in a car accident. Suddenly life gets extremely complicated and incredibly upsetting. You cry. You become sad. You're emotional. You haven't cried like this in YEARS. You experience a loss you have never experienced before. You feel a pain you've never experienced and just cannot seem to explain. You think you're OK, but you're not. Deep down you're truly struggling. Then another family member passes away just weeks later. Now you are into the holidays, and you're realizing the depression truly is back. THIS IS MY LIFE RIGHT NOW.

I have literally had the highest of highs this year, the best days of my life, days that I will cherish until I die. The fact that I got out of a toxic relationship is more than a lot of people can say, and I am TRULY so proud of myself for that. But with the good, I think always comes the bad, and this last half of the year hasn't just been bad, it's been HELL. But if I all did this year was survive, I'm OK with that, because at this point that's what it feels like.

At what point does a person step back and tell herself she can't handle anything else? A terrible marriage. A bad breakup. I walked out on my husband. A bad, beyond bad, divorce. A pet dying. A divorce that's now never-ending and putting me in major debt. A family member's death. Now another family member's death. All of this should break a person, and I'm pretty sure I'm very close to that breaking point now. My happiness this year feels like it's been shattered, even though I truly know it hasn't. It just feels that way.

This particular blog is honestly just me venting for once. Not me explaining what I think is right or wrong, my beliefs, my viewpoints, opinions, whatever. It's me venting because I feel like I need to. I've accepted the fact that grief comes in waves, and this is one of those bad waves. I know each and every one of you can relate. At one point in every single one of your lives, you've had to grieve. Whether it be over a friendship lost, someone who made fun of you, a death, a breakup, whatever—grief is grief, and if I've learned anything this year, it's that grieving is OK. Grieve at your own pace because everyone does this differently, and do not ever be ashamed of how you grieve, because that is your personal coping mechanism. Do not EVER let someone make you feel bad for that either!

No matter what happens, I know I will be OK. I always am. This is certain. If I can survive almost ten years of mental abuse, with the "Megan" I once knew being ripped away from me, I know I can survive anything. I know who I am deep down to the core, and I'm always going to stand by that. I know what this bitch is made of, and I will never stop trying when it comes to being happy! And damnit, I've come this far! I've survived many nightmares, and this is just one that seems to be a little harder than most. But as I said, one thing's for certain: I will survive, and if all I did today, this week, this month, this year, was survive, I think that's perfectly OK.

Love, a fighter AND a survivor,

Megan

Shelli Marie Gray: Part 3

December 6th, 2019

This day, one month ago, my family and I lost someone. One split second and our whole world was turned upside down. It's not something you always think of, or even want to think of, but it truly goes to show how fast life can change.

I remember this day pretty vividly, as if it were some significant event like 9/11 or something. I woke up in a terrible mood for a stupid reason, I was standoffish with my boyfriend that morning for really no reason at all other than my emotions getting the best of me, and then I spoke to my lawyer about my divorce, got some good answers, and felt good about the day around noontime. I texted my boyfriend around 6 p.m. asking when he'd be home.

11/06/2019

Megan—6:06 p.m.: When will you be home? I just talked to my dad and he asked me if you liked to go hunting. I told him no but that you like to shoot. And he said he would take you out to do some target shooting if it's not super cold when we go to Iowa for Christmas.

A—6:12 p.m.: Should be leaving soon. Also, that's great!

Megan—6:13 p.m.: He never takes me out to shoot anymore!

A—6:41 p.m.: Well, I'm excited about it! I love shooting!

. . . .

At the same time this was happening, I get a random text from my sister. One that will stick in my brain forever.

. . . .

11/06/2019

Sister—6:46 p.m.: MEGAN

Megan—6:46 p.m.: What

Sister—6:47 p.m.: Shelli got into a really bad car accident I guess so pray for her, Grandma just called us.

Megan—6:47 p.m.: What happened?

Sister—6:47 p.m.: She doesn't even know

. . . .

Megan—6:55 p.m.—My cousin was just in a bad car accident. I can't talk right now, I'll see you when you get home.

A—6:55 p.m.: Oh my god, that's terrible! Are they OK? I'm on my way home, leaving now!

. . . .

At this point I was frantic. I was calling everyone I could to find out what was going on. I truly didn't think it would be that bad. She had to be OK, right? She HAD to be OK! Life wouldn't rip away someone like Shelli! Not like this. Not in a matter of a split second. NO! "She's fine," I kept telling myself. "I'll get a call soon, and everything will be fine! She may have some bumps and bruises during the holidays when I see her at Christmas, but she's fine!"

I called my mom, I called my grandma, I called my aunt, no one could tell me what was going on! But when I finally did get hold of someone, all they could tell me was that she was in critical condition, and I was still in denial, telling myself there's just no way. Maybe it's not even Shelli! Maybe it's someone else. CLEARLY IT HAS TO BE SOMEONE ELSE, RIGHT?

. . . .

Megan—7:10 p.m.: I've tried calling everyone and no one knows what's going on or how bad it is!!

Sister—7:14 p.m.: Mom will call you.

. . . .

A split second later my mom called, and I took a deep breath and answered.

"Hello?" and the next two words I heard changed my life forever. "She died."

. . . .

I didn't know what to do. I didn't know how to feel. I could barely cry because I was still telling myself it wasn't her, IT COULDN'T BE HER. But it was. This was real.

I couldn't even talk. I was in complete shock, and then the tears started rolling in. I started hyperventilating. All I could get out between breaths was, "I cannot even believe this." In literally a matter of twenty minutes, everything changed. It was her. This did happen. This is happening. She is gone.

I like to think everything happens for a reason, but really? WHAT THE FUCK.

WHAT.

THE.

FUCK.

Life being unfair is one thing, but this is something completely different. How dare you take someone like Shelli? How dare you take such a kind-hearted soul who only had positivity to share and love to give? How dare you take someone close to me away? How dare you steal the happiness of a husband and three kids? HOW DARE YOU, HOW DARE YOU! I will never understand this one. Never. I can always find the reasoning in something, even if it's a harsh reality, but this is something I cannot and will not ever be able to fully comprehend.

This is the stage of my grieving where I'm angry, and I'm not ashamed of that. It's unfair, and that's the reality of it. It really just goes to show you that in the blink of an eye you can lose everything. This is something I always took for granted because we all seem to think it'll never happen to us—until the one time that it does happen. And that right there is a very harsh reality of life.

So please forgive often. Love with all your heart. Always hug someone goodbye and tell them you love them. Laugh a lot more with everyone, cry if you need to, and hug someone a little longer. Because you never know when it'll be the last time you get that chance.

I love you, Shelli. I see your signs you've been sending me. Believe me, they don't go unnoticed. It's a reminder that you're out there somewhere watching over us and helping us cope with the loss of your beautiful soul. But I will say, it doesn't take away the pain. I miss you. I miss my friend. I miss my cousin. I miss talking to you. I miss our venting sessions. I miss your spunk, and I miss your sass. What I wouldn't give to have you back in our life right now for the sake your friends, your kids, your husband, your family, all of us. You truly were a beautiful soul taken FAR too soon.

I don't have the words for a clever goodbye today,

Megan

The Truth On Losing My Child.

December 8th, 2019

If I had a dollar for every time I thought about writing this blog but never did, I would be rich. This is a topic that is NOT up for debate, and before you read this, I need you all to know that I will NOT stand for the harassment or judgment that will come with writing this. Please understand that despite anyone's personal beliefs, this is the very harsh reality of a very serious situation that happened, and to judge someone regarding this isn't just morally wrong, it's not going to be tolerated.

· ·

In August of 2013 I had an abortion. I was forced into it by my ex-husband. I've built my following on being open and honest about life, life's struggles, life's happenings, and helping those who need help with topics not always generally discussed. Abortion is a topic I never have discussed, until now, but I'd like to be open and honest about it. There are many reasons why I haven't talked about this. Many would say it's because I regret the decision and am paying for what I did, but sadly that's not the case. Let me start this by saying I am extremely PRO-CHOICE. I, personally, believe wholeheartedly that what a woman decides to do with her body is up to her and no one else, and let it be known that no matter what your opinions are on this topic, no one is going to change my mind. With that said, I believe women should have a choice in what they do when and if they become pregnant, and I wish this had been my choice, but it wasn't.

In May of 2013 I moved down to St. Louis, Missouri, to be with my boyfriend at the time (who eventually ended up being my husband, and obviously, we all know him now to be my ex-husband, and for good reason). We had been dating for a year and both felt it was the right time for me to move in with him. The week I moved down here, I caught him cheating on me—and not with just one other woman—oh, no, that would be too easy! I caught him cheating on me with six women, probably more than twenty times. If you think I'm exaggerating, I truly wish I was. I realized very fast that I'd made a mistake in moving eight hours away to be with someone I had just learned I couldn't trust. But, like anyone who's young and dumb, I stayed. I thought things would change. Two months later I felt different. I was very tired all the time, my breasts were very tender and sore, and to my surprise, I missed a period. I took the dreaded pee test in a Target bathroom one day before work. I purchased two tests to be certain, and I went to the bathroom right from the checkout lane to find out as fast as I possibly could. Sure enough, the test proved positive. I was pregnant.

I called my mom first. I'll never forget the feeling I had. I walked out to the parking lot, got in my car, drove to the very back of the parking lot in tears, and decided to park my car there and call her. I cried. She cried. But for some reason, deep down, I wanted it to happen. I don't know if subconsciously I thought maybe this would save our relationship? Maybe timing is everything and this could be a good thing? Maybe I was being forced into parenthood because the universe had bigger plans for me? Hell, I don't know, but I can tell you in that VERY moment, I was scared but excited. I went to work right after that and began thinking up scenarios of being the perfect mom, with the perfect family. Picking out names, not even knowing what was going to happen, and talking to my mom to figure out the next steps. The next day I went to the doctor to confirm the pregnancy. Sure enough, there was a baby in there! I had an ultrasound and saw my baby as a tiny dot on the ultrasound screen. I remember thinking this is what I always have seen in movies; this is the part where I cry tears of joy, seeing my baby for the first time and hearing its heartbeat. But I remember thinking how nice it would be if the father could be there with me, but sadly he didn't know yet. The nurse said I was about five weeks along, and it was very early, so I shouldn't be surprised if we couldn't find the heartbeat quite yet. Sure enough, there was no heartbeat yet, but it was a viable pregnancy. She instructed me to have the talk with my boyfriend and then to come back in a few days to gather the next steps in moving forward. I got in my car and left, trying to figure out how to tell him. I ended up texting him that we needed to talk, but I needed to talk to him in person. He told me he was busy at work and asked if it could wait. I told him no. I called him and immediately burst into tears saying those dreaded words: "I'm pregnant." There was a long pause. All I remember after that is him saying, "Well, that's pretty unbelievable considering you are on birth control." He said this in a tone as if he thought I was lying. I wasn't lying, and this was actually happening. And yes, I was on the pill. However, I was only twenty-four at the time, and to be honest, wasn't really keen on waking up at the same time every day and remembering to take a pill. I know, my fault. Young and dumb, remember? But lo and behold, this was very real, it was very much happening, and it needed to be believed because there was a confirmed baby inside me. He said we'd talk more when he got home from work.

I think in my head I always pictured the perfect scenario. I always pictured this happy couple finding out they were pregnant, the tears of joy, the "surprise!" when the test gets a positive, the tears they both shed during the first ultrasound when they first see their baby, when they hear the heartbeat together and realize what an amazing milestone this is in their life. But I got none of that. He came home from work, and all I remember is crying while he told me, "You realize you have a choice in this, right? You don't have to go through with this." And in that instant, I realized how big a mistake this truly was.

As I stated before, I am very pro-choice. I believe women have a choice! I believe women should be able to do whatever they feel is right when it comes to their body and their life. But I wish this could have been my choice. He made it very clear that he didn't want this baby and that I didn't have a choice in the matter. He basically gave me the ultimatum to have this child or watch him walk away. I researched how to have an abortion in the state of Missouri, and it turns out you CAN have one here, but you have to make two separate appointments. The first one is to basically tell them you want an abortion and have them try to talk you out of it before you go home and sleep on it, then the second one to actually do it. I knew that wouldn't be a good route because if I were given more time to think about it, I would change my mind. I researched a place in Illinois, right over the river, where you could do it all in the same day, so I called and made an appointment.

Leading up to this appointment were the worst few days I've probably ever dealt with. I had so many questions. I was so indecisive. I was confused. I couldn't make up my mind. I ran through every scenario I possibly could on what I should or shouldn't do. I went back and forth on my decision on a daily, sometimes hourly, basis. Then some weird things started to happen that made me really question his sanity. One night we were goofing around having a tickling fight—you know, like normal cute couples do—and usually when this would happen I would kick or hit him jokingly, but this time he slightly hit me instead. I normally wouldn't have an issue with it, as I know this is how we would joke around, but his "hit" was directed right at my stomach. Was that an accident, or was it preconceived? As always (young & dumb), I thought to myself he couldn't possibly have done that on purpose, so I went on with my day. The next night I went through his computer. Judge me all you want on that, but fact is, that's how I caught him cheating on me in the first place, so excuse me for being scared and making sure it wasn't still happening. What I found on his computer was scary. I don't know why on earth this wasn't a huge red flag for me. He was literally searching "how to give your girlfriend a natural abortion." As in, he was looking up certain teas he could give me, certain pills, certain foods— anything that would kill my child "accidentally on purpose," more or less. At that point I knew the goofing-around punch in the stomach the day before was real. He knew what he was doing, and that's when I realized this child didn't deserve a father like that. So I made the decision to go through with it. And every day leading up to this, he would remind me that we WERE going to that appointment, and he would remind me how many days were left, as if in his mind that would keep me at bay and make me do what he wanted in the long run.

I remember driving there and still wanting to turn back. I remember getting out of the car and wanting to lock myself in. I remember seeing the protesters out front and wanting to turn around so they wouldn't harass me. I remember getting called a "slut" even though this was my boyfriend I had gotten pregnant by! I remember how dirty those people made me feel, and in that instant, I just wanted to die. I wanted to run away and die. I wanted to turn around, but I didn't have that choice. We walked into the building, and I was asked to fill out some paperwork. They specifically asked him to wait in the waiting room while they brought me to another room to fill out paperwork, and the first question on the paperwork was exactly what I dreaded: "Are you being forced to be here against your will?"

I hesitated... but checked "no."

I immediately knew why they put him and me in different rooms, and I thought, *Here is your chance to back out!* But I didn't. Then they took me to another room where a nurse read over my answers in front of me and reiterated that first question. I kept giving her the same answer, but it was almost as if she could tell the truth. Then the waiting began. I waited about four hours before an ultrasound could be done to verify the pregnancy. Once again, a new nurse asked me the same question: "Are you being forced to be here?" and I kept saying no. Then another three hours went by and I was moved into the final room where I would meet with the doctor. I chose to do a medical abortion since I wasn't too far along. A medical abortion is when you take an abortion pill versus having a D&C. They brought me into another room, where I waited another hour for a doctor to finally come in. Finally she came in, gave me one pill to take right then and there, and told me to take the second pill at home the very next evening. She also gave me pain pills and instructed that I use them because, she said, I WILL go through labor and contractions. She made it very clear that if I take this first one but back out on the second one, fetal defects WILL occur and I WILL have a disabled child. I took one long, deep breath, and took the pill. And that was that. I remember being sad. I remember wanting to puke it back up minutes after I took it, but I didn't. We then got in the car and left, and his first words to me were, "Damn, I didn't think this would take eight fucking hours. I'm starving." I thought to myself, that's really all you have to say right now? Not an "I'm sorry this happened"? or "If you need to cry, it's OK"? Nothing like that. Just, "I'm starving. Let's find a McDonald's."

The next night came the hardest thing I've ever had to do. Take that second pill. I took it with the pain medication, and within two hours I started having contractions. The doctor was right—these were full-out labor pains and contractions! The contractions started like period cramps, nothing too terrible, but as the minutes went by, they became worse and worse until I was suddenly getting them every sixty seconds, and it felt like I was dying. I was on the living room floor crying out in so much pain. Those who know me also know I have a high pain tolerance. But nothing prepares you for labor, let me tell you! And I wasn't even pushing a baby out. This was the worst pain I have ever experienced, and I don't say that lightly. It was EXCRUCIATING! The whole process lasted about eight hours, although my brain seems to only remember about two. I think there's a huge mental block that happened during the majority of this, and I guess, in a sense, I'm thankful for that because this isn't exactly something I want to remember. I remember calling my mom, screaming in pain. At this point my mom knew what was happening, but I lied to her, telling her I was having a miscarriage instead. There's nothing in life I am more ashamed of than lying to my mom about this, because she was genuinely so happy to be a grandma. And for that, mom, if you're reading this, I am so incredibly sorry. Words cannot even describe how sorry I am to have lied to you about this, and I hope you'll forgive me after you read through this whole blog. I cried to her in pain while it was happening, and she just kept telling me to go to the hospital. All the while this was happening, my boyfriend sat on the couch on his computer. The only thing he did for me was fill the bathtub with hot water, but only AFTER I begged for him to help me with this pain. I vomited about thirty times when the contractions started to really kick in. About once every two minutes I was in the bathroom puking. I finally got myself in the bathtub and fell asleep. That hot water was the only thing that even remotely touched the pain I was in. I got out of the bath, who knows how long later, and I remember feeling like I had horrible period cramps and needed to sit on the toilet. I sat down, almost as if I needed to have a bowel movement, and when I looked down it looked like death. It was death. I was passing all of the tissue. The amount of blood was horrible. I remember thinking there shouldn't be this much blood, but it was normal. I had passed my aborted child. After about an hour of full-on heavy bleeding, with the pain and contractions finally subsiding, I vomited about another fifty times and realized this whole process had just come full circle, and it was now done. My boyfriend had already gone to sleep, as it was now four a.m. and he had to work in the morning. I then went to bed.

I woke up the next day in so much pain, but every time I texted him, he didn't answer. Then the next day he left to go to Indianapolis for a drum competition that he "could not miss." Yes, my friends, this man left me alone for the next five days. After everything that my body had just gone through, he thought a drumline competition was more important. He was not there to help me physically and sure as hell wasn't there to help me emotionally. I was left alone after just losing my child, all because of him. I begged him to stay, but he didn't budge. This competition was more important than helping his girlfriend with the loss of THEIR child. Then, to make things even worse, I went through his computer again, only to find out that when I was lying on the living room floor screaming in pain, while he was on his computer, all he was doing was watching porn. I can't make this shit up you guys. HE WAS WATCHING PORN WHILE HIS GIRLFRIEND WAS SCREAMING BLOODY MURDER, IN PAIN, ON THE FLOOR THREE FEET IN FRONT OF HIM, GOING THROUGH AN ABORTION. Let that sink in, and read that one more time.

I struggled a lot with this for a long time afterward. I was so unhappy with myself that I didn't even know who I was anymore. I shaved my head. I got breast implants. Anything to make me somewhat feel good about myself, or somewhat normal. I was depressed. I struggled with this decision for years after it happened, and to be honest, I'm still hurt over it. Having had all the labor pains, contractions, everything, but no baby to show for it. I read help books over the loss of a child, I watched videos, and I searched countless hours trying to find some kind of help out there, but nothing was the help I needed. Nothing out there was available for someone who purposely went through an abortion and felt bad about it. Nothing was out there about an abusive relationship where you were forced into something you didn't want to do. I struggled so hard over this because I couldn't find help, and I sure as hell couldn't talk to anyone about this. Please know, that this is exactly why I'm writing this blog. You may ask why, after so many years, I am finally coming forth with this. It's simply because I know there are COUNTLESS women out there who have been in my shoes. And there are countless women out there who I don't want to see this happen to, but if it does happen, I want them to find the help they need.

I still cry about this, to this day, seven years later. I cry every April knowing my child would have had a birthday. I cry around my own birthday in August every year because it was that same week when I had the procedure. My birthday for the rest of my life is now tainted because of this, and it's very unfair. It's unfair that I had to go through this. It's unfair that anyone would have to go through this, and this is something I wouldn't wish on my worst enemy. I struggle every day knowing I could have had a child when I so desperately wanted that baby, and even though I now know it was for the best, it doesn't take the pain away.

To make it worse, six years later, we got married, and on our honeymoon I wanted to have the conversation about trying to have another baby. You know, the normal talk of newlyweds? We were on our honeymoon in Barbados, in the pool at our resort, and I brought up the topic of wanting to talk about kids. I wanted to see, you know, since we were now married, if I should think about getting off birth control, if I should wait, what our timeline looked like, and so on. I wasn't meaning I wanted to go make a baby right that very second, but I wanted to have a conversation like any adult would do, especially those now married. What he said to me in that pool will forever be engraved in my brain. And this is where our marriage suddenly went downhill fast. "You have to be fucking kidding if you think I'm going to allow you to bring a child into this!" And he laughed in my face, LOUD, for everyone to hear. I was hurt. I was sad. I cried. I was pissed. I was embarassed. For someone who once told me, "You'll be a good mom when the time is right," to this... was that all a lie to make me feel better about you forcing me to kill my child? I was dumbfounded. Truly. That night, I also found him talking to his ex-girlfriend. Again, I can't make this shit up! And for those who wonder where our marriage failed, this was basically the start of it.

At this point in my life I've come to terms with it and made peace with it, but I'm still sad that it had to happen. And what truly kills me is the idea of having children now. Will I ever be a good mom? Will this decision haunt me for the rest of my life? Will I even be able to have children someday? Will my kids resent me for this? Do I have to explain to my kids that they could have had a brother or a sister? Do I even want to go down the route of getting pregnant again for fear that it'll be too hard on me mentally? The questions are never ending—and that, my friends, is one of the MANY things my ex left me with that will forever haunt me.

So there you have it, folks. No more secrets. The only secret I've ever had is now out there for all to read.

As with all of my blogs, I don't write them to gain pity. I don't write them looking for advice or backlash. I write them because this is real. This happened. And I know this is happening to others out there. I write this because I want you to know you are not alone, and this is OK to talk about openly! Yes, it's embarrassing. Yes, I feel ashamed most days. But you know what? I'm done trying to hide from it. I need to make known exactly what I went through in hopes that someday it may help just one other person. Judge me if you must; at this point I couldn't care less. But if you think I'm a terrible person for what I went through and was forced into doing because of an abusive boyfriend, I beg you to think again. I beg you to understand that this could have been you, or your daughter. This could have been anyone, and sadly this happens every single day. Please open your eyes and understand that abuse isn't always in the form of physical bruises. This is just ONE of many occurrences that happened with my previous relationship that ultimately left me with no choice but to leave my husband. I appreciate you reading this, and if you do decide to unfollow me based on my decisions, that's understandable. But I do hope that someday you can choose to see the bigger picture here and just be open-minded enough to realize I am not the villain here. No way, no how. And think about this the next time you judge a woman based on her decision with her body. Thank you.

Megan

Do What You Love, And You'll Never Work A Day In Your Life

December 10th, 2019

My dad used to always tell me this quote growing up: "Do what you love, and you'll never work a day in your life." I never really took the time to understand it until recently, and it has proven true.

Two years ago, I started working with a company on a complete whim that has changed my life forever. I was unhappy with my regular job, I was coming home crying every night, I was depressed, I wasn't making the money I felt I deserved, I was busting my ass for no reward, and I felt I was being bullied at work. I started with this company, and within a month I was able to quit that normal job and work from home. I will be forever thankful. But the stigma of working from home or being a stay-at-home mom goes one of two ways. Either people love it, or they have a lot to say about it. They either love that you stay at home with your kids or work from home to provide for yourself and your family, or they think you are the laziest person on the planet who gets to stay in their PJs all day while sitting on their couch doing nothing. It bothers me when people think that we who stay at home don't do anything with our lives. I want to prove this stigma wrong.

I, for one, can tell each and every one of you right now that I have never worked this hard in my life. The last two years, I have worked harder than I ever have. There have been far too many sleepless nights to count. I have made more money in the past two years than I have in my entire life, and my hustle sure can prove the success in that! But the battle of working from home, living that "American dream," doesn't come without the work put into it. For me, this didn't just happen overnight. I put in a LOT of hard work, blood, sweat, and tears to get where I am at today. Worth it? 10,000 percent—but it's hard, damnit! There have been so many nights where I go on fifty-plus hours of being awake, just to nap for a few hours and do it all over again. Day after day, week after week, month after month. There for awhile I was literally killing myself! I wouldn't change it for the world, but I will not let anyone tell me I'm lazy just because I work from home!

I absolutely love when people ask me what I do for work, because that gives me a chance to brag about myself for a moment, and I'll be honest here, there hasn't been a lot in my life that I like to brag about, but this gives me a sense of happiness! I worked SO freakin' hard to be here, so hell, yes, I am going to allow myself to brag for a moment! But when someone asks what you do for a living, and you tell them you work from home, then their next response is, "So what do you exactly do besides sit around at home all day?"—that rubs me the wrong way.

You see, people don't see the hard work that goes on behind the scenes. They don't see the blood, sweat, and tears put into businesses like this! When I owned my own clothing line, which has since closed its doors, I would go on fifty-plus-hour runs with no sleep, nap for a few hours, wake up, and do it all over again. Because I worked from home and was the CEO of a successful company with only ONE other employee, I was the one who had to micromanage everything, and it killed me. I had NO life. I was only one who responded to every email, every Facebook message, did the six-hour shows every other night, packaged orders every other day, sent out two hundred or more invoices every night, separated orders by name, did inventory counts, ordered $8,000 of inventory every week, carried ten ninety-pound boxes down the steps every week when they showed up, separated inventory, ran the customer service side of things, shipped one thousand packages a week—all while trying to have a life and be married at the same time. No wonder my ex-husband cheated on me, right? (That was a joke; stop taking everything so serious.) But for real, IT'S HARD! I grew my social media platform to 50,000+ followers in one year, had almost half a million dollars in sales in one year, and did this all on my own—all while ALSO running a thousand-person team in the direct sales business I was still a part of.

You see, working from home isn't just sleeping in until noon, showering once a week, drinking coffee and eating snacks all day, living the life. It's HARD WORK! Don't let anyone tell you otherwise! And this goes for stay-at-home moms too! You stay at home, taking care of the kids, cleaning the house, getting the groceries, running errands, all while your husband pulls in the income. Although I can't say I allow one person to make an income for me, and although I do not have kids, I feel this! I am the person who cleans the house. I am the person who gets the groceries. I am the person who cooks. I am the person who does all the laundry. I am the person who takes the dogs for walks and runs all the errands. Staying at home is a full-time job within itself, and whether you actually pull money in at the same time or not, it's HARD!

Honestly, you deserve a life and a business that makes you happy. If working from home or staying at home with your kids makes you happy, THEN DON'T LET ANYONE TELL YOU ANY DIFFERENT! I, for one, work from home because of a few reasons. I dropped out of college because of my depression and my learning disability. I never could hold a job because of my anxiety and my learning disability. I never felt like I fit in anywhere because I didn't have a college education. So what did I do? I made something of myself with the resources I had. I came out of a slump in my life of depression and a really bad financial rut. I'll be damned if someone is going to judge me for bettering my life, even if I stay at home in my pajamas all day!

Moral of this blog, in my opinion, is that if you make an income, provide for your family in some way, pay your bills, and are living life to the fullest, why should you be judged for that? And in all honesty, WHO CARES EVEN IF YOU DON'T DO ANYTHING ALL DAY, AND PAY YOUR BILLS FROM ROYALTIES FROM SOMETHING ELSE! WHO AM I TO JUDGE? Because you know what? You are living YOUR best life, and that's all that should ever matter. THAT, my friends, is living the American dream. MY American dream.

I've said this many times. Joining this particular direct sales business was a big stepping-stone into what my life's purpose is, and I'm so thankful I was able to realize it, watch it grow, and get to where I'm at now. I mean for real. Joining a company as only a side hustle just to pay my car payment, to then making a large enough income to pay off every dime of debt in my name, to then opening my own clothing line, to now getting ready to write a book. THIS IS MY DREAM! And it's happening right before my eyes!

Take that risk. Be that risk. DO WHAT MAKES YOU HAPPY! Work so hard that your enemies ask if you're hiring! Work so hard that your Monday morning cubical is actually your bed! Work so hard that you get to decide where your office is for the day—Cancun, Jamaica, your living room couch, WHATEVER! It puts a whole new meaning to "casual Friday," am I right?

Now, this isn't some stupid "plug" to get you to do what I do. But what I do want you to do is do something that makes you happy. For me, working from home is something I never thought was attainable because I grew up in an era where you were forced to believe college was the only way, and if you didn't get that degree you weren't worth shit to society. I am here to prove that wrong.

So before you judge me based on what I do to pay my bills, ask yourself if you are truly happy at your job. And if you are, GREAT! But if not, don't judge me based on mine. Capeesh? And this goes for those stay-at-home mamas, too! KEEP DOING YOUR THING, BOO BOO! YOU ARE DOING AMAZING! Do not let ANYONE tell you otherwise!

So while y'all have something to say about how I pay my bills, what I do to pay my bills, what I do on my spare time, or whatever, just know that I'm going to continue to take five hundred selfies a day, because I can. I'm going to continue to sit in my pajamas as long as I can, because I can. I'm going to continue cleaning my house the way I always have, because that's what I have to do. And I'm going to continue to cash in those paychecks, because I FUCKING HUSTLE! End of story! :)

Love, your friendly hustler who doesn't know how to stop,

Megan

A Letter To Him

December 14th, 2019

> "I knew you were the one when you walked into my chaos
> and never left."

I believe things happen the way they're supposed to in life. Some of us like to call them stepping-stones, coincidences, fate, destiny, whatever the case may be, or whatever you choose to believe in. But I believe that things will always happen the way they're supposed to happen, and what's meant to be will ALWAYS find its way. When I met you seven years ago, it didn't occur to me that you were placed in my life for a reason. It didn't occur to me that you were what I truly believe to be my soul mate. It didn't occur to me that you'd be placed back into my life so many years later to help me with something I couldn't even help myself with. But here you are.

When I first met you, I was immediately connected to you, and I know now by our recent talks that you felt it too. Something about you radiated in a way that my soul felt connected to yours, and although I couldn't explain it at the time, I understand it now. You were genuine, you were sincere, you actually held a conversation with me, unlike anyone else there that night. You had me thinking about you for months after we had met because of that weird connection I had felt that I could not seem to explain. Fast-forward seven years, and that connection was made once again over margaritas. This time I just needed a friend. I needed someone to listen to me without judgment. I needed someone to vent to, even only just to hear myself say it out loud that I was truly in a bad situation. You opened my eyes more than you'll ever realize. You saved me. You allowed me to speak openly about things I had never talked to anyone about before, and somehow it just came very easy to talk to you, and in that moment I was able to realize my truth and my worth. In that moment I was able to see just how badly I was being treated and how the red flags I once ignored could no longer be tolerated. You saved my life, and that's the honest truth.

This exact time last year I was confused. I was disoriented. I was hurt. I was broken. I didn't know what to do and had not a single person to talk to about it because of the embarrassment I felt. This time last year, I had been secretly searching for divorce lawyers for about a month, but couldn't pull the trigger for fear everything I worked so hard for would be taken from me. I was scared I would have to continue with the mental abuse if I brought it up, so it was easier to just keep quiet. I was scared. I was alone. I was nervous. I was sad, and I was angry. I had dealt with far too much, but deep down I knew there was more to life than this, that I was worth so much more, but I just couldn't get myself to say it out loud. You helped me realize that my worth was so much more than that and that not a single person on this planet deserves to be treated the way I was being treated.

I want to thank you for the endless amount of love you've given me over the past year, even when I'm the biggest pain in the ass on the planet. I know I am hard to death with, and I know I come with a lot of baggage, but within all that, somehow, you make me feel normal. Somehow you make me forget about all this bad shit, and I'm able to focus on the good. You make me forget I was once labeled "crazy" for things that are just, in reality, normal for people to deal with. You make me forget that I was once told I needed to be admitted to a psych ward because of my past. You make me forget that I once felt so unloved, so used, and so mistreated that I can go back to being a woman again. You make me feel beautiful, when I was constantly told there was better out there. Thank you for allowing me to open my eyes to see the abuse I was suffering. Thank you for helping me get the courage to leave an unhealthy, abusive relationship. Thank you for allowing me to see I was worth more than the way I was being treated. Thank you for allowing me to constantly vent to you, without making me feel terrible for it, because—let's be real—had some of these venting sessions happened like this in the past, I would have been called names, talked down to, and bullied for the fact that I had "feelings" within certain situations. I could never open up to my ex because of how he always made me feel. I was called "crazy" more times than I'd like to admit, and because of this, I've always felt my emotions are a bad, bad thing. Thank you for allowing me to realize feeling emotion is normal. Thank you for allowing me a shoulder to cry on through the death of a pet, to the death of a family member, to just being my emotional self. Thank you for binge-watching stupid TV shows and playing board games with me every night. Thank you for treating me like an individual instead of holding me to some unreachable standard. Thank you for allowing me to be me without judging my looks or my actions. Thank you for treating me like a queen even when I don't think I deserve it. And thank you for seeing that dark side of me, the one I don't share with anyone, and still loving me anyway.

Our relationship may not be as traditional as most, and it may have started out in a way that it shouldn't have. People can have their opinions on this, but the reality is that I needed a friend, and you were what the universe handed to me. There toward the end of my marriage, I found myself praying, and I'm not even religious. I found myself begging someone up there to help me get out of this hell I was living in, because I needed out and had no way of doing it. I cried so many nights there at the end just begging for the universe to give me a sign that this was the right thing to do. Then randomly you popped in, and after talking to you that night, everything changed. And that, my friend, is exactly what saved me. YOU saved me. YOU saved my life. I will be forever grateful for that. You, my friend, are a gem—a very rare gem. I joke about how you are the male version of me, and I know myself—I am a very rare breed! I used to think how crazy it would be to meet the male version of myself, but here you are! You tell it to me straight, you tell it like it is, no sugar coating. You give me the straight and honest truth about everything in a way that never makes me feel bad about my decisions. You feel so deeply about things that I also feel so passionately about. You relate to things much like I can, which is why I trusted you from the beginning. You give me a reason to be thankful each and every day, and words cannot even begin to describe the reality of that. I know now the universe put you in my life seven years ago for a reason, and it brought you back into my life at the moment it did because karma was finally catching up to me and allowing me something good for once. Hell, I deserved it finally! And I think you did too.

You and I are an interesting find. We don't argue; we don't compete. We just allow ourselves to be ourselves in a world where society likes to show its true colors. You know who you are deep down, and I love every single part of that. Never once have I judged you for anything you've said to me, and in return, to my surprise, you've never judged me, even when there's SO much you could be judging me on. You have never made me feel like an outcast, you have never been unsupportive with my ideas. You have always supported everything I do, to the point where I actually feel proud of my accomplishments, when I used to hide behind them because a certain person couldn't stand my success. You truly make me feel like I am someone who is worth something in this world. Someone good. And I've honestly never felt that before.

You see, before you, I was clearly broken. I was a different person. You saw a side of me that not many people have seen. You saw a version of me that was hidden so far down that I couldn't let it through anymore because of the pain from my past. You saw how trapped I was. You saw the mental anguish I was going through, and yet you still gave me the love I had always craved. In my mind I was so lost. No one would ever find that part of me again because it was so buried deep within the wounds of my past. It was so far down that I didn't even think I deserved to find it again, and I was not in a position to find enough self-love for myself to ever allow it to resurface, so I was just lost. The "me" I once knew was gone because I had been abused for far too long and was too scared to speak out. But you allowed me to see myself in a better light.

You once told me that in order to love someone, I had to find love for myself. And at first I didn't want to believe you because I didn't think self-love was possible in my case, but I made it a mission to prove to myself that you were right. And just like that, when I found that self-love I had always wanted, you came with it. I allowed myself to find such a love for myself, love that I never thought I'd find, and in turn, by allowing myself to love myself again, I allowed myself to love another person again, in the truest, most pure way. REAL love. Not the kind that's been battered and abused for years. Not the kind where I walk on tiptoes every time I talk. Not the kind that's forced. And not the kind that breaks a person down mentally, physically, and emotionally. That was not love, even though for so many years I thought it was. You have allowed my heart so much more. You allowed me to love another person again, when after everything I had recently gone through, I shouldn't have loved at all.

You have given me light back in my life and have allowed me to see myself from someone else's eyes. Just hearing you tell people about what I do, and listening to the words you use to describe how I help so many people, is enough to make me cry. Why? Because I've never gotten that recognition before. I know my life's purpose here, but to hear someone else be proud of it and show how much they love seeing me do this is just so inspiring, I sometimes forget it's me you're even talking about.

I am just so incredibly thankful for you this past year because of all this. I am finding it hard to even put into words just what you mean to me, but at the same time I feel like I could write a book. You mean the world to me, and even if this relationship doesn't end up where I'd like it to, I will always cherish the fact that you gave me so much light in my life. Light that I had thought I'd lost. Light that I never thought I'd gain back. You saved me. And I will continue to say that until the day that I die. YOU. SAVED. ME.

So here's to us. Here's to the year 2020. I will continue to spoil you with vacations around the world. I will continue to encourage you to fulfill your dreams. I will continue to make you laugh at my stupid jokes or play board games with me every night even if you don't want to. I will continue to be there for you through the good and especially the bad, even if you don't understand why. I will continue to fall in love with you more and more each and every day because I feel like I can just look at you and in that moment realize just how lucky I am. Thank you for allowing me to remember what butterflies feel like. Thank you for allowing me to see my true worth. Thank you for not mistaking my past as "crazy" but realizing it's just a part of me. Thank you for standing by me even when life gets a little too hard for even my strong heart to handle. Thank you for loving a person the way they deserve to be loved. Thank you for taking my pets in as your own. And thank you for just being you... because YOU are everything to me.

Thank you.

I love you.

Megan

A Christmas Without You

December 16th, 2019

This weekend I attended my family's Christmas gathering, and someone wasn't there. Someone who I had always looked forward to seeing was gone, as if it was just the new norm. Sadly, the reality is that it IS the new normal, and that's a hard concept to wrap my head around. No contagious laugh, no glass of wine in her hand, no funny jokes, no storytelling. Nothing. The house felt very empty even though people filled up every seat.

This weekend was a hard one. I had a bad mental breakdown that I wasn't ready for when we came home that night. I let out a lot of built-up tears and anger that needed to come out. I pride myself in being strong during the hardships in life, but at some point I think I forget that it's OK to be human. I stand tall to help everyone and all of you, but I forget to help myself most days. I hold it in until it gets bad, and even though I know it's unhealthy, that's just what I do.

I'd been waiting for the mental breakdown moment but just thought maybe I wasn't there yet or maybe it had already happened to me. I feared maybe it was coming soon but kept telling myself not to let it out as I feared the embarrassment it could leave me with, or that I'd lose someone close to me because of how much emotion I felt. Unfortunately, it came this past weekend. I truly don't ever remember crying as hard as this. I was hyperventilating to the point where I couldn't control any of it. The amount of emotion I was feeling was overwhelming. I cried out of sadness, out of anger—I couldn't breathe. I missed her. I started contemplating what death felt like, what it felt like to her, where a soul goes when you die, where you go when you die, what happens during that final breath.

You see, I've always been terrified of death. It's always been one of my biggest fears. I don't understand it, I can't wrap my head around it, and after last month, I am even more scared of that "unknown." I found myself crying so hard that I couldn't breathe, and I just kept crying in pain and saying it wasn't fair. I found myself screaming that I missed her, and needed her back. I found myself so mad, so angry at the world. After about two hours I finally was so exhausted from the amount of emotion my body was feeling that I passed out, just to wake up three hours later with a headache from hell because of the amount of crying I did. Tension headaches follow my tears all the time, but this was a whole different level of pain. I woke up wanting to find death so that I could stop thinking about it, so that I could be with her, or at the very least so I could hug her one last time. Obviously, I'm OK now, but bottling these emotions up is so, so unhealthy. I know that, you know that, we all know this deep down, but yet we continue to do it. I do it because I am a healer. I try to help everyone except myself because it's more important to me that others get the help they need before me. This has usually worked out fine, but in this situation I really needed to respect myself and my body and give myself that healing it deserved.

All of this emotion was bound to come out sooner or later, and although I felt, at first, TERRIBLE for allowing my boyfriend to see me like that, I realized it's very normal. Thank God for him; he's a savior for me right now. As embarrassing as it is to have to lie on the bed crying so many tears, screaming in so much mental pain, hyperventilating because I have so much emotion running through my body, I'm thankful I have someone who can talk me down off a mental ledge and get me to realize this is normal and this is OK. I'm not ashamed of the way I grieve, but it's not something I care to have anyone see.

I've said it before and I'll say it again, don't ever let anyone tell you how to grieve. Don't let anyone tell you there's a timeline. And don't let anyone make you feel bad for it. My grieving may be different from the next, but this is one way I'm coping. And even when it gets this bad, to the point where I let it all bottle up inside until I lash out, that's just how I do things. No matter how you choose to grieve through a death or a loss, just know that it's normal, and it's OK. Just please do me a favor: please be healthy about it. Take time for yourself, and allow yourself tears and pain. It's OK. It's normal. And at the very least, you feel a tiny bit better about it when you're finished.

To all of you who have lost someone around the holidays, let me take the time to say I am so immensely sorry. This has been one of the most painful things I've ever had to deal with, and being close to the holidays makes it so much worse. To those of you who are missing someone at your dinner table this year, please know you are in my thoughts. This is such a tough thing to go through, but I know you'll get through it. They're there with you: that I can promise you. Open your mind a bit and see the signs. The signs she has been sending me have been my saving grace. They allow me the reassurance I needed to know she's OK and that I'll be OK. So to those dealing with a loss this holiday season, please know I am thinking about each and every one of you as I too am sitting down at the table with an empty seat next to me. You're stronger than you realize, dealing with situations like this, I promise you. Please have a Merry Christmas and remember the new year is right around the corner. The new year is where every single one of us have a chance to push that "restart" button.

Much love to all of you,

Megan

The Ornament I Didn't Think I'd Have To Hang

December 18th, 2019

My mom gave me a beautiful ornament this year for Christmas while I was in Iowa this past weekend. A rainbow bridge ornament with a photo slot for Kitty. I buy Christmas ornaments every year when I go on trips, or when something significant happens. It's a weird little tradition I started for myself when I moved out on my own. Eventually I want a tree full of useless ornaments that my grandkids ask me what they're for! Last year, for instance, I purchased a turtle ornament from Mexico to signify saving the baby sea turtles while in Cozumel. This year I got myself an ornament from Jamaica that says "Happy Birthday," since it was a trip on my birthday; an ornament from Cancun that's a cell phone with a palm tree on it signifying the first trip I ever did turning my phone completely off (it's an accomplishment, don't judge me); a globe ornament for the traveling I did in 2019 after leaving my ex-husband; and a four-wheeler from Greece because of the excursion my friends and I were able to do while there. This, however, was not what I wanted to signify my year.

I never thought I'd be getting a memorial ornament, because I never thought this would be actually happening. I never thought I'd have shrines around my house talking about the rainbow bridge, losing a loved one, losing a pet, photos of my pets, urns, and memorial necklaces. My house seems to have a lot of "death" in it now. But, that's life.

So here we are now, half a year after Kitty has passed, and I do truly wish, like the ornament says, that the rainbow bridge had visiting hours. I sure could use a could cry with you, Kitty.

Those of you who have lost a pet know the pain I'm feeling. It doesn't seem to get any easier after months go by, but we learn to cope, much as with any loss. I do find myself waking up wishing you were next to me, getting an extra food dish out to feed you when you're not here, or thinking I hear your meow. I find myself crying over you when I don't mean to. And overall, I just find myself missing you and wishing I could have just ONE more day with you. But all I can do is wish. I know you're in a better place, suffering no pain. That truly gets me through the day, but damnit, no one ever wants you how hard this would be. No one prepares you for the truth.

The end of 2019 has proven very hard for me, and it would mean so much just to come home one day, see you on my couch, and have a good cry with you like I used to do. But you're not here. I know Ivy sees you on a daily basis. I watch her reactions to seeing something, and suddenly she does something you used to do. I know you're teaching her things, so I know you're here. I just miss you. That's all it comes down to. I miss you, Kitty. A lot.

Megan

It's OK To Live A Life People Don't Understand

December 23rd, 2019

How often do we go through life with judgment?
How often do we make decisions that other people like to have terrible opinions about?

How often are we forced to make a decision to better ourselves, only to hear the backlash other people feel the need to give?

It happens FAR too often. I can say it happens on a daily, sometimes hourly basis for me. From the platform I have on social media to my personal decisions here at home, I am judged CONSTANTLY. How I choose to react to these comments and opinions are on me, though. And although I used to be incredibly defensive when it came to this in the past, I no longer feel I have to be because I know who I am deep down. I know why I did what I did, and I knew I had to better my life some way, somehow.

People like to form opinions. People like to cast judgment before knowing the whole story. Every time this happens, I tell myself in my head, "If they knew the whole story, they'd be proud of me." And it's the truth. I'm not here to get you or anyone else on my side. I'm not here to prove who I am to ANYONE out there. But what I am here to do is show you that YOU do not need to live your life according to someone else's standards. Live your life according to YOU. Be YOU. Do YOU. And do what YOU need to do in your life.

I left my ex-husband this time last year. I was a mess. I was so confused, so disoriented. I was embarrassed to be living with such abuse, but I was also embarrassed to admit I was wrong in marrying the abuser.

I was scared. I was alone. I didn't talk to anyone about this because of that embarrassment. So, on the outside, it looked like I just up and left for no reason, but in reality I had been thinking these thoughts since before the wedding even happened. Before I had even walked down the aisle. I told myself for MONTHS that things would change, that things would get better, that it was "normal" to start getting cold feet before a wedding—but in reality it was my brain telling me this was all wrong. I knew it deep down but could never admit it. I lived like this for years, and each day was harder than the last. Each time he broke me down, he took a little more out of me. Each time he called me "crazy" pushed me back a few more steps than the last. Until one morning—one morning I woke up and realized enough was enough. What seemed sudden to 99.9 percent of my friends and family had been years of abuse built up. People talked. People judged. People had some choice words to say about my decisions. People started rumors that I was cheating when I wasn't. People listened to one side of the story instead of hearing the truth. But walking out of that door was the best thing I've EVER, in my entire life, done for myself.

It's OK to live a life people don't understand. I'm not here to live a life for anyone but myself, and I knew I was being mistreated. I knew I was being abused. And I got out. For those of you who couldn't understand that at the time, it's OK. I would have been confused right along with you. But when abuse is happening, as most of you know, people rarely speak up. I didn't speak up. I was embarrassed by it, much like many other men and women out there who have been or are being abused.

It's OK if people don't understand your reasoning for leaving a job, coming to work late, leaving a relationship, getting a divorce, cutting certain family members out of your life, what you chose to spend your money on, or anything you do. It's OK that they don't understand! Why? Because that's YOUR life to live, not theirs. It's OK to live that life that people don't understand because you know your truth deep down. You are the ONLY person who knows truly what happened and what you suffered from. You know you bettered yourself, and that's all that matters. In my case, I bettered myself by walking out of an abusive marriage, and I will forever be thankful for waking up that day and realizing enough was enough, but I'm not here to prove my reasoning to anyone. If someone wants to hear my story, I'll gladly tell them. But for those of you who don't understand why I did what I did, that's OK, because I didn't walk out of a marriage to benefit YOU. I did it to save my life.

Not everyone will understand.

Not everyone will get it.

Not everyone will be OK with your decisions in life.

But knowing it's not about them will give you clarity and happiness in life.

What do I always say? Life is hard, but happiness shouldn't have to be.

Your decisions in life are your decisions.

NEVER let ANYONE make you feel bad about it.

Love, a friendly soul who makes a lot of bad decisions and still doesn't care!

Megan

Another End Of An Era

December 26th. 2019

I suppose it's truly an end of an era when you get a memorial tattoo, right? Part of me is sad, though, realizing this truly does mean she's gone. I'm so thankful to have spent twelve years with her. She was my rock. My friend. My pet. My saving grace for so many years. I never imagined spending days without her, so the last six months have been incredibly hard. Thank you, Derek at St. Louis Tattoo Co., for once again bringing my tattoo dreams to reality. You never disappoint. The pain this tattoo gave me was NOTHING compared to the heartache of losing her, but you've truly made it a beautiful memorial piece for me.

It's really weird. Somedays it's like she never left. Other days, I feel so heartbroken, as if I can't wake up in the morning. I suppose that's part of the grieving process, right? Some days are harder than others, and that's just normal. I know they say "time heals all wounds," but I don't really believe in that. I believe time allows a person to cope, but it doesn't heal. At least not for me.

Kitty, I still swear I hear you meow every so often. I still find myself getting up in the morning ready to grab your medicine and food to feed you. I still find random ponytails all over the house, in places I forgot to look when I cleaned, knowing the last time these were played with was when you hid them there. Or maybe that's some sort of subtle sign that you're still here playing with them. Somedays I swear I see you in your bed. I swear I can smell you near me when I sleep. I wake up thinking you're in my arms cuddling like you always were, only to find you're not there.

It's hard, man. Real hard. And I know I've said this a hundred times, but no one truly prepares you for the loss of a pet. It's something you think of as every year passes, but no one prepares you with what you're supposed to do after they're gone. Where's the self-help book for that?!

For now, I'll continue to look at your urn every morning, as if I'm telling you "good morning" every day like I used to. I'll continue you touching your urn every so often, as if to let you know that I'm still here hurting, but comforting you so you know it's OK. I'll continue dreaming of you, like you're still here, not in pain, acting like the crazy creature you once were. And I'll continue crying every so often because I really am just sad. I miss you so much. And as I sit here and write this blog, the tears just won't stop. What I wouldn't give to have one more day with you. One more hour. One more hug. Thank you for watching over us. I know you're there. I can sense it. But I wish I could just reach out and pet you one last time.

Megan

Pleasing People

December 30th, 2019

I've always lived my life trying to please people. I don't know why. I have no reasoning, truly; I just am one of those people who would rather make other people happy before herself. Everything from what to make for dinner, to eating dinner last so everyone else can eat, to the way I look or dress, or even sometimes how I act. I put other people ahead of me, and I think lately it's taking a toll on me. I think I'm starting to realize that I do this, though, and I've been trying to come up with ways to conquer that.

Some days, I feel I do so much for people that I wake up feeling not good about myself. And honestly, this is the first time I have talked about it out loud, so maybe this is a stepping-stone for me.

It's probably hard for me to explain in a way that you guys will understand, but in my head I know what I'm trying to say! I just know that I am a healer, so I try to heal everyone in any way I can. Even if people aren't dealing with any sort of issue, even if it's just something that I know would make them smile, I do it. I think I tend to forget I don't always have to be that healer. I don't always have to please someone just to make life easier. Sometimes I fail to remember it's OK to have my own opinions on things and do what I like versus doing something to make someone else happy. I'm realizing that I do a lot of that lately, and I can't seem to pinpoint why I don't just stop it all together. It really puts me in a funk when I let it control me like it has.

I woke up a few weeks ago kind of sick with myself for doing something I maybe shouldn't have. But I did it to please someone. I knew that if I did a certain thing, it would cause less headache later, so that's what I did. But that's not me, and I can't seem to figure out why

I continue to do that. Maybe that's why I've had multiple relationships fail (both partners and friends)—because I aim to please too much. I need to remember there is such thing as just letting shit happen and going my own way! But I never do that.

Part of my healing is making sure people are happy and taken care of. This includes friends, family, romantic partners, pets, and coworkers. I go out of my way to do what they'd want me to do or simply to make them happy. But I think it's turning me into a pushover. And lately it's making me really mad at myself. And then I start thinking back to my previous relationship, where all I ever did was try my best to do what HE wanted, and in return, I dealt with a LOT of narcissistic abuse, him having this crazy "control" over me, and me just dealing with it because that's all I knew how to do. Whatever made him happy, I did. Whether that be sexually, emotionally, physically, whatever—I did what I KNEW would please him because I didn't want to piss him off. And I find myself doing that every single day now with other friends, partners, and so on.

Is this part of my PTSD from my previous relationship? Will that "control" ever go away? Because to me, it really sucks that I still feel tied to his leash after all this time being away from him. I still feel he has 100 percent control over me, and it's really hard for me to understand. He manipulates this divorce, his lawyers, my company, and my previously owned business. He uses his manipulative tactics when he talks to people about me and about us. He fucked with my head SO much the past ten years that I am still suffering even after leaving him. What's a girl to do?

New Year's Eve

December 31st, 2019

Last year on this exact day, I stayed home on New Year's Eve for the first time in my entire life. I was completely confused, disoriented, broken, torn apart. I had ended my marriage and had yet to tell my friends or family.

This very night last year I cried on camera while watching the ball drop during one of my online facebook shows. New Year's Eve has always held a special place in my heart. I get a little nostalgic because I used to spend the night with my grandparents playing board games, dancing in the living room with my cousins, and drinking sparkling grape juice. But more importantly, New Year's Eve to me is a restart button. Pushing restart on your life, on your year. No matter what happens from the year prior, you get to put all of that in the past and move forward to bigger and better things.

I told myself, when I finally made up my mind that I was leaving my ex-husband, that if I was finally going to do it, I had to actually do it. It was hard, you guys. The hardest thing I've ever dealt with in my life. I was embarrassed about being married for only a year and a half. I was sad because I didn't want to put him through this. I was angry with myself for not realizing things sooner and doing something about it. I was confused because I still didn't know which road to take. But partway through the video I recorded that night, I had made up my mind, and about thirty minutes after I filmed it, I opened up to my mom. My mom was the first person who knew.

I remember the guilt I felt in that exact moment. I remember the heartache I felt. The tears that were shed this very night last year were some of the more painful tears my eyes have ever felt. But I knew that

124

the restart button this year would be the biggest restart I was ever going to need, and I was right.

I told myself if you're going to end this marriage, you need to do it for yourself for yourself. You've lost so much of yourself these last ten years and you need to somehow get that back, and the first step is to walk away from the abuse that held you back for so long.

So here we are exactly a year later, and what have I learned?

I learned that I was right. I needed to find myself. I had never been able to find myself or find love for myself, and suddenly with the push of that fancy restart button we like to call New Year's Eve, I was able to accomplish this. Was it hard? Yes, the hardest thing I've ever done. Was it sad? You bet. It tore me apart in so many ways you all can't even imagine. Was it scary? Hell, it was terrifying.. But was it worth it? I cannot begin to tell you this enough: IT WAS THE BEST THING I EVER DID IN MY LIFE. I had so many doors open up for me this year, and my mind has been opened right along with it. My heart has opened up enough to find not only love for myself, but love for someone else in the process. Someone who deserved my love for once. Someone who isn't abusive, controlling, or manipulative. It allowed me to travel the world, see the world, find inspiration from different parts of the earth.

Looking back at the video I made last year, I'm truly seeing the growth I went through. And god damnit, I am so fucking proud of that, despite what anyone else may think.

So CHEERS to 2020! Use this new year, new decade, as a restart and a refresh. Do what YOU need to do in life because life is so very short. Get your goals in order. Make them happen. And never, EVER stop believing in yourself.

Auld Lang Syne,

Megan

Anxiety

January 2nd, 2020

Someone asked me recently what my anxiety entails, and that's always a hard question for me to answer. Simply put, it's hard for me to even figure it out. There are a lot of "issues" my anxiety stems from and a lot of responses that my anxiety creates. Issues from childhood, past friendships, PTSD from abusive relationships, being cheated on more times than I'd like to even count—you get the point. One specific example we discussed was the fact that I can sing in front of forty thousand people, but when it comes to meeting someone face to face I have the utmost WORST anxiety. I can't answer the phone, I can't answer my door, I can't meet someone to pick something up, I can't sell on Facebook marketplace because that requires meeting up with someone. It's a hard thing to deal with! Then they asked me if I knew what the issue was regarding the fact that meeting people scared me. I said there was a difference between my anxiety and being scared or nervous. Being scared or nervous allows you to still do things. With my anxiety I literally can go into anxiety attack mode. And I told them that I think a deeply rooted concern is the fact that I have a rather large social media presence, and I'm, I think, secretly scared that I won't live up to people's expectations of me. Which is weird, right? Why care what people think? I literally make a living preaching how to be yourself and how to live YOUR life not according to anyone else. It's a strange dynamic. Sometimes it's even hard for me to comprehend, and to be honest, I really have no idea when or why this ever started. I'm sure somewhere along this screwed-up life I dealt with so much emotional abuse, bullying, and so on, that I'm scared to be made fun of, I'm scared to portray someone I'm not, and I'm scared to let people down.

This is obviously a work in progress. It's something that's taken years to marinate in my brain and will take even more years to truly figure out. But please know that if you, too, suffer from this, you are not alone. If we ever meet in person, please let me know that you, too, suffer from similar anxiety strains, and I promise you I will hug you until you want me to let go.

I say this a lot, but I never had anything or anyone to turn to for help with scenarios like this. This isn't something you can just type into Google or look up on YouTube and find people sincerely talking about it. Let this be your safe haven. Let this be your place. Because that is what I'm using it for. Hearing your stories helps me more than I think I help you. So always, ALWAYS know that you are not alone. But with that said, if you come ringing my doorbell, just know I will not answer!

Love, your fellow hermit,

Megan

The Engagement Story

January 3rd, 2020

Story time!

Five years ago I traveled back to New York City for the first time since I had visited originally in high school, which was in May 2006. I had longed to go back to the city that never sleeps because of the pull it had on me. I had only dreamed of going there when I was young, seeing the city lights, the giant buildings—it was all just a dream to me until our band and choir trip in 2006. Ten years after that, I made the choice to return, traveling solo.

I was in a rut. A major depressive rut. I felt incredibly used and abused and didn't know what to do. I think deep down I knew I was being mistreated, yet I couldn't say it out loud. Traveling was always a passion of mine, but at the time I hadn't done much of it, especially not alone. It was February of 2015. It was negative seven degrees in New York City that day I arrived. I cried while flying over the city in the plane because I was finally back to the city that had my heart. My job was draining, my relationship was failing, and I wanted more out of life but couldn't find it. Traveling alone, to me, sounded like it could be very inspiring, so that is what I did.

I booked the trip on a whim, asked for the time off from my boss, and left about five days later. During the week leading up to this my ex and I had a huge fight. I don't remember exactly what it was about, to be honest, but I remember thinking if I didn't get my shit together, I was going to leave. But leaving was something I knew I couldn't do either, so I felt entirely stuck. I remember feeling the desire to get married, but I knew he would never go for it from previous conversations we'd had at this time. This man couldn't settle down, but for some reason I made it a mission to prove him wrong time and time again. I'm assuming the fight we had previous to this trip probably had something to do with that, but I'm sure it dealt with a lot of other issues we had at that time too. Wanting to be married, his cheating coming back into play, the abortion (this was two months before I would have given birth, so as you can see I was not in a good mindset and needed a big restart to life). Nonetheless, this trip was very needed, if only for me to find myself for a few short days and regain something back in my life. I wasn't sure what that "something" was at the time, but I desperately needed it.

The night before I left for my flight, I wrote him a letter. It was a very long letter about what he meant to me, why I needed to do what I was doing, and how he truly was the love of my life. So whether he believed it or not, I was fighting for him. I shouldn't have been, but I was. You see, I always thought I could change him. I believed I could soften him. I believed I could make him believe in love for once, even though at this point we had already been together for about three years. I believed deep down that I could make him stop being a womanizer, settle down, and have a happy-go-lucky life with me. I became fixated on helping him come to the realization of a normal life instead of helping myself, so in turn, I lost myself entirely. Every little thing he did wrong, I was always standing behind him knowing that someday he would change and I was going to help him, because if I didn't help him, who would? And for some stupid reason, I really thought it was possible. (Note to self: it's not possible to change someone this far gone. Read that again.)

I arrived in New York City and spent the day walking around in negative seven degree weather without a care in the world. I made a promise to myself that when I arrived, I was going to shut my phone off. I wanted that time to myself, and I wanted no distractions. But also, part of me didn't want to see his response to my letter. I cried seeing those buildings once again. I cried knowing I got myself back to the place where I last was happy, ten years prior. I cried because that city had done SO much for little ol' me, and here I was again. I cried because I was proud of myself for once for doing something I wanted to do, and something for me for once! It was such a great experience, and to this day I tell people it was my most memorable trip.

Backtrack. I haven't told you what was at the end of the letter I wrote. It was that I wasn't sure I was coming home. Obviously, I knew

I couldn't afford to live in New York. Not alone, and probably not ever. But still I thought maybe that would be a good way to show him I was truly serious about us. This fight we had the week prior, and every other fight we'd had up until then, I was still here, and I was here to stay, but I knew deep down that I didn't want to come home. New York was my happy place, and even if I could only spend a few days there, I was going to milk that for all it was worth, because after that weekend, I knew I'd have to return home. Return back to the hell I was living, the day-to-day life that I hated so much, with a man who didn't love me and forcing a relationship I knew wouldn't work.

So here I was, day two in New York. I was doing some sightseeing, and for some weird reason I had the urge to turn my phone on. Nothing showed up from him. I thought he must have gotten the letter, right? For sure he read it, right? I decided to reach out to him just to make sure. Heck, maybe he hadn't seen it. He responded that he did read it and wanted to talk more when I got home.

Day three in New York was my last day before I returned home. I had purchased tickets to see a musical with my favorite Broadway singer, Idina Menzel. The musical was called *If/Then*. I knew very little about it, but obviously I had to see it while it was still showing on Broadway. It was about life and what you'd do "if" this happened, and "then" what would happen next. The butterfly effect in a sense. It really had a lot to do with my life at that moment and what I had been going through and contemplating, so it seemed very fitting. I didn't have much planned for this day, other than the musical that night, but I was up all night thinking about this dang letter I wrote and contemplating what to do moving forward. Why this next thing popped into my mind, I still have no idea, but it sounded like an amazing idea at the time, and I for some reason thought it would help our relationship. I wanted to buy a ring and propose when I returned home. Maybe deep down I thought this would open him up more. Maybe then he would see how serious I was. Maybe then he would stop the shit he was putting me through and actually WANT what I was giving him. SO SO SO stupid, but it's what was running through my head at that moment.

So I woke up the next day, took a walk through Central Park, and contemplated this move I wanted to attempt. I was pretty poor at the time, so this was not really an easy task for me, on top of not even knowing where to go or where to look. The obvious jumped into my mind: Tiffany's. Plus, it would be cool to walk through the store, right? So I walked to THE Tiffany's of all Tiffany's—Fifth Avenue, New York City. The shopping mecca of all shopping. And expensive shopping at that. I should have known I didn't belong in a store like that when I had to be escorted into the elevator by a private doorman just to go from floor to floor! When I got to the floor with men's jewelry, I quickly was knocked back into reality when a simple black tungsten band was over $2,500. So I left. Back to the drawing board. I went to a couple pawn shops just to see what they had to offer, but I didn't find much I liked. I looked up a Kay's Jeweler on my phone and found one like twenty blocks away. It was a nice day out—cold, but the sun was shining—so I thought, Why not? I made the hike to the store, found a ring, and told the store clerk that I would be back in a bit to purchase it. Really, I just wanted a little more time to think about it, so I went to grab some lunch.

At this point, my mind was made up. I was going to ask him to marry me. I couldn't afford this, but I wanted it. I wanted this cool moment of me proposing to him, us crying and telling each other how much we loved one another, and finally being this happy couple that everyone saw us as on the outside. I guess, maybe, that's just the hopeless romantic in me. So, I went back a few hours later and bought the ring. I headed home the next day, extremely worried and scared, but a part of me was excited. Excited that finally the cheating would stop, excited that he finally could see just how much I loved him, excited that his parents could help us plan a wedding, and excited to tell my parents this part of our love story! But that was very short lived.

Upon getting home that night, he sat me down on the couch to talk about the letter I wrote him. I honestly don't really remember much of what was said or talked about that night, because I just kept running over what I wanted to say in my head and figuring out precisely when to pull the ring box out that was hiding in my sleeve. Eventually, he made me cry. And not in a good way. I was getting emotional and a little frustrated, so I said something along the lines of wanting this relationship to work because I loved him so much, and I knew he loved me too, even with our problems... and then... "Will you marry me?" It came out. I pulled the ring box out and handed him the box. He laughed like he thought I was joking, until he opened it. I remember he sat there looking at it for awhile, and I really didn't know how to read him in that moment. He eventually started crying, and he said yes! But the next words out of his mouth left me uneasy. "Yes, I will marry you, but let's not tell anyone yet." I guess maybe I thought he was kidding. Maybe I thought he meant not until the weekend or something. I didn't realize what he really meant until later on.

That next morning on my way to work, I called my mom, I called my dad, I called my grandma, and I told all of my coworkers. I came home to tell him how happy everyone was, and he said, "I thought we weren't going to tell anyone?" Now I was confused. Why wouldn't you want to share this awesome news? Why wouldn't you want to scream to the world you're engaged? I guess men and women are different in that sense.

Weeks went by, then months. He told me not to put anything up on Facebook and not to tell anyone else. I remember asking him why he hadn't told his parents yet, and he just said he would in time, but it wasn't the right time yet. Months went by, and I eventually sat him down and asked him why we couldn't tell anyone our news, and if we waited too much longer, we'd have no time to plan anything. "No time to plan anything?" he yelled. "We have our whole lives to plan this!" I remember thinking, *OK, no we don't!* Weddings take some serious time to plan. Picking out a day, then finding a venue that works for that day, and I wanted a fall wedding at the time, and fall was fast approaching. I eventually stopped the argument because it wasn't getting anywhere, but what really hurt me the most was him basically hiding this. Why did he want to hide this? Why did he want to hide me? This was supposed to be a happy time in our lives, and it was incredibly depressing!

More months went by. It was now November, and I started telling him I wanted to get this all figured out so we could get a venue booked for the following fall. He told me that we were NOT having a fall wedding, because that would be in less than a year, and we'd have no time to save or prep. UMMM, HELLO! THAT'S WHY I WANTED TO START PLANNING IN FEBRUARY! YOU KNOW, WHEN WE GOT ENGAGED? And let it be known, he still hadn't told anyone about the engagement. I started thinking maybe he had some master plan to actually buy me an engagement ring for Christmas, so I started throwing him ideas. I even won a prize for one thousand dollars off an engagement ring from a local jeweler, but that didn't seem to faze him. So Christmas came and went, and nothing landed on my finger. He kept telling me it was too expensive, and he wasn't going to purchase anything large like that right now. I kept reminding him I not only had a gift card for one thousand dollars toward an engagement ring, but also the local jewelers had a twelve-month, no-interest plan, so literally it wouldn't cost him anything to finance something. He did not approve. I even found out he purchased a six hundred dollar Batman Playstation console in the midst of all this and literally hid it from me in the basement after every time he'd play it. I caught on to that act pretty quickly and called him out on it, but he showed no remorse. Then we hit February, the one-year mark. We had been engaged for a year, and still no one but my family and coworkers knew about it. Not a single one of his friends, not a single member of his family, none of his coworkers. It was truly like it never happened. He still told everyone I was his girlfriend. The word "fiancée" had yet to come out of his mouth.

That year (2016) we decided to go to New York City once again, but this time for his birthday. We had a big fight leading up to this trip about the engagement, and at this point I was so frustrated with the situation that I didn't even know if I wanted to be married anymore. It had been over a year and we still hadn't told anyone or picked a date, he never wore the ring, he didn't get me a ring, NOTHING. He told me in the midst of this fight that HE wanted to be the one to ask me to marry him; he didn't want people to know I asked him. Stupid excuse, but clearly he couldn't have that on his ego, right? He told me he had planned to get a ring and do it while we were in New York so that we would have this awesome surprise when we came home. OK, fair enough. Well, the New York trip came and went. No ring.

At this point, I was pretty much done. It was now clear to me he didn't want this to happen. So another fight erupted. We ended up in a screaming match, which resulted in me throwing my phone at him in a frustrated crying fit. He told me he didn't want to marry me and that he was never going to change, and I should just move on. I threw my phone at him, cried on the staircase for an hour, and tried sleeping on the couch. That should have been my cue to leave once and for all, but I was young and dumb and STILL thought I could change him. He eventually came out to console me, saying he was sorry, and he knew what he was doing was shitty, and he felt bad about it. He said I was right, this shouldn't have been prolonged as long as it had been, and this weekend we would go look at rings. So that is exactly what we did, finally. And that next week we announced our engagement.

I was happy, I admit it. I finally felt loved! I finally felt like things were falling into place! I finally knew everything I did leading up to this was for this reason, and it just felt so perfect!

In 2017 we were married. At the end of 2018 I walked out on our marriage and filed for a divorce.

The Packer's Game

January 4th, 2020

I've gotten to a point with these blogs where I've pretty much said all of my secrets. Now it's just a matter of digging deeper into the stories to show fellow victims how abusers truly work.

Remember the abortion story? Of course you do; how could you forget? I'm sure you all read it and became as disgusted as I did while typing it all out. It's almost as if I relive it little by little as details arise, which normally would hurt me. However this time I feel it's a relief. It's finally a relief because I feel I can finally talk about it and help others out with similar situations. It's not always an easy topic for me, because the majority of people judge me INSTANTLY based on the words alone, forgetting there is a person behind the story that was truly hurt by it. So be it.

Tuesday, August 6th, 2013, was the appointment date. August 14th was my birthday. Three days after the appointment and procedure, my ex-husband left to head to Indianapolis for a drumline competition, leaving me helpless. I was still in physical pain from going through labor, I was still heavily bleeding, and I was not in a good mental mindset, as you can imagine. He left me for five days alone. I begged him to stay, but this was more important than his girlfriend who just had labor pains and contractions for ten hours, plus bled out what seemed like a lifetime's supply of blood and tissue, AND was emotionally unstable from going through such an experience. Thoughts of suicide ran through my mind as he left. I didn't want to live. I was sad, embarrassed, and hurt. This man I was with truly disgusted me. How someone could just leave a person like that, days after a procedure, I will never understand.

When he returned home, late the night of the 11th, he still showed no remorse. I even remember texting him while he was gone telling him I was still in a lot of pain and wasn't sure if it was normal or not, and I'd really like him to come home just in case I needed to be brought to the hospital. He said, "You'll be fine." He came home that night, not asking how I was doing, not consoling me, nothing. He went right to the couch and said he wanted to relax after a busy weekend.

August 14th was my birthday. I had purchased tickets to the pre-season Packers game here in town. I have always been a huge Packers fan, and although I'd lived in Packer country for about four years, I had yet to go to a game. The team coming through town was super exciting to me, although with everything going on, I felt less than thrilled to be going. I didn't even want to go, let alone with him, but I felt a little better as the days went by. I was really embarrassed to go to the game, honestly. I had not showered in over a week, the last thing I wanted to do was my makeup, I was sick to my stomach, the thought of food disgusted me, and I was still bleeding heavily. I had to wear extra-large pads to help with the blood, as, for obvious reasons, tampons were a no-go for something like this. It was just embarrassing. I felt ugly. I felt gross. I didn't want to be out in public.

That day I woke up, and he told me he wanted to bring me out to eat to somewhere I had never gone before. We ended up getting ready to go, and I felt somewhat excited again because for once he was giving me some attention. He brought me out for sushi, and at this point in my life I had never eaten it but had always wanted to try it. He told me to get whatever I wanted, his treat! He bought dinner and drinks, and we headed to the Packers game where he also wined and dined me some more, as if nothing had ever happened.

Leaving the game, I was happy with him. I felt connected again with him. But something felt weird. Something was missing. Did he somehow just FORGET everything I had just been through? Was he purposely ignoring the elephant in the room? No. He was buying his guilt. He knew if he did something nice, I would forget about the disaster that had just gone down. Sadly, I didn't forget, but it was a nice way to redirect the attention, I suppose.

You see, when abusers abuse, they will deflect the abuse any way they can. This particular instance, a little wine and dine never hurt anyone, so he played that card quite well. This tactic happened so often in our relationship, it's sad that I didn't realize it sooner. He would justify everything with "I love you so much, let's go out to dinner!" or "I'll take care of you!" That was a big one for him—"I'll take care of you"—even though he never really cared to take care of me. It's like he knew the right words to flip a switch in my brain to love him again, and I was too young and stupid to catch on. This behavior never really stopped; it only got worse.

Advice From Friends

January 5th, 2020

Do you ever wonder what life would be like if you had just sat your ass down and listened to your friends' advice? I do. Life would have been a hell of a lot easier, wouldn't it? But something I wholeheartedly believe is that YOU have to make the decisions in your life. No matter how many people tell you something is a bad idea or isn't going to work, YOU have to be the one to consciously figure that out, and until then, things will not change.

So many simple examples run through my head with this. It's hard for me to take my own advice even though I've known this for a long time. I have a friend who will go nameless for the time being. She was dating a guy who really had no interest in her other than sex. She knew it. I knew it. Her friends and family knew it. She called me numerous times to vent about her situation but she found herself still lying in his bed at night. No matter how many of us told her it was a bad idea and that what he was doing to her was not OK, SHE had to figure that out on her own. Another occurrence: a friend of mine got into some hard drugs. She probably knew deep down this wasn't such a good idea, but she continued to do it anyway. No matter how many of us begged her to stop, she didn't stop until one day she was arrested and thrown into jail. It took something pretty significant for her to say out loud that she needed help, and from there on out, after SHE made that conscious decision, she was done. I couldn't help her for years before that, and neither could her parents, her boyfriend, or the rest of her friends, but once she figured it out, everything changed.

That same concept applied to myself. There were many red flags that I ignored, and so many people I ignored right along with them. Here and there I had a few people tell me, family 105my attention on a cruise we went on together. I didn't see it. I didn't WANT to see it. People didn't see our reality! Or did they? Did they see what I couldn't all this time? Yes. Yes, they did.

After the split, some of his friends told me how proud they were that I up and left such a toxic relationship. HIS VERY OWN FRIENDS! They could see from the get-go that this was just not a healthy pair, and it was incredibly interesting to hear their side of things once they came out and talked to me. Most said they saw it right away—the emotional abuse he put me through, him treating me terribly in public, and more. Most knew it right away, some figured it out eventually, but the majority of people who reached out after we split up told me it wasn't their place to open their mouth at the time. I guess that's fair.

It's reassuring to hear such comments after you walk out on someone, confused as hell, wondering if this is the right thing to do or the wrong thing to do. You feel embarrassed because you don't want people to judge you based on months married, you don't want people to see the real side of this—at least, not yet. It's hard! And when people start coming forth with the truth that THEY saw with their own eyes, it's reassuring because suddenly you know you did the right thing. Especially when those people are acquaintances of said abuser.

My point is that no matter how many people tell you something is wrong, YOU have to be the one to make that decision. And only then will you come to terms with it. You could have nine hundred people tell you not to do something, but until YOU decide not to do it, nothing is going to stop. So sit yourself down and really ask yourself if it is worth it. If it is worth the heartache, the stress, the abuse, whatever the case may be. This could be a relationship, a marriage, a friendship, something to do with a family member, maybe even your job, drinking alcohol, drugs, sex, addiction in general—WHATEVER THE CASE MAY BE! And maybe it's as simple as you just making the decision to buy a new car and no one else agrees! Catch my drift? Once you figure it out for yourself, you'll figure out the direction you need to go. Until then, nothing will change. So if you're reading this and constantly finding yourself saying "She's right," I beg you to ask that question deep down to yourself. Life is so hard, but happiness shouldn't have to be. Find your happy. Don't let ANYONE take that away from you.

Kind regards,

Megan

I'm Sorry I'm Never Good Enough, But I Really Do Try

January 9th, 2020

Lately I've been struggling with something. It's something that I dealt with in my past for a very long time that has, for some stupid reason, resurfaced. My life has drastically changed in the past fourteen months. Leaving a toxic relationship was something I never thought I'd have to do, but lo and behold, I suffered way too much abuse to stay.

I never felt good enough in my previous relationship. I was always being compared to other people, other scenarios, told I wasn't what he wanted, what he needed. Years of that takes a toll on a person, and sadly, those past feelings are once again resurfacing. I don't know if it's just memories getting brought back up, memories that I wish I could forget, or maybe part of the PTSD I suffer due to my ex-husband's lack of empathy, or maybe it's simply because I'm in another serious relationship and I'm just terrified. Whatever the case may be, I'm struggling.

The thoughts of never feeling good enough are truly enough to break a person down mentally and physically. Whenever my ex and I would go to the mall, he'd make sure to point out the Victoria's Secret models in the windows of the store. When we'd watch movies together, he'd always point out whether or not someone was attractive. He'd ask me, "Why don't you do that?" when something would happen in a movie, or in front of us at, say, a baseball game. He pointed out my flaws CONSTANTLY in such a twisted way that you couldn't tell if he was joking or serious. He picked on me numerous times for being gay. He knew the words to break me down and used them often. He, on numerous occasions, asked why I didn't dress certain ways, act certain ways, why I didn't like sex like most people do. He told me I wasn't normal for the feelings I had toward sex, toward pornography. He had opinions on clothing or shoes I'd wear that I felt comfortable in but didn't really fit his taste, and let's not forget the fact that he cheated on me multiple times with multiple women, saving photos of them in his phone for him to masturbate to later, making me feel like the ugliest woman on the planet when I found out. Stupid me, thinking I was good enough, right? Stupid me for being ME and not trying to act like every other fake female out there. Stupid me for understanding individuality rather than conforming to social norms. Everything I did was wrong to him. Everything I liked or didn't like was wrong to him. It made me feel completely worthless, unattractive, and just never good enough on an emotional or physical level. So what did I do? I shut down and let the abuse continue.

People have asked me numerous times, back when I was still with him and after I had left, why I stayed with him if I had those types of feelings. My answer: because I didn't feel good enough for anyone after that. When someone brings your self-esteem down so low, picking apart your physical traits, your personality traits, making fun of you for certain things, and flat-out calling you NOT normal for your feelings, you truly begin questioning your sanity. Sure, it's easy for me now to stand up for myself, but back then when it's all I knew, he knew he had me trapped in that sense. A true narcissist will do this to you. They will break you down until nothing else is left, because at that point they know they have you trapped. They know you'll never leave because they know you won't feel good enough for anyone else out there. Maybe that's why the cheating continued. He knew he could get away with it because where was this broken individual going to run? He owned me. He controlled me. He spoke for me. He manipulated me. This, my friends, is abuse.

So recently I've still been struggling with this. Like it's resurfacing. I still don't feel like I am good enough for anyone. I have so many shitty quirks about me that aren't exactly fun to deal with. I have massive PTSD from being cheated on and abused in previous relationships. I have CONSTANT anxiety, thinking every person I come in contact with is going to treat me just as others did in the past, and because of that, I refuse to get close to anyone. I feel like I can never please anyone on a physical level because my sex drive is nonexistent some days due to my past with sexual abuse, and my past with my ex-husband making me feel completely abnormal for the thoughts I had regarding sex. I've actually never had a super high sex drive; thank the person who raped me when I was seventeen for that one. But my ex-husband couldn't understand that. He never had an ounce of empathy for my past regarding sexual abuse. He constantly told me, "You are not normal for not liking sex!" "Do you know how unhealthy it is that you don't want to have sex with your husband?" "Do you realize I've resorted to touching myself every morning, feeling like an old pervert, because my wife won't have sex with me? Do you know how that makes ME feel, Megan?" He made me feel crazy. He made me feel so guilty. But, god damnit, why couldn't I have feelings in this matter? Or are a woman's feelings invalid in times like this? To him, they were. So he resorted to porn and cheating. I constantly felt betrayed. I constantly felt ugly. I constantly felt worthless. Seeing him watch porn all day and hearing him in the bathroom every morning really got to me, and to this day it is one of my biggest triggers with my PTSD. And these triggers follow me now, making my life a living hell, making this new relationship of mine so, so hard, and making me still just constantly feel worthless.

You see, he ripped that part away from me, and I'm not so sure I can ever fully get that back. That "uniqueness" you have that you love about yourself, those parts of you that make someone fall in love with you. He ripped that away from me almost ten years ago when we first started dating, when he chose to cheat on me with MULTIPLE women, multiple times. But dumbass me still stayed. And then I moved in with him. I was then stuck. I stayed because he was all I knew. He was what, supposedly, made me happy. Even with him treating me so badly and making me feel like a terrible person on a daily basis, that was love to me. He was the best, and even though maybe deep down I knew I deserved better, I told myself I wouldn't ever find better because I didn't deserve better. It's one of the many things he stole from me. My uniqueness. My individuality. I will say, it's definitely shaped me into who I am today, that is with 100 percent certainty, but I wish I could feel good about myself sometimes. I wish I could feel worth it to some people. I wish I could feel like I am enough and be enough for everyone. That's one thing I haven't been able to accomplish yet. I found my happiness, I found my truth, but yet the PTSD from this fucked-up marriage is still there to haunt me, and part of that PTSD is feeling like I'm not good enough. What I have learned, though, and I suppose this is the silver lining here, is that if you're lucky enough to be different, you shouldn't ever change. I have come to the realization that I am a VERY different individual. I think I'm different than most, I dress different than most, I speak different than most... I AM different than most. But when it comes to being enough for someone, it is a CONSTANT battle in my head.

I hate to even write about this because it's going to make it seem like I'm not happy right now. Let me make something very clear: I have never been this happy in life—like, EVER. The man I am with treats me so good, you guys. SO GOOD. I don't even know how I deserve it most days. But, in terms of never feeling good enough, I'm constantly asking myself why I can't do more. Why I can't provide more than I do. Why I can't be someone's "perfect person." Although we know "perfect" doesn't exist, I guess I believe that we should still try to be the best we can be, right? I'm so sorry for anyone else who deals with this. I'm so sorry for anyone currently dealing with this. It's a hard pill to swallow, knowing that you probably will always have these feelings in the back of your head, and we all have that one person to thank for it. So for now, let's all throw out a big FUCK YOU to those who hurt us. Those who ripped a part of us away, a part of us we won't ever get back. FUCK YOU to those who degraded us and made us feel like the lowest people on earth. It's because of YOU that we are like this. And what YOU don't realize, is although we got away from you, and you can live your life happily ever after, we are stuck with the everlasting effects of this trauma. So let's all come together as men and women and just remember we ARE worth it. Even if it's hard to remember some days. Know your worth, then add tax. Then add shipping and handling, and labor too!

Love you guys!

Megan

Children

January 12th, 2020

It's incredibly hard for me to look at my friends and family who are having children recently. I'm at that stage in my life where "baby fever" is a real thing, and at almost thirty-two years old, I have been feeling as if something is missing in my life.

About six months ago, I stopped at a local Starbucks to grab some coffee and have a "date day" with myself to get my mind off of some things. It was nice out, so I sat outside and people watched, one of my favorite things to do. A mother with her three-year-old daughter came up and asked if it was OK if they sat next to me. There was only that one table left open outside, and of course I said yes. It almost seemed as if the mother thought her daughter would be a nuisance to me, so she had to ask permission to sit down just in case. I couldn't help but stare at them for the next twenty or so minutes. The mother was around my age, and the daughter was this cute three-year-old with a brightly colored dress on. She was eating her fruit from Starbucks while her mom sipped her coffee. They had a cute relationship. The daughter and her mom had these cute little conversations that made me giggle every time the little girl opened her mouth. She eventually finished her grapes and wanted to play. The mother stated she could play right next to her in the grass, but not to go any further than that. You could tell this mom just wanted a date day for herself too. Maybe it was her day off work, or maybe she was a stay-at-home mom and really just thought the weather was nice enough to go outside for a bit. The little girl danced and spun around in circles, making her dress all poofy. Every time someone walked out of the building, the little girl did another spin to show it off. I couldn't help but sit there with a kind of jealousy hanging over my head. I was stripped away from that gift in life—children—and I thought to myself how I really, truly, would have been a good mom despite the shitty circumstances, but we'd never know because of what he did to me.

When I see children out and about, it's an immediate reflex in my head that makes me wonder how I would be as a mom. I know things happen for a reason, but to this day I still wonder why I had to suffer such an extreme loss. Maybe that's why this void seems to be very present in my life. Maybe that's why I seem to have more "baby fever" than others lately. I'm at that age where I should have a child, but I'm pained to say I don't. I want children, but I was stripped of that privilege, and I'm not so sure I'll ever have that opportunity again.

It's a sad realization every April, when my child's birthday would be happening. I count the years every year, thinking to myself how old they would have been. In April 2020, they would have turned six. It's a little crazy to imagine life with a six-year-old, but sadly, they aren't here.

I continue to ponder what it would be like to have a child. I'm sure someday it will happen when the timing is right, but the loss that I still feel is incredibly hard. It's devastating. It's something that time won't ever truly heal. I still cry over it every once in awhile, although it's easy for me to talk about now. It wasn't easy for awhile. I purchased a couple things to help the grieving process, one of which still sits in my house today. It's a willow tree figurine of a female holding a child. My mom got it for me after it all happened. Though at the time she thought it was a miscarriage, she now knows the truth after reading this book.

The figurine sat in our house for a few days before my ex noticed what it was. After he noticed it, he hid it behind the TV, as if I wouldn't notice. I brought it up one day and asked why he moved it. He first lied to me, telling me it wasn't him, although I knew the truth. Eventually he said he moved it because it was stupid to have in the house, and a piece of wood wouldn't heal me from anything. Come to find out later, he hid it because he had friends over that night and didn't want anyone to see what he had done to me or have anyone question why Megan was mourning the loss of a child. I told him it was a way of coping for me, to have something I can look at and remember, since I had no ultrasound photos or anything. He told me that was the stupidest thing he'd ever heard, and I needed to find other ways to cope. I cried and told him I was leaving the figurine out, whether he liked it or not, but he made me move it to another shelf.

The loss of my child was something I hope I never have to experience ever again, and I do truly hope that one day I can have a child with a man who gives a fuck. A father who wants his child just as much as I do. A father who adores me and the baby. Someday I'll be able to have that moment in the doctor's office where we hear the heartbeat together and see their little fingers and toes on the ultrasound screen. Someday I'll be able to find out if it's a girl or a boy with my partner, and cry tears of joy when they are born. Until then, I watch others become happy mothers and wonder why on earth someone thought it was OK to take away motherhood from someone and think everything was OK.

Girl 1

January 13th, 2020

It was the fall of 2012. I had just gotten home that past week from making the trip to St. Louis. I went down there once or twice a month via the Amtrak train since I was, at the time, living in Milwaukee, Wisconsin. It was pretty inexpensive to travel by train, and I just slept most of the time, so it was an easy ride. I remember that it was still warm enough out to wear a tank top to bed, but cold enough out that dew on the grass felt cold if touched. These types of details I remember very vividly. I had just gotten home from a great weekend with my ex, but put a few days in between us and a Friday one-night stand, and there you have it.

I don't know what part of "long-distance relationship" sounded appealing to me at the time we started dating, but we tried to make it work. Or at least I did. The past few weeks leading up to this I noticed he was getting tagged in photos with another girl a lot. We will call her "T." As much as I want to throw him under the bus for everything he did to me and other women in his life, I don't believe in harassment, nor do I believe in bullying. So, as you can see throughout my writings, I have yet to call him by name, and to follow suit, I will not use anyone else's names in the matter to further hurt anyone. T tagged photos of the two of them at bars, baseball games, and random parking garages. It seemed weird, but they were hanging out together a lot. There was another girl that also was tagging a ton of photos and status updates with him around this time period, but we'll talk about her another time. On this random Friday night, the tags were strange. Baseball games, bars... what was he doing with her? I asked him numerous times leading up to this particular day who those girls were, but he always assured me I had nothing to worry about. So, as any trusting person will do, I trusted him. But this particular night was different. I had a VERY strong intuition something was wrong. I don't remember having a panic attack before this in my life, until this very moment. I was hyperventilating, packing my bag for some reason to go find him, I could not stop crying, shaking uncontrollably once I started to piece it all together—it was a full-fledged panic attack.

I remember watching TV that night while scrolling through my phone and seeing statuses of them pop up and then be instantly deleted, as if he didn't want to be tagged in them. I called him. No answer. I called him again. No answer. I called him one more time. Straight to voice mail. I received a text message saying, "What do you want? I'm at a bar, it's loud and I cannot answer." I told him he needs to call me right now because I need to know what the fuck is going on! But he never called. I continued to be a psycho and call nine hundred more times, thinking eventually he will get tired of this and answer. I kept texting him saying I was freaking out, I was crying, I was in full-on panic attack mode, and he didn't respond. So, I told myself FUCK IT, I'm going to drive the eight hours and see what he's really up to. I kept calling him but got no answer. I texted him telling him I was on my way. He finally decided to text me back, telling me not to come, it wasn't worth it. I knew something was happening, though, and I was on a mission to prove it. I got to the Chicago area around midnight, and he randomly texted me, "Please turn around." I said, "Too late, I'm already in Chicago." He said, "Good, then you aren't even halfway and you can still turn back." Mind you, he had yet to answer any of my phone calls. I told him, "I will be there around 5 a.m." He responded, "I have to work in the morning, so if you could get a hotel that would be good." Why on earth I didn't see that as a red flag is BEYOND me! I kept telling myself the entire car ride there that I KNEW what he was doing, and no matter what he told me, he was NOT going to change my mind. I got to a cheap hotel outside of St. Louis, slept for like three hours and texted him as soon as I woke up. He asked if I really came down there. I responded, "Yes." He said he had a wedding to go to that night, some casino south of Missouri along the river. I said something along the lines of, "I drove eight hours to see you, you didn't mention anything about a wedding. Can I come with you? I'll go shopping and get some nice clothes now." He told me, "No, I already RSVP'd, and it was for only one person." OK, fair enough. So I wasted an entire day bored out of my mind because he was at work, and then he went to this so called "wedding."

I finally got a text that night around midnight saying he would be home in about an hour and if I wanted to stop by, I could. Of course I did, but in the back of my head I knew he wasn't at the wedding, I knew he didn't want me at his house, I knew there was someone there, I just couldn't prove it. I wanted to show up earlier just to watch her walk out his door, but the thought of "knowing" and "seeing" him do this to me was too much confrontation for me to handle at that moment, and I guess I told myself that maybe it was better not to find out this way. So I drove to his house, parked in a parking lot, and waited for him to drive up. I sat there staring at his garage for about twenty minutes but never saw his car pull up. I then received a text saying he was home. Weird, since I had never seen him come home, but you know, I was clearly very young and very naive. I walked to the apartment through grass that seemed to be a foot tall, soaking wet in dew from being so late at night, and my feet were only in flip flops so it was FREEZING. I had gone shopping that day to pass the time and ended up getting these cute little PJs, so I wore them to show him. I knocked on his door, and he was in his boxers. Clearly he had been home for awhile. This proved that theory. I sat my stuff down, and he instantly started getting frisky with me. Hands all up and down me, kissing my neck, leading me to the bedroom. I didn't even get a "hello." He only wanted sex. The second I kissed him, I could smell another girl. I could instantly tell he had given oral sex to someone right before I had arrived. I'm not fucking stupid, but he clearly thought I was. I still couldn't get myself to ask him what that was all about, though, so I ended up sleeping with him anyway, like the young, dumb, broad I was.

The next morning we woke up, and he told me he had a family BBQ to be at. I remember telling him, "Dang, you have a lot of stuff going on this weekend that you failed to mention," and he just laughed like it was no big deal. He walked me out of his apartment, and I looked him in the eyes and said, "Are we OK?" He smiled and said, "I don't know, are we?" while kissing me once more. In my head, I wanted to ask him a hundred questions, but my mouth simply just said "yes" instead. I asked him if he wanted me to come to his family BBQ with him so we could spend a bit more time together before I headed back the eight hours to Milwaukee. He told me no, and that was that.

T and him had a lot of one-night affairs. And after a few years of the cheating, I eventually contacted her about it to give myself a clear conscious. She said she asked him multiple times about me, but he told her I was just a friend who wouldn't leave him alone. Real cool, right? They slept together off and on the entire first year we were dating, and I was too stupid to say anything, because I was scared. He had a reign over me unlike anything I'd ever felt before. I felt I'd be punished if I brought up the truth because any time I'd ask, he would get so defensive that it scared me. So I learned to keep my mouth shut most of the time, even though I knew what was going on.

I'd come over to his house other times and see receipts on his desk for two people eating at Denny's, and I'd chalk it up to him and his mom on a lunch date. I caught him with another girl the night before I came down there a different time, and he took all the bed sheets off the bed saying they stunk, and he didn't want me to smell that he hadn't washed them in so long. Upon assessing his laundry basket, I saw there were bodily fluids on them. And yes, I smelled them, I know what sex juices are—again, I'm not stupid. Little things like this added up for a very long time, but I was too dumb to bring it to his attention, so I just allowed the cheating to continue.

Years later, I realized there was no casino along the river south of St. Louis. He never went to a "wedding" that day. Also, come to find out, there was no family BBQ that next morning.

The Silence Of Spousal Abuse

January 14th, 2020

Each day after I walked out on my ex-husband I became more and more open about my secrets, and each day it became easier. And the more it came out, the easier it became to uncover the truth.

I honestly thought for awhile, right after I left, that I was still to blame. I was at fault for everything he did to me. I couldn't open up like I wanted, but I knew my story had to be told. I also knew I wouldn't ever get what I wanted out of leaving this relationship if I didn't take some time to myself for a bit. I needed to find the Megan I once was, even just to regain an ounce of that part of me back. It was hard. INCREDIBLY hard. So many tears were shed, so many words were screamed, so many thoughts were happening in my head pulling me in nineteen different directions. Some days I was at peace with leaving, knowing I was ready to conquer the world, but other days I lay in bed for forty-eight hours, not wanting to wake up. I wasn't suicidal, but I also didn't want to face reality for awhile. I was scared to live on my own, pay my own bills, take care of my pets alone, live by myself. Most of all, I was scared that I was going to be an embarrassment to my family. I took to writing. I didn't have this blog right away, but I wrote a lot of journal entries, and I posted a lot of long-winded posts on Facebook. Eventually I had someone tell me I was good at writing, so I let it all out for anyone who wanted to listen. Slowly the secrets started coming out. Slowly I was beginning to realize that this was my new reality, and I needed to man up and talk about it. Once I started opening up little by little, it became easier to uncover the truth to people, and people latched on. I took a lot of pride in standing up for myself, figuring out my life on my own, and walking out of an abusive marriage. I was proud of that. And I wanted other people to get to that point in their lives too.

For the first few months, I didn't even tell anyone I moved out. I think it may have been March before even my family knew that I had gotten my own house. But by this time, I had come to the realization that this was my new life, and I wasn't ashamed anymore. At that moment, I started talking about it and opening up little by little.

I have so many blogs that haven't been published, so many words that I want to say, but I'm not there yet. There are things I cannot talk about yet because it's too hard for me to get them on paper. There are things I want to say but fear people won't understand. I promise you, one day it'll all come out, and when that day comes, I want each and every one of you reading this to understand how hard this has been for me. You see, I own a platform that includes more than sixty thousand people via social media. Being open and honest has always been my "thing," but this was a very hard transition. It went from me being open and honest about life's struggles to suddenly me being open and honest about something that actually happened to me and that I was currently going through. It was partially healing for me, though, to come out and talk about this, because in doing so, I realized my readers saw what I couldn't see. My friends came forward with their thoughts on my ex-husband. His friends came forward telling me their stories of him and his past with women. Some of his own family even told me they were proud I left because they saw how he treated me. And when things started getting deeper, I realized I was helping people out there with similar situations.

After I released a recent blog, I received about forty messages from people within the hour saying how much it touched them. Which is ironic, because a few weeks ago I had a phone call with a psychic medium, and she told me I need to stop thinking I never help anyone, because I help many more people than I realize. These blogs may never reach millions of people, but the few hundreds that it does reach, and the ten or so people that they seem to really help is worth everything to me. I will always be your voice, I will always stand up for what's right, and even when it means breaking down my walls to let my deep, dark, past come to light, I'm willing to do that for you guys. Why? Because this is important to me. Domestic violence is abuse. Both mental and physical. I am going to talk about things some people warned me would be too much for some people. I am going to let out things I've never told a single soul. Be ready, because this "silence" has been broken, and I will not be silenced any longer. And remember, if you knew the whole story, you'd be proud of me.

Until next time,

Megan

The Wedding Night

January 15th, 2020

Ah, marriage. Something that every little girl thinks of the moment they start understanding what "love" is. We plan it in our heads down to the colors, the dress, the flowers, the cake. Every little detail. I remember in high school, we even had a class where we went over wedding details. Ironically, the same class that gives you the fake baby to take care of and hope and pray that it lives through the weekend. From the moment I asked him to marry me, I had everything planned in my head. What I wanted my dress to look like, the venue space, the time of year, the color scheme, the flowers—EVERYTHING. Sadly, I had to wait a year to start the planning process because of him keeping this a big, dark secret. But planning it was fun to me! That seemed to be the only fun part.

In short conversations in passing, I'd talk to him about what I wanted with our wedding, trying to get his input on what he wanted. He made it very known that some of my ideas were downright stupid, too expensive, and ugly. He didn't want a fall wedding because it was too soon, yet he waited over a year to tell anyone we were engaged, so we didn't have time to plan or save money. I told him I wanted to wear chucks under my wedding dress because that is literally the ONE clothing item that everyone knows me for. He told me it was going to be incredibly tacky. I mentioned to him once about wanting a pantsuit instead of a dress, and he brought up lesbian stereotypes, poking fun at my bisexuality and telling me everyone would think I'm gay. He had harsh opinions on food, photography, decor, but yet didn't want to pay much for anything. But, as with anything, everyone has a right to be picky, right? After all, this is a wedding, a once-in-a-lifetime thing that normally people tend to think about over the course of their lifetime.

Leading up to that day, I felt excitement but yet a ton of fear. My fear wasn't normal cold feet, yet I chalked it up as that. I told myself that feelings of not wanting to go through with this were normal—that that's what everyone says, anyway. That the whole "cold feet" analogy actually happens to a lot of people, and once you get through the day, you'll be good! I also dealt with a lot of stress planning this wedding because I did everything on my own. He didn't help me, his parents didn't help me, my parents couldn't help me because they were five hours away... it was rough, and I told myself it was because of all that stress that the cold feet started happening. I guess I didn't know it at the time, but those "cold feet" feelings were reality. I really didn't want to go through with this wedding, but I was too embarrassed and scared to admit that. I don't know of a single person who openly admits to NOT wanting to marry their fiancé. And had I come clean about that, I would have been entirely embarrassed. You see, my family paid for the majority of this wedding, and although we tried to do things as inexpensively as possible, it still was VERY costly. How was I supposed to tell them I didn't want to marry him anymore after they forked out tens of thousands of dollars? I couldn't. I couldn't EVER do that to them. So I kept reminding myself that this was all normal. Everyone goes through this, and it too will pass. Although the constant fighting and dishonesty was still happening in our relationship, I just kept telling myself that I can get through this... it's stress related... it'll all calm down... once we are married, everything will get better... he will get better... he will change.

When the weekend of the wedding came, I didn't feel the excitement that I wanted to. Everyone started to come to town, and I started getting excited to see all of my family in St. Louis for once, because no one ever really came to visit me other than my mom and my sisters. But that excitement definitely reigned over the excitement I still wasn't feeling for the actual "wedding" part of the weekend. It was almost as if I knew there was a wedding, but I knew it wasn't mine. Once again, I told myself this was all normal. Maybe I was so focused on making everyone else happy that I forgot that there was an actual bride and groom involved. I do think that at some point, with wedding planning, you eventually start planning a wedding for everyone else and not yourselves. Somehow, somewhere in the mix, people forget what a wedding truly is about, and they lose sight of the marital part of it. I was planning a party for basically our friends and families to meet, and that was about it.

On the wedding day, I felt detachment. I felt as if I were a part of the audience, watching someone else's love story. It was beautiful, don't get me wrong, but it felt incredibly forced and written, like a damn Hallmark movie. The vows were beautiful, but they felt forced. The scenery was beyond incredible, but it felt like a movie set. And everything that anyone did felt like it was all made up. I felt people could sense my hesitation on a lot of things, but of course I will never ask them to find out the truth of that. I felt as if it was some kind of paid acting gig, honestly. You show up, look pretty, do your thing, and be done with it. To be honest, I didn't even have a good time. I drank a couple glasses of champagne here and there but was incredibly exhausted by about 8 p.m., and when everyone was packing up the reception hall, and ready to head to bars or karaoke, I found myself just wanting to go to bed. I wanted to go back home with my dog and cat to cuddle. We got up to our honeymoon suite in the hotel where the reception was held, I sat on the couch and ate a big bowl of cold, leftover pasta from the reception, and we went to bed. We didn't even have sex. I didn't want to.

I had so many hesitations about this wedding, to the point where I almost called it off more times than I'd like to admit, but I told myself this was normal, so stick it out because that's what you are supposed to do. What exactly ARE you supposed to do when you have feelings like this? I couldn't talk to him about it—no way! He'd call me crazy. That was always his go-to. He'd call me crazy, make me cry, yell at me about what a stupid idea that was, go to bed, and try to apologize in the morning. I couldn't talk to my family about it because they paid for the majority of the wedding. I couldn't rely on friends, because if I was as crazy as he made me out to be, I didn't want them to see it. And to be honest, I really just didn't want to end up like the movies where you pay all this money, spend so much time and energy planning this massive event, and then be the asshole who leaves their fiancé at the alter because they wanted out. I didn't want to be that person. No one in their right mind WANTS to be that person, but yet, here some of us are.

Weddings, to me, are so beautiful. I cry every damn time! They should be a love story of two people falling madly in love with each other, so head-over-heels in love that they can't stop looking at each other the day of, seeing how beautiful each other looks, knowing they are each other's person for the rest of time. The vows are beautifully written, the decor is beautifully placed, and they dance the night away happy as ever. I love weddings, I truly do. But I couldn't love mine. I couldn't love a wedding that seemed as fake as the groom standing at the end of the aisle. I remember thinking to myself, "Why am I not crying more while walking down the aisle?" I thought something was wrong with me! My dad cracked a few jokes to make me laugh as he held my arm while walking down the aisle to "Tale As Old As Time" from *Beauty and the Beast*. He was always good at that. But something still felt weird to me. I wanted this to be so beautiful, I had worked so hard to make this beautiful, we spent so much money on how beautiful it was on the outside. But to me, it wasn't beautiful. It was fake. Our love story wasn't love at all. I knew that, and he knew that. I was just too stupid to say it out loud.

I often wonder what it would have been like had I met someone different. Had I chosen to marry someone who cared. Had I chosen to find someone who loved me the way a person deserves to be loved. I could have had the wedding of my dreams and celebrated US instead of everyone else. I could have walked down the aisle with my father and my grandfather, the way I had always dreamed of. But it didn't happen that way, and I'll never gain that experience back. Yet another "thing" in life that I truly feel I was stripped of. Something every little girl dreams of and plans for. And it's a very sad realization when you tell yourself you will one day have to tell your children that their dad wasn't your first marriage.

The love I have for my current partner is something I only had ever dreamed of with my ex. Especially after this divorce, he's the best that's ever happened to me, and I truly don't understand how I deserve someone so amazing in my life. But the thought continues that I wasted that precious life experience on the wrong person, and you can't ever really get that back. And to me, it's completely unfair. It's unfair that if there ever is a next time, I can't have that excitement like I should. It's unfair that I didn't give him the love I gave someone else, someone else who was worth so much less to me. The love I once could offer before I was tainted with hate, cheating, disgust, and abuse. But, I suppose with anything in life, life can just truly be very unfair.

Estate Planning, Life Insurance, And CPA Meetings

January 15th, 2020

Early in 2018, my ex-husband quit his job to stay at home and help me with the leggings business. This was something we had talked about for months leading up to it, but he hadn't pulled the trigger until February of 2018. Everyone thought we were nuts, but he hated his job at the bank, and I was making enough money to keep him home, so why not? It was great at first. I was incredibly proud of the fact that little ol' me made enough of an income to provide for two of us, keeping us both at home, and he could help me with the business in the process by helping me organize stock, get orders out fast, and do other odd jobs. He sat me down and talked numbers with me, including how much I should be paying him. He told me we should really start doing things the right way and have a paper trail, so that if we ever get audited, we have everything for proof, and everything was done correctly. I agreed. He worked out the numbers for me and told me that he wanted him and I both to have a salary of $80,000 a year. I don't really know how he came up with that number or why he thought we both needed to make the same amount, but I never argued it. I had never made that kind of money in my life, so it all sounded great to me at the time. I also knew he wasn't entitled to that much, but if I argued with him, it would start a whole separate argument that I didn't even want to deal with. So he made just as much as the CEO did in this successful company. That CEO being me.

A few months later he got very serious about us going to an estate planner and an insurance brokerage and getting our life insurance and estate planning figured out. He made good points about how if one of us ever had something happen to us, the other would be set up for life. It made sense in my head, but the numbers never did. I knew I was never good with numbers, though, so I always trusted that my husband knew what he was doing since that's essentially what he went to school for.

We went to an estate planner and talked to her about what we'd like as far as a trust, a will, and so on. It was an awkward conversation. I remember pretty vividly not wanting to be in the same room with him because he seemed to be making all of the decisions for me. When the estate planner would ask me a question, he would answer. When she would ask me a personal question regarding who I want my money and property to go to if I were to pass away, he always felt the need to chime in or question my answers. For instance, I wanted to split my money between my mom and dad if I happened to pass away while they were still living, but I also wanted money to go to my sisters and my grandparents. He didn't love that idea. It was almost as if he didn't understand that they come first in my eyes. He had something to say about every idea I had that day, but I just let it go. I remember he even wanted to put it in the trust and will that he was part owner of my business. I remember thinking we had discussed this one time prior to the meeting, but we never fully decided on anything, and never signed any paperwork regarding it. Three thousand dollars later, we had our trusts and wills put into place, half of which I didn't even agree with but knew better than to argue about with him.

A few weeks went by, and he was still on this idea of getting everything figured out for insurance, taxes, estate planning, and all the rest. Whenever he got an idea in his head, there wasn't really any real way of talking him out of it, so I just let him do his thing if it made him happy. I wasn't going to argue with him because it really never helped. He brought me to an insurance company to get our life insurance figured out. He wanted a million-dollar life insurance policy for each of us. I asked him one time why we needed such high policies. His response was, "Well, if something happens to me, I want to make sure you are taken care of. Plus, Megan, we can afford it." I didn't disagree, but it seemed high for just two average people with no kids. So I agreed to go to the meeting and see what the payment options would be. When we got to the meeting, it wasn't to go over payment options; it was for me to sign papers saying this is actually what would be happening. I didn't have a say in it. But, as always, I trusted his judgment. And I paid more than three hundred dollars a month for life insurance because I didn't know any better. He couldn't wait to brag to his parents.

We ended the week by going to meet with a CPA. We needed a CPA for owning a business; that was obvious to me. He had one that he was referred to by a previous client of his. So we went to meet with him. At the meeting, the CPA went over how we could save some money with taxes, and one idea was to become an S corporation or "S-corp" instead of a limited liability company, or LLC. Now, when I started the business, I read up a little on laws for small businesses, and the safe way for me to go at the time was to file as an LLC, so that's what I did. I didn't really know what an S-corp was, and to this day, I'll be honest, I still don't get it. But the CPA told us if we wanted to both be partners of the business since we were married, this would be a smart route to go because it would save us some on taxes at the end of the year. I agreed because I wanted to save money, but I was concerned on the partnership split. After we got home, I remember telling him that I wasn't so sure I wanted to split my business with a potential partner. He got a little defensive about it, stating that he was my husband and that's what people do in business, but it rubbed me the wrong way. I will agree, I was selfish about it. I started this company, I ran this company, I was the face of this company, and everything this company stood for and did was MY idea, so I will admit, I was selfish and wanted that to myself. I'd worked hard for something that really took off, and I'd made a name for myself. I didn't want someone to come in and ruin that or take part of that away from me. So I just stopped talking about it in hopes that he would forget it.

In October of 2018, eight months later, he brought up that it was almost the end of the year, tax season was going to happen, and we needed to get ready for the taxes we owed. We saved 30 percent of each paycheck into our own personal savings account for taxes, so that when tax season did come around, we would already have the money that was owed. But he told me he wanted to make sure we saved as much as we could, and he wanted to further the S-corp idea. He called me upstairs one day while I was packaging orders and said, "Hey, I need you to sign something." It was a bunch of paperwork saying he filed for my business to be an S-corp instead of the LLC without me knowing. I had to sign papers stating the original LLC would be shut down and re-filed as an S-corp. After about ten signatures, the final paper was the partnership agreement. He told me once that Steve Jobs had a 70/30 partnership with Apple, and this man was OBSESSED with Apple, so that's apparently how he came up with this agreement. I would own 70 percent of my business, he would own 30 percent. I wasn't in the right mindset to fight with him because I had one thousand packages that had to go out that week, so I signed the papers to be done with it and went back to work. Nothing more was ever said.

It always rubbed me the wrong way that he wanted some part in the company that I initially started. It's almost like he couldn't bear the thought that I did something better than him for once in my life. Up until that year, he was the breadwinner, and he for sure made that known. Now suddenly, his wife makes triple his income, and he couldn't handle that. I paid him an $80,000 salary for hardly doing anything. He helped me with taxes, and helped me package items at night, but at the end of the day, even a high-paid CPA doesn't make that much. I did the live shows every other day, I packaged the orders in between shows, I ordered the ten thousand dollars' worth of inventory every week, I organized all of the inventory as it came in, I unpackaged everything as it came in and I repackaged everything as it went out, I was up for fifty-two hours at a time some days, just to nap and do it all over again the next morning, I took care of the customer service side of things, answering emails and phone calls. He helped with quarterly taxes and helped me package for two hours a night. I ended up paying him way more than he was worth, but in my head, it was my way of taking care of my husband and keeping him at home. It wasn't about the success or that his wife was doing something awesome in helping women with body issues and sexism; it was about money to him. He bought a new car, tinted the windows as dark as possible, purchased these million-dollar life insurance policies, wanted a huge house for no reason whatsoever, talked about wanting to buy stocks all the time and investments, and wanted everything fancy and expensive. In no way, shape, or form was he proud of me. He was proud he was WITH me, because of the amount of money he could throw around. And he had NO problem telling people what he made for an income from there on out, especially now that he was a partner in this.

This Is C

January 19th, 2020

This past weekend I was fortunate enough to attend my company's annual convention in Nashville, Tennessee. Convention is always something I look forward to. I get to see friends I haven't seen in awhile, let loose a little bit, get to know new team members, and become motivated by hearing inspirational stories from guest speakers, while broadening my knowledge of the industry with useful training. This year was a bit different, though, from any other year I'd ever been there. I've been struggling lately with understanding the reality of how many people my blogs have actually helped, and in a recent conversation with a psychic medium, she told me that I help more people than I realize. I think that was proven to me this weekend.

Because this blog is public, I won't mention her name, so we will call her C. C was the nineteen-year-old daughter of one of my teammates. I had seen her there with her mom the whole weekend, but on the final night, awards night, her mom came up to me and wanted to introduce me to her daughter. She said, "This is C, and I would love to introduce you to her. C has read your blog religiously, and you have helped her so much through the PTSD that her father left her with." Instantly I had tears in my eyes, and so did she. This young, beautiful soul was suffering. I told her I was so thankful they came up to me. We talked a bit, and then I had to excuse myself to get something done for the corporate staff, but I couldn't get her off my mind.

At the end of the night, I ended up having a line of people in front of me who wanted to talk to me or take a photo with me. This is a little weird to me considering I'm really no one special, but it truly made me FEEL special. My boyfriend just stepped aside to watch it happen. It was a pretty cool experience. I felt like a rock star signing autographs! But C and her mom were among the people in line again to say something to me. Once it was their turn, I hugged C again and told her thank you so much for coming up to me and telling me her story. She started crying while hugging me, and I said, "This is just part of your story! This is YOU. And it's OK to be YOU!" Her hug meant so much to me. Her words meant so much to me. I could feel the pain that she was dealing with, the struggles she was dealing with, her tears that she seemed scared to shed, I wanted her to cry for me! I told her, "It's OK to cry! Because I cry A LOT!" At that moment I just felt like this is what she needed. She needed to meet me and hear that it was OK to feel the way she felt. I then told her, "When I publish this book, the first copy I get, I'm going to sign it and send it to you," and the poor girl just cried, as if that's all she needed to hear. It wasn't the fact that a free book would be given to her, it's that someone finally heard her words, and someone finally understood her.

THIS IS WHY I DO WHAT I DO. This is EXACTLY why I am out to tell my story and be open about every single one of my struggles. Life is hard, but happiness shouldn't have to be. Thank you, C, for this weekend. You left more of an impact on me than you'll ever know. Keep being that beautiful soul you are, because you, my friend, are a rare find. You are a gem. Do not let anyone define you or tell you different.

Love,

Megan

G and S

January 21st, 2020

In 2017, when I joined my direct sales company, I began growing my team very quickly. Recruiting was something I was good at. People seemed to flock to me, wanting in on the fun. I began growing very close to people on my team. I set a dynamic within my team where we all show love and support for each other, and I found people to live out that mission with me. Two of those people slowly became my best friends. But while that friendship was blooming, my ex-husband's jealously was blooming as well.

G and S were suddenly two of my very best friends. We hung out almost every weekend, talked almost constantly, met each other many times for lunch, and just truly had a great friendship. I had never gotten close to many people, so those I did connect with were rare, and when I did feel comfortable with someone, they were practically stuck with me! G and S both joined my team around the same time, and the three of us grew very close very fast. G was an openly gay man, married, and had two beautiful children. We connected in an instant, and I considered him like a brother to me. S was a married woman with four kids, had the resting bitch face of a god, and lived in the same area as G. We all were pretty surprised we all lived within about forty minutes of each other, so we all hung out a lot during this time. My ex-husband, however, didn't approve.

December 31st, 2017. My ex-husband and I had no New Year's Eve plans, and that was weird to me because New Year's Eve is my favorite holiday. We didn't have anything planned because we wanted to save some money. I told him a week prior to this that G had invited us to his house for a small New Year's Eve gathering with some friends.

He didn't like the idea from the get-go and told me he would rather go to the casino. I didn't have a ton of money at the time, so I really didn't want to go to a place where all I would do was spend money. I told him the morning of New Year's Eve that I didn't really feel comfortable spending money right now and that I would rather just go to G's house. He gave me the silent treatment for a couple hours, as if that would make me change my mind, and then eventually told me his thoughts on me going to his house. He did NOT want me to go. At the time I didn't understand why he didn't want me to go, but he clearly was upset about it. I wasn't going to let that ruin my New Year's Eve plans, because as I said, this was my favorite holiday and I wasn't about to stay home all night, so I ended up going to G's house alone. S was there as well, and so were about five other people. We had snacks, champagne, and played games all night. I actually had a LOT of fun! G and I stayed up all night talking about girls, boobs, men, relationships, makeup—everything! The benefit of being friends with a gay man is that you can have "girl talk" without another girl! And I find great beauty in that, as I really don't like many girls out there! We ended up not going to bed until the sun came up because we were just so deep in good conversation. I ended up going home around noon. I walked in the door, and my ex-husband continued the silent treatment the entire day. You could clearly tell he was VERY jealous of my relationship with G, but I had nothing to hide. I'd invited him to G's house with me NUMEROUS times, but he never wanted to go. I invited him for New Year's Eve, but he didn't want to go. He clearly had it out for G. At one point, he asked me, "So, what, are you gay for G now?"

S and I had a quirky relationship. We both are very outspoken individuals. She never judged me for my craziness, she was a very salty human being like myself in most situations, and she was just hilarious to be around. I loved hanging out with her because we connected on a weird level that I rarely found with anyone else. We would do lunch every so often when I had some free time, go downtown for drinks here and there, and talk pretty consistently. One time I mentioned to my ex-husband that I was going to meet her for drinks. Immediately he said, "So, what, are you two lesbians now?" No. We were just two girls hanging out like normal friends do. Again, the jealousy was bad for him. He always scolded me for being a very jealous person, but I had never been jealous over friendships of his. He had no reason to be concerned or jealous of mine, but yet it was very concerning to him. And he always loved to belittle me by bringing up my sexuality. It was earlier this same year that I came out to the world as a bisexual, which clearly bothered him more than he ever liked to admit.

Months went by, and our marriage started going downhill slowly. After our honeymoon in August, when I caught him talking to his ex-girl-friend again, it started going downhill even faster. He questioned where we went wrong numerous times, and during one of our arguments he had the audacity to tell me, "I've been trying to pinpoint where we went wrong, and the only thing I can come up with is that you changed when you started hanging out with G & S." He literally was telling me I changed because I had friends. I changed because suddenly, after eight years of living in Missouri, having no friends whatsoever, I connected with people who I actually cared about instead of sitting in my house all day like a hermit. He couldn't handle sharing me like that. He couldn't handle knowing I had friends now to pay attention to other than him. This couldn't have been further from true, so of course I became very defensive. How dare he say this about me! How dare he question my happiness! I had been living in Missouri for eight years with no friends other than one coworker I was very close to, and he had the balls to blame me for our marriage failing simply because I had friendships that he was jealous of.

In December of 2018 it went further. He swore up and down that I was cheating on him because I'd been thinking about divorce. As if just thinking of getting a divorce meant I was having an affair. This is what narcissists do. They know what THEY did wrong in the past, and they will continuously blame someone else for their own mistakes. He cheated on me, so clearly that's what I was doing to him, right? No.

S and I decided to go out for drinks one night because I needed to get out of the house. He had gone through my computer earlier that week and found me searching for divorce lawyers. I had nowhere to stay, so I was still living under his roof. I needed to have a night out with friends, away from him, so S invited me out for drinks with her and her friend. We went to get tacos and margaritas and then went out for kara-oke afterward. When I got home, he decided to yell and scream at me, asking why I was out so late with S. He said he saw photos and videos of me doing karaoke and was very offended when he saw a photo of S and me together. At this point, my friendship with S was two years old. He had nothing to be concerned about with S, but what he threw in my face next was something COMPLETELY unnecessary, and frankly, it was downright offensive. He asked me if I was having an affair with S. I was completely taken off guard! Like, REALLY? S was a thirty-nine-year-old, happily married woman with four kids. Not to mention she's not even into women! He didn't even make it a question, like, "Are you having an affair?" It was him telling me he KNEW I was having an affair with S, and there was no changing his mind. He even threw in, "Well I know she's bi like you, so obviously this is happening." There he goes again, belittling me for being bisexual. He did this a lot. Only this time it was completely unjustified. She was as straight as an arrow!

My ex hated when I had friendships like these. Any relationship in general he couldn't handle. Why? Because suddenly he was losing his control over me, and he couldn't handle that. He couldn't handle my attention being somewhere else; he couldn't handle no longer having that "leash" on me. When he decided to pull that card out on me that day in December, claiming I was having an affair with my best friend, all while he cheated on me time after time after time, I knew right then and there that I had to get out of that house, and I knew this was my sign for a divorce.

"I Believe All Women Are Beautiful Without Makeup, But With The Right Makeup, We Can Be Pretty Damn Powerful." —unknown

January 22nd, 2020

Something I've always been super NOT confident in is my skin. I was bullied for years for my terrible skin, and even to this day I rarely go out without foundation on because of the scars that bullying left me with. I recently posted a side-by-side photo of myself with and without makeup on, and I had a lot of interesting feedback. Please know that it takes a lot out of me to post stuff like this because of my past.

Those of you who say, "You don't need makeup; you're beautiful!"—please know that although I appreciate that, being able to "cover" something that everyone sees as "disgusting" really is a wonderful thing. Had it not been for makeup, I would have been in a bad place back in middle school and high school when the bullying was at its peak. I thank my lucky stars every day for having something in this world that gives me confidence. And that is makeup.

Although makeup is something we view sometimes as "materialistic" or "hiding the real you," to me it's confidence. And it's art. In 2011 I went to school for skincare to help people with similar skin issues so that they wouldn't have to grow up being bullied like I did. I had a major focus on makeup because I considered it an art. In fact, when I was a makeup artist I always used the catch phrase, "I don't sell makeup, I sell confidence!" And girlfriend, if you have the confidence to wake up every morning and walk out that door owning the world like the badass that you are, you can do anything!

Your friendly confidence booster,

Megan

Direct Sales

January 24th, 2020

Remember how I said social media is a job within itself? This is what it looks like.

The past four days, I have gone back to my roots of growing a page via social media and hustling like crazy to grow it as fast as physically possible. Why? Because I have to. People ask me every single day, "How do you do it?" My answer? I woke up and got shit done. When I started this business two and a half years ago, I was motivated to succeed because I had no other choice. I was forty thousand dollars in debt, my bank account was negative, I had a job that I hated, and my depression was at its worst. I succeeded because I had to. Today is no different, I'm pushing my business because I have to. My ex-husband has put me through a whirlwind of emotions, abuse, and pain for the past ten years. And now I'm in another world of debt with the divorce. I walked out on my marriage one year ago last month and haven't looked back. But with that comes a hefty fee. My lawyer bills aren't stopping, and neither is he. But here I am, paying my bills and making a name for myself. This past year alone I brought in a six-figure income BY MYSELF! Do you think I could have done that half-assing it? NO! I wake up every day and I GET SHIT DONE!

My hair may not get brushed today. Lord knows it hasn't been washed in four days. Hell, I might not even shower! I'm wearing the same PJs I wore two nights ago because I haven't even stepped foot outside my house. Laundry from this past weekend still needs to be done, and my house, for some reason, hasn't figured out how to clean itself!

I'm on my phone nineteen hours a day, and I'm pretty sure my boyfriend hates me. Wanna know why I'm successful? Because when someone tells me GO... I GO! I'm willing to put the time, effort, and consistency in when others would have quit. I'm willing to give it my all because I HAVE TO. I'm willing to go further than most because my level of "HAVE TO" is much more than most.

Hi. I'm Megan Besler, and I'm on a mission to change lives.

Girl 2

January 25th, 2020

Early in our relationship I thought everything was too good to be true. We had met each other back in 2005 and become incredibly close. We had that brother-sister type of relationship. He came to me for things, I came to him for things. We had a unique friendship, but it never went anywhere. Then 2012 rolled around and we both suddenly became single after some hard relationships, so we decided to meet halfway in Chicago and hang out for a bit. About a month prior to this, I had spoken to him and confessed that I'd had a huge crush on him all these years. He did the same. So meeting in Chicago was more of a "let's see where this goes" type of date. After Chicago, I knew this was too good to be true, but my feelings had grown for him. The only downside was the eight-hour distance between us. I was still living in Milwaukee, Wisconsin, and he was in St. Louis, Missouri.

I knew deep down that the distance factor was going to suck. I knew I'd have a hard time trusting what was happening eight hours away, but for some reason it felt right, and it felt worth it to me. We saw each other maybe twice a month for the first few months. I would drive down there for the weekend, and every once in awhile he would make the trip up to see me, even if it was just for one day. It felt good to know he cared. It felt good to have this sort of "love" that blossomed over seven years. And to me, it felt like he was "the one."

I remember telling someone I worked with at the time that I knew I was going to marry him someday, and I'd never said that about anyone else I'd ever dated. I knew that someday he was going to be my husband, and I knew that my intuition was rarely wrong. On the flip side of that, I also felt something was off. I knew he had a not-so-good reputation when it came to women he dated. And that scared me. My intuition was trying to warn me, but I didn't listen to it.

As you have read in an earlier blog, I had warning signs about women he was seeing, but I chose to ignore them even though they were blatantly obvious. Receipts on his desk showing he went out to eat with someone, his bedsheets being washed every time before I'd come over, the posts he was tagged in and then suddenly deleted, the way he talked about certain women around me—so many red flags, and I ignored them. One of these women, named B, was someone I was VERY threatened by. He spoke about her openly to me, which I always found weird, but he never made it known that he was sleeping with her. He would just always brag about knowing a "model" and how they hung out a lot, how she was hot as hell but was only a friend.

I questioned her a lot. I knew they were sleeping together but I could never prove it. I knew he hung out with her when I wasn't in town, but I never had any hard evidence as proof, and if I ever questioned him, he turned it around on me, making me feel like a terrible person for not trusting him.

In May of 2013, I finally made the move to St. Louis. I packed up all my stuff, including my cat, and headed down to be with him. We lived in a one-bedroom apartment outside St. Louis. Our apartment complex was older but had a pool and a fitness facility that was quite nice. He was really into fitness at this point; he wanted to bulk up, so he went to the gym almost every evening. Exactly one week after moving down here I noticed that he left his phone on the counter while he went to work out. Something told me to look at it; I don't know what. I saw a message from B. B asked how he was doing lately, and she wondered when they could hang out next. I shouldn't have opened the message, but I did, and what I saw has forever traumatized me.

I scrolled through their messages, almost a year's worth. I saw naked photos of her sent to him. I saw photos sent from him to her of him in his boxes showing more than I'd like to remember. I saw messages about them going to bars, her talking about giving him oral sex on the way home one night, a photo of her that HE took of her in his bathroom in her underwear posing, him asking her how her vagina felt after a rough night of sex.... You guys, I had just moved my life to St. Louis seven days prior to this. I was shocked, I was hurt, I was confused, and more than anything, I knew I was stuck. I brought it to his attention, and the first thing he did was get mad at me for going through his phone. This was his usual rebuttal on me, even up until last year when I caught him texting his ex-girlfriend on our honeymoon. It was never about me catching him cheating, it was about me going through his phone, and how I was now the bad guy for it. He could never be the bad guy; he always had to be the victim. He didn't give a shit that he had been cheating on me for over a year; he wanted to throw it in my face that I went through his phone and didn't trust him, and that made me out to be the bad guy. I was so hurt. I had never cried this hard until I saw those photos and read those vulgar messages. I thought I was in a lot of trouble considering I had just moved down here, had no money to move home, no job, and no place to go. What on earth was I supposed to do now? One month after this all went down, I found out I was pregnant, and we all know how that ended for me.

There were more girls involved in his cheating games. I caught on to three but confirmed there were at least six that he physically slept with during the time we were dating. But the number of women he had sexual conversations with, sent nude photos to, and spoke to every night were far more. One of his friends even reached out to me once saying they hung out with him at a bar, and he was showing them a hidden folder on his phone of all of these naked women he fucks on the side and saves their photos as trophies. He bragged about it to them. He bragged about the model he had on the side who had kids at home. He showed them photos of these naked women, saying "look who I took home last night," all while he had a girlfriend. This kind of behavior, no matter how you look at it, is not OK. And this was just the beginning of his abuse. Had I chosen to walk away when I had the chance, I wouldn't be so bruised and battered, with such emotional PTSD right now. But I chose to stay, and I stayed for eight long years. The abuse never went away. It just kept getting worse. And the longer I chose to stay, the more he knew he had that kind of control over me.

Emotional Abuse vs. Physical Abuse

January 25th, 2020

This is a topic I've thought a lot about in the past year. It's something I've truly tried to understand and study. The psychology-oriented brain of mine constantly wants to dig deeper and find out WHY. WHY people do what they do. WHY people think what they think. My boyfriend will tell you, even the darkest scenarios, the darkest most harmful situations, I sit here and ask "why." Murderers, rapists... I want to know the psychology behind it. So when I realized I was being abused, I tried to dig deeper and figure out the underlying issues behind WHY it was happening. Not that I ever truly figured it out in my situation, but in studying this a lot more and really coming to terms with it happening to me in this scenario, I began realizing why emotional abuse is sometimes worse than physical.

Now, disclaimer: abuse is abuse. Domestic violence is a serious thing. Whether you were physically harmed or emotionally fucked with, abuse is abuse and IT IS NOT OK. I am truly not saying one is worse or better than the other, I'm simply explaining my opinion on the matter.

Emotional abuse is defined as a form of abuse, characterized by a person subjecting or exposing another person to behavior that may result in psychological trauma, including anxiety, chronic depression, or post-traumatic stress disorder. Physical abuse is abuse characterized by an intentional act causing injury or trauma to another person or animal by way of bodily contact.

Abuse, in my opinion, is abuse. No matter what shape or form. I don't necessarily think one is worse than the other per se, but I will say this: after the bruises go away, what are you left with? Emotional ties. Mental anguish. Mental abuse. I truly feel like the mental part of any kind of abuse continues to linger long after the bruises go away. I feel fortunate that I never truly had to deal with severe forms of physical abuse, but the mental side of abuse has truly fucked me up. PTSD is a very real thing when it comes to abuse. A lot of people associate PTSD with soldiers who have fought in wars, but the actual definition shows that PTSD is a very serious mental condition that people develop after a shocking, terrifying, or dangerous event. These events are called traumas. After a trauma, it's common to struggle with fear, anxiety, and sadness. People have trouble sleeping, have upsetting memories pop up, have anxiety over the littlest things, have disturbing flashbacks, emotional numbness, angry outbursts, feelings of guilt, and so on. PTSD causes your brain to get stuck in danger mode even when you are no longer in danger. So when the bruises go away from physical abuse, you are still left with the mental aspect of it, and I truly believe the mental side of abuse is the hardest part. Bruises go away over time, but in my experience, mental issues do not.

I remember an instance recently when I was talking about this on a live show of mine on Facebook. I had stated my feelings on mental abuse. I didn't even mention the fact that I had dealt with severe mental abuse for the past eight years of my life, but someone offered me their two cents. They said in a comment to me that mental abuse is something people just make up to make themselves sound less crazy. I was mind blown. I AM NOT CRAZY! So ever since then, I've kind of been on a mission to prove this wrong. We aren't crazy, you guys. No, sir. People think you're crazy because nobody can see your physical pain. And until you have a bruise for proof, no one bats an eye or wants to help. I remember thinking numerous times within my marriage that I was being emotionally abused, but every time the thought entered my head, I didn't know what to do with it. It's almost like I didn't know how to talk to people openly about it because I didn't think people would believe me. How would they believe me? I had no proof. I couldn't go to the cops because they would want to see physical proof, like bruises or black eyes. I remember wanting to tell friends and family, but they would just think I was making it all up in my head. With the history of my friends and family telling me to shut my mouth back in high school when I was raped, this wasn't going to offer a different ending. I was physically RAPED and people told me to shut my mouth. How would they ever take me seriously if I told them I was being mentally abused? They'd simply tell me to stop being so sensitive and get over it, which I guess in turn, is a form of mental abuse on their end as well. So all these years I just figured it was easier to keep my mouth shut. I found myself wishing he would hit me, so that I would finally have the proof I needed to come forward, and that is NOT a healthy way to live.

Eight years of this, and it got worse and worse as the years went on. And I fully think if I had stayed and let this continue longer, it would have turned into physical abuse. I got to a point where I was scared some nights, because I thought it was going to turn physical. Thank god it didn't, but I will tell you I was scared. The cheating started it all, then eventually it got into gaslighting and being controlled. I felt like I was on a tight leash and had to obey every command.

Once, a few months after we had gotten married, we were picking up a friend for breakfast. This friend of ours sat in the back seat of N's car and was in mid-conversation with N when he noticed my wedding ring and said how beautiful it was. He then asked, "How does it feel to be Mrs. _____ ?" In an instant, N chimed in, laughing and saying, "That's right, I own you!" I laughed because to me, it was a joke. But it really wasn't. I had fallen complete victim to his abuse, and this proved it. After I left N, this friend of ours brought this story back up to me and told me how uneasy that response made him feel. N was in such control over me that at the time it didn't even occur to me that what he said was very alarming. He had such control over me that I was in a delusional state and very much in denial. Now I see the danger in that, and if someone told me that now, I would GO OFF on them!

He may have never hit me, other than that one time when we found out I was pregnant, but he destroyed everything I ever had. I don't know if I even realized at first that it was abuse because it wasn't physical. I think I eventually figured it out, but I was in such denial over it that the thought merely entered my mind, and I realized I couldn't say anything to anyone about it, and then it left.

Because of years upon years of this mental abuse, I am pretty fucked up, to say it bluntly. I have severe PTSD that I think the majority of my friends and family can now notice, my boyfriend included. I constantly apologize because I'm so used to being criticized excessively. I hide my feelings because I'm used to being blamed for them and having them go unnoticed. I break down over the smallest disagreements because they trigger flashbacks for me. I need a TON of reassurance because I'm used to being constantly reminded that I'm not good enough. I have MASSIVE anxiety over everything because I'm terrified it will all happen again. Our divorce has allowed us to go our separate ways and live two separate lives, but I'm left with PTSD for the rest of my existence while he is out there doing this to the next woman, and truly, it's very, very unfair. But, as always, this is part of my story, and I'm not ashamed of it. I think the minute I truly realized I didn't deserve that kind of torture anymore, that was the day I decided I was done. Two months later, I walked out of his house and our marriage.

Gaslighting

> "A narcissist's mindset. That didn't happen, and if it did,
> it wasn't that bad, and if it was, it's not a big deal, and if it
> is, I didn't mean to do it, and if I did, that was your fault."
> —*unknown*

I often, in recent months, have been examining how I control my emotions. I've always been the type of person who hates arguments. Part of it is the fact that I hate confrontation, but the other part of it is me just really believing that fighting isn't necessary. As adults, I believe we should have civil conversations. Now, I know life isn't all happy rainbows. It's completely unrealistic to think we can go through life without arguments or debates. But FIGHTING, to me, is unnecessary. We're all adults here; let's act like it. I believe when there is something to be argued, a good debate is a beautiful thing. But I don't believe in fighting or raising your voice, I don't believe in belittling people, and I don't believe in attacking someone, whether it be in person or behind a computer screen. I just don't believe fighting is healthy. What I do believe in is a civil, adult conversation. A healthy debate. An "agree to disagree" end result, because at the end of the day, we still have to go on with our everyday lives, and fighting is just going to ruin a person over time.

N wasn't about the "civil conversation" outlook. We would fight pretty consistently, and his rebuttal was always picking on me to a point where I would feel backed in a corner. These fights would end in one of two ways. 1) I would cry my eyes out because I felt picked on, cornered, and torn apart. 2) I would be so mad that I would leave and stay at a hotel for the night. Neither is healthy. I would catch him in so many lies, which would create a huge argument with him trying to prove that I was crazy. And after so long, I truly believed he was right.

Whenever I caught him cheating, he turned the argument around me on, making me to be the crazy one and turning the conversation into me being the bad guy for catching him. And whenever I would catch him in a lie, the gaslighting kicked in. His rebuttal to catching him lying was always that my memory sucked and I never knew what I was talking about. I knew I had a terrible memory, but I also knew what I saw and heard. But when someone gaslights you, you begin to truly believe you're crazy, and that is the hardest part about dealing with a narcissist.

Gaslighting is a form of psychological manipulation in which a person seeks to sow seeds of doubt in a targeted individual or members of a targeted group, making them question their own memory, perception, or sanity. N's patterns developed over time, and even though I caught on to it, I didn't do anything to stop him because his leash got tighter and tighter on me as years went by. Whenever I'd claim we had spoken previously about something, he legitimately told me I was making it up, to the point where I started to believe him, thinking I really did have some sort of bad mental disorder where I made up scenarios in my head. One time, at his parents' house, we were simply having a normal, everyday conversation, and something got brought up. To be honest, I can't even remember the topic. I was so incredibly embarrassed by the situation that I know I put a mental block on the day because this was the first time he did this to me in public, and I felt incredibly ashamed. His mom said something, and N responded something else. I remember saying, "We talked about this other day; don't you remember?" and N got very defensive about it, stating, "I think I'd remember that conversation. You truly don't know what you are talking about." I responded calmly, "No, seriously, we had this conversation the other day. Don't you remember me talking about this in the living room while we were watching a movie?" And what he said next had me almost in tears. It was something that literally made me feel like I was a puppy being scolded and had to go to my kennel for time out. He said out loud to his mom and dad at the kitchen table, "You have the world's worst memory, and now you're literally making up stories in your head that never happened!" and laughed about it while his mom and dad chimed in their laughs with him. I remember feeling defeated. I remember shutting up right in that very moment, because deep within their laughs, I felt bullied. I felt like they were picking on me because I had a terrible memory. Yes, I do have a terrible memory, but I did not make up an entire conversation in my head about whatever we were talking about. But suddenly, to his family, I was a joke. I was a mental case. I remember wanting to cry. I remember wanting to just disappear. I was being bullied and picked on by people who didn't even realize they were doing it, and although it was something so simple, it really REALLY hurt. And right then and there I realized he truly was a narcissist. I had contemplated him acting like one for a long time, but gaslighting me in front of his family just so he wasn't wrong was a huge eye opener for me.

After that day at his parents' house, I picked up on him doing this to me over and over as the days, weeks, and months went by. He did it in front of his friends, in front of his family, in public at the grocery story, everywhere. His gaslighting technique was designed to make me doubt myself to the point where I thought I really was crazy. And, well, it always worked.

Our arguments were bad. They'd end in screaming fits. And as someone who truly doesn't believe in fighting, this was very hard for me. I hated the person I'd become. I hated screaming at someone just to prove my point! But my point would never be proven with a narcissist, so the arguments became worse and worse over time. I always gave in to our fights, however, because I hated going to bed angry. So although I usually felt like I was in the right, I would always apologize because at the end of the day, I just wanted his love. To me, it was easier to just say sorry and move on than to deal with trying to prove my point to someone who would never listen. Unfortunately, that gave him leverage. He knew every argument he would win, and he used that against me numerous times. When you're that much in control of something or someone, you know you'll always win because the other person will always give in. And that, my friends, is a true form of mental abuse.

My Coming Out Story

January 30th, 2020

I've always known I liked both men and women. I never talked about it growing up because I lived in a tiny conservative town of five hundred people with a huge amount of judgment. But after moving out on my own and really figuring out life, I came to terms with the fact that I was pretty sure I was bisexual. Still, even in college, it wasn't something I talked about. At this point in my life I hadn't been with a woman; I just found myself attracted to them in the same way I was attracted to men.

In 2018 I had a thriving business, where people came to me for advice, people came to me with their problems, people opened up to me who didn't even know me from Adam, and people were even coming to me at fifty years old saying they were in fact gay but didn't want to tell their family. I was really inspired by the amount of courage these people had, to the point where I decided to rebrand my business. I sought after a new logo, new branding, and a new mission.

In June of 2018, my then-husband and I took my sister to New York City for her sixteenth birthday. June is obviously pride month, so I chose this month to relaunch our newly branded business. I didn't tell my then-husband everything I had planned to do, but he knew about the new logo, the new mission, new packaging, and he approved.

I've always been fascinated with the rainbow, to the point where, as a young girl, whenever someone would ask me what my favorite color was, I'd literally say "the rainbow!" without batting an eye. In fact, for my high school prom, I even wore a crazy obnoxious rainbow dress! I guess maybe that was my sign. But while we were in New York that June, I decided THAT'S when I would relaunch the business. We had just hit twenty thousand followers, and being in New York City for Pride month, I had the overwhelming inspiration of using this as my coming-out story. So that day, my sister and I went to a random tattoo parlor, and I got myself a rainbow tattoo to commemorate this part of my journey—my coming out story. I told her I was pansexual, and she was the only one in the family I had told. I expected her to be a little concerned, but she stood by me in every way. The next day, I did a relaunch on my newly branded business. This is what I posted.

· ·

I originally planned on waiting a few more months before officially announcing this, but the 20,000 follower mark happened way before we ever expected! Never in a million years did I expect to hit my one-year goal in just over six months! This is an insane accomplishment for a small business owner and I'm just so damn proud!!!! As a small business, and as a woman who owns a small business, this is just so rewarding to me! I want to share a little story with you guys before I announce our big news.

I always have expressed my love towards rainbows. When asked as a little girl, "What's your favorite color?," I would always answer "The rainbow!" because it literally was just that. A rainbow! I just cannot choose a favorite color simply because I like them all! You guys have heard me talk about "Team Rainbow" for my online business, and my reasoning behind naming it that.... Every color to me is something unique and special. Just like every one of you. We are all unique, we are all special, we are all weird, we are all beautiful. It doesn't matter if you're male, female, black, white, gay, straight, big, thin, WHATEVER! We are who we are, and when we as humans can come together and realize that, that's when something truly beautiful happens. You are a color of this rainbow, just like I am. My goal with this company was never to be huge, never to become rich, never to be a company that doesn't get to know its customers.... My goal has always been to make people feel comfortable in their own skin and be proud of who they are! Whether you feel uncomfortable in public because society has labeled you as "fat." Whether you are thin and society has labeled you as "anorexic." Whether you are a gay man and society has scared you from coming out. Whether you are picked on, looked down upon, talked about, bullied... YOU are unique! YOU are beautiful. YOU are a rainbow! Thank you for allowing me to be a rainbow with you!

We can officially announce, we have rebranded our company to now show our true mission! To allow everyone to feel as special and unique as they truly are!

When I first came up with the idea for Mad About Leggings, it truly kind of happened overnight. I didn't think it would work but I thought it would be fun. A few weeks went by after opening this store, and messages started flooding in. Messages from people I've never met... messages stating:

"Your clothing has finally made me feel comfortable in public. And as a bigger girl, that's hard for me to say!"

"These leggings and shirts have helped me get back to living life. I suffer from nerve damage and cannot wear heavy clothing so I'm rarely able to go out in public."

"I started buying your leggings under a fake profile because I didn't want you to know I was a male. I finally got the courage to order under my regular page and never once did you judge me. I'm a 56 year old gay man. I have since gotten the courage to finally came out and admit that to the world. Thank you!!"

"I'm going through chemo, and don't have a lot to do with my life sitting at home all day. You give me not only something I can wear and be comfortable in around the house, but something I can look forward to."

"I get made fun of for being a very petite girl. I've dropped out of college because so many people think I'm anorexic. I would get made fun of every time I took a trip to the restroom because people assumed I was going in there for other reasons. Hearing your inspiring story of how you started this has made me determined to start school back up!"

At some point, it occurred to me this was no longer just a retail clothing store. This was so much more than that. What I was leading was a movement. A movement with power. A movement with force!

As a feminist, I can honestly say I truly believe every individual, male or female, is beautiful... and you only have one life to show it! And as a fellow member of the LGBTQ community (yes, this is my coming out story), I want to announce to the world that I, too, am unique. I, too, am important. I am a pansexual woman, and I am beautiful. Only a handful of people actually know this about me, but because of you guys, I am ready for the world to know who I truly am. Again, thank you for allowing me to be a part of this rainbow with you! I owe you guys so much for giving me a safe haven to not only sell my products, but to be who I truly am.

So with that said, I introduce to you our new branding!

- *We had our new logo designed with you in mind! YOU ARE A COLOR OF THIS BEAUTIFUL RAINBOW! Clothing tags and business cards will sport this logo, as well as all of our internet platforms! (Website will be updated when we get back home.)*

- *We have new mailers thrown in the mix, rainbow themed!*

- *New packaging for boxes with new rainbow wrapping!*

- *New photos with our rainbow watermark!*

- *NEW PRICE STRUCTURE! (I will go in detail in a video about this soon!)*

We hope you enjoy, and we truly hope you see our vision here at Mad About Leggings!

If it's something you, too, feel strongly about, please share with your friends! Thank you!

#spreadlove #nohate #tastetherainbow

. . . .

In coming out to the world, I was scared, I can't lie. I hadn't even really talked to my family about this yet, but it just felt right. I had the best support system I could have asked for with my friends and my customers, and that, to me, made it very easy for me just tell it like it is and be my true, authentic self. My then-husband was cool with it. At least at first. He seemed to support me in what I was doing, and he and I had had conversations in the past about me being pansexual/bisexual. But things ended up going south pretty fast.

It never really occurred to me, I guess, that he would feel weird about me coming out like I did. I say that because he and I talked about this numerous times. He knew I liked both men and women, and never once did he tell me it bothered him. But after coming out publicly, I could slowly see it did bother him. He would pick on me and mention it a lot. Saying unnecessary comments about people I was close with, making fun of me, and even getting really inappropriate about it. One time, we were on vacation with my company on a cruise, and someone who I am very close with brought her husband. Her husband and I really hit it off since we both deal with a lot of the same issues in life, like anxiety and depression. We hung out a lot because this couple were among the few people I really got along with and felt comfortable around. We were at the casino one night, around everyone else, and I happened to be in a conversation with my friend's husband, when my ex-husband came up to me and asked if I was ready to head to bed yet. I calmly said, "No, I am talking to F right now." And he responded, "What, are you gay for F now?" Like, really? I can't have friends who are men? Also, why bring up gayness? Is that REALLY necessary? I also once told him I wanted a suit for Christmas. A women's suit and tie. I just thought it would look so good on me, and I never thought anything looked good one me. The minute I told him this, he responded, "What, so people will think you're more of a lesbian that you already are?"

Another instance that really rubbed me the wrong way was once on vacation in our hotel room when he started getting really touchy with me. You could tell he wanted sex, but I was not in the right mindset for sex at that point. We never had sex. It was like I physically wasn't attracted to him enough to want him like that, and I wasn't emotionally connected to him anymore, and for me to lay myself down and be that open and vulnerable with someone, I HAVE to have that emotional connection. I physically cannot have sex with someone without that emotional connection. So at this point in our marriage, I was already gone. This particular instance, he started getting very hands-on and touchy with me and clearly wanted something. I remember him touching my breasts and me just bursting into tears because I truly didn't want this, but I knew he was my husband so if I didn't give in, he would be mad at me. He started asking me really inappropriate questions dealing with my celebrity crush, who was female. He said, "If KM was here right now, what would you do to her? Tell me in detail." I refused to tell him, as I was very taken back by this question and just laughed at him, thinking maybe he was joking. Months later, this happened again on our couch one night. We were watching a movie, and out of nowhere, he asked again, "Tell me what you would do if KM was here right now." I said, "I don't know how to answer that." He replied, "Come on, if she were here right now, I want to know what you would do to her." I said, "Well, I mean, if you're asking in sexual terms, and if I'd have sex with her, yes, I would." He responded, "Yeah, but like what exactly would you do to her? I want to know." At that point I was a little disgusted. I felt this was a very inappropriate conversation to be having, and I wasn't comfortable at all in giving him an answer. I kept telling him no, but he kept asking. Eventually I started crying and getting myself all worked up over it, and I finally asked him to stop because I felt it was incredibly inappropriate to talk about. He got up and went to bed. I couldn't help but feel violated, and I didn't even do anything.

Another time, he told me the reason we didn't have sex anymore is because I was only after pussy. I felt very betrayed in that moment. How dare my HUSBAND, who I thought supported me in all this, belittle me for what or who I loved? I was obviously with him, I loved him, and I wasn't out to be with a woman. Yes, I was attracted to both men and women, but I wasn't out to have a girl on the side by ANY means, but he had the audacity to basically tell me I wanted a woman over him. He had the balls to pick on me all the time over this. Numerous times he would bring this stuff up, and honestly, it made me feel like the worst wife in existence. I knew it was OK to love both men and women, but he made me feel like it was NOT OK, and that, my friends, is why I didn't come out sooner. He was doing the very thing that society does to people of the gay community, and having truly thought he supported me in this, it was heartbreaking to know my husband DIDN'T support me in being bisexual. So at this point, I regretted ever coming out at all, and I felt pushed back in a closet and suddenly knew the feeling everyone else in the world feels when they are shunned for loving who they choose to love.

Love wins,

Megan

Letting Go Of Other People's Expectations

January 31st, 2020

"The greatest gift you can give yourself is letting go of other people's expectations." —*Rachel Hollis*

There was a time in my life, not too long ago, where anything that was said about me or done to me bothered the hell out of me. I'd become incredibly defensive, making myself look like an idiot. I would resort to bullying back because I felt so deeply about defending myself and my name. Today, however, I couldn't give a fuck less. What changed? My life. I guess that's the best answer.

I have dealt with bullying in all shapes and forms since middle school years. I still, to this day, get picked on, maybe even more so than I did in the past. I own a public platform where I talk openly about a lot of stuff, I'm not scared to be vulnerable, and I take far too many selfies. I open myself up for the hate to come my way, and as far as I'm concerned, I welcome it. I've gotten to an age where I just don't fucking care about drama anymore, and I sure as hell don't want to be a part of it. I've dealt with enough BS in my life; drama is the last thing I want. You see, to me, defending yourself and your truth takes so much time and energy. Just to type out a paragraph to a cyber bully or a troll on my page is five minutes of time that I will never get back, and I'm sorry but I have a lot of shit to do—that five minutes is precious to me! I have a damn empire to build, and your childish remarks toward me and my acne-prone face aren't going to grab my attention! I have nothing to prove, I know my truth, and that's honestly all that matters in this game. Yes, I could try to teach these people less hateful ways to go about their day while living in their mom's basement, but it would take me five minutes to write that paragraph to them, then another forty-five minutes of debates back and forth on who's right and who's wrong, I just don't have time for that, nor do I want to fit that into my agenda!

If you care about what other people think and let it bother you each and every time they have something to say, you will always be their prisoner. And I'll be damned if I'm going to let someone have that much control over my body and my mind again! When you stop caring about what other people think or say, you will see this inner beauty in yourself that you never thought you had, and once that comes out, girl, you will be UNSTOPPABLE! People envy those who stand their ground. And even more so, those who stand their ground in a professional matter where stuff truly just doesn't even faze them! I mean let's be real, you can't make everyone happy—you're not tequila! But holding your head high and just doing you without getting involved in the drama is such a gift. If you want that respect, respect yourself first. And respect yourself enough to know you are better than all those haters out there who have shit to say. You value yourself enough to know that keeping your mouth shut does more damage to those bullies than being defensive and stating your opinion will EVER do.

The bad news? You can't make people like, love, understand, validate, accept, or be nice to you. The good news? IT DOESN'T FUCKING MATTER. Go be great—because your unique self is what makes ME love YOU.

Love, your favorite (annoying) selfie taker with no shame in her game, Megan!

The Topics I Talk About

February 3rd, 2020

Someone recently told me that the topics I talk about are not going to go over well if I decide to write a book, because the majority of the topics I discuss can be considered controversial. And although I agree, I want to point out a couple things.

Yes, I have a blog, as well as a YouTube channel where I talk about rape, abuse, divorce, depression, abortion, the LGBTQ community, and so on, all while throwing the f-bomb a few hundred times. But here's the truth. Do I want your young daughter to watch and hear that stuff? Of course not. But what I do want your young daughter to know is that she's not alone. And while she might not deal with these types of struggles right now, it's likely that at some point in time in her life she will encounter some type of similar obstacle. Whether it be bullying, or breakups, family issues or whatever, my hope is that if and when she does encounter this in her life maybe, JUST MAYBE, something I said will help her overcome it. Similarly, maybe later in life she will have a friend who was raped, for example, and something I said gave her what she needed to help her and her friend overcome it, or at the very least allow them BOTH to realize they aren't alone. You see, I don't do these blogs or these YouTube videos for attention. I don't want fame from them. I WANT TO HELP PEOPLE. I truly have an obsession with helping people. I want these topics talked about. I want people to openly discuss these taboo topics that everyone else keeps hush-hush. When I was sexually assaulted, I didn't have anyone to talk to. Those who I did try to talk to about it told me to keep my mouth shut. I would have LOVED to have YouTube as a "thing" back then! Where I could type in "I was raped" and find real stories of real people. I would have LOVED to have a channel to watch where someone understood where I was coming from when it came to being made fun of and bullied.

Growing up, everyone has always told me that speaking my thoughts and being so open was a bad thing. I have been shamed NUMEROUS times by friends, families, coworkers, and previous bosses telling me that what I post is not OK. Telling me my opinions are not valid and if I don't keep to myself, I'll be fired. Telling me that what I talk about is not OK, and people are going to view it differently than I do, so it's better if I just stop talking. I'm here to tell you IT IS OK! AND NO ONE SHOULD BE SILENCED!

BULLYING IS A REAL THING.
ABORTION IS A REAL THING.
ABUSE IS A REAL THING.
DEPRESSION IS A REAL THING.
DEATH IS A REAL THING.
ANXIETY IS A REAL THING.
DYSFUNCTIONAL FAMILIES ARE A REAL THING.
DIVORCE IS A REAL THING.

And guess what, all of these "real things" can be openly talked about, believe it or not!

So just because you have a son or daughter who is ten years old and you don't really appreciate me throwing the f-bomb around and teaching them what a rainbow flag means, that doesn't really make me the bad guy here. Let me be the voice for them, since no one else will be. Let me allow them to see life for what it really is, instead of a sugar-coated version of it. Let me teach them that IF they are bullied, they are not alone! Let me teach them that IF they ever have a toxic relationship where abuse is happening, they can walk away before it's too late.

That is the purpose of this channel, and I will not stop because this is something I am EXTREMELY passionate about—helping people with their struggles in a way that makes them feel safe.

If you don't approve, you can kindly go elsewhere,

Megan

Finally Deciding To Leave

February 5th, 2020

In November of 2018, I officially decided to leave my husband. I didn't actually leave until two months later, but that's when the thought entered my head and finally stayed. When the thought came up this time, instead of pushing it out of my head like I did time and time again in the past, I decided this was actually going to happen. When I left, I knew if I was going to leave, I actually had to do it this time. So many times I threatened to leave but always came back, and he knew that. He knew I wouldn't leave, and every other time I threatened leaving, even I knew deep down I wouldn't actually leave for good because he had ingrained in my brain that I was worth NOTHING. I would never make it on my own. I had a shitty job, I was crazy, and no one would ever love me for me, and he always made that very known. The eight years we were together, he had me hating myself more than I had hated him, and I wish I had noticed this sooner, but the sad reality is that I was young and naive and just truly thought he would change.

I often wondered if all marriages were like mine. I had thoughts of not wanting to go through with the marriage over and over, but I always told myself this was normal, that everyone goes through this. But were other marriages like mine? Does every marriage cover up secrets and hide the skeletons? I realize now how not normal this all really was, but at the time, in my head, this was all what was supposed to happen.

But in November of 2018, some kind of light bulb went off, and I woke up one day ready to file papers. People ask me all the time how I ever got to the point where I knew leaving my husband was a good idea, and truly I just tell them that I woke up one morning and realized I didn't want to be treated like this any longer. I knew my purpose in this life finally, and being under his leash was not a part of that. I was tired of being abused and mistreated, I was tired of being unhappy, and for once in my life, I was tired of not feeling my worth. And once I finally figured all this out, there wasn't anyone who could change my mind and stop me. I couldn't believe how stupid I had been this entire time.

So I started looking for divorce lawyers secretly on my computer night after night, and I started pricing out houses and saving money in hopes that I could somehow get out of his house sooner than later. He caught on quick. Went through my computer, found my search history, and didn't understand. In my mind, I couldn't comprehend how he couldn't understand, because he was the abuser all these years, but he didn't get it. He never will get it. And as months went by, you'll see why he still never could understand it. In fact, when he brought it to my attention that he saw my computer's search history, he made me feel terrible, made me feel like the bad guy. He played the victim card, crying at my feet and not understanding where all of this came from. He kept questioning how it came so out of the blue, saying I MUST be having an affair, which was far from true. He couldn't be man enough to sit down and realize that eight years of living under his abuse finally got to me. The sad part was, he couldn't understand the severity of his abuse all these years and that the reason I needed out was because of him. Because he was a cheater in the past, he figured I had to also be a cheater in the present. He couldn't take the blame for something like this, so he constantly shifted the focus on my so-called adultery, when he was the root of these issues all these years. A true narcissist for you.

I took the next month to figure out what was next. I needed to get my finances in order to move out, I needed to find a house, I needed to move out all of my belongings, and I needed it all to happen FAST. I went to a hotel for a few weeks here and there, trying to gather my sanity and make sure this was a real-life decision and not just another breakdown moment of my "crazy."

In December I was able to find a rental company that would purchase me a house on a rent-to-own basis. The home was perfect for me, but I had to wait until the home was closed on and actually purchased, so I had to really bide my time until then. I hung out with my friend S a lot. She tried to get me out of the house as much as possible for fear of further abuse happening now that the separation was in order. I hung out with another friend of mine, A, who seemed to be one of the few people who listened to my story without judgment. I continued to stay in hotels for a bit and had a company convention during this time period, which also got me out of the house. Come January, the home I wanted was finally closed on, and I moved in. The lies continued, the narcissism continued, and the abuse continued.

When I moved out, I left him all the furniture and appliances. I only took my personal belongings and my pets. I decided it was easier if I just furnished my own place myself, so we wouldn't have to fight over any material items. I forked out fifteen thousand dollars to furnish my new home while leaving him everything.

I was incredibly busy one weekend right after I moved, getting furniture put together on my own and trying to run two businesses. I asked N if he could watch the dog for the weekend, just to give me a little time to get everything situated. He told me he was busy with a video shoot, so I let it go. Monday rolled around, and I found photos of him tagged with his ex-girlfriend in Illinois—the same ex-girlfriend that he somehow rekindled his relationship with on our honeymoon. When I confronted him with this information, he still lied, which ended up in a screaming match on the phone because of his ability to twist the story and still think he knew what he was talking about. Why is it that when cheaters are confronted with real information, they still feel the need to cover it up? I never could understand that. I guess, coming from someone who truly hates to lie to people, I just don't understand. Had he just been open and honest with me all these years, we maybe wouldn't even be in this situation where I leave him, but here we are.

After I moved out of N's house, the abuse continued. The narcissism was at an all-time high, and I was more mind-blown on what continued to happen after I left than anything that was happening while I still lived with him.

At one point in February, I received a call from my mom. I answered normally but could hear in her voice that she was scared of something. She immediately said, "Are you OK?" I was incredibly confused, but I answered her. She then said that N contacted her on Facebook and told her that he was scared for my mental sanity. That a bunch of my friends had reached out to him scared for me, and he thought it would be best if he got me the mental help I needed. He then proceeded to tell her that his parents agreed that putting me in a mental institute would be best right now, considering I was suicidal. NONE OF THIS WAS TRUE! I was 1,000 percent NOT suicidal; in fact, it was incredibly offensive to me that he thought that was OK to joke about, considering my past, and that he told my mom that he and his parents decided that putting me in a psych ward was a good idea, and that my friends were reaching out to him to help me! None of this was true. No one reached out to him, I was not suicidal, and I honestly at this point in time, was not even in a bad spot. I was actually loving my life, so happy to have gotten out of that house, and finally finding love for myself that I had never had before. But that was challenging him. To him, it was a slap in the face. How dare I go out and live a good life without him? How dare I be happy without him? So, what's a narcissist to do but to manipulate more people and try to get them on his side.

A

February 6th, 2020

I had become pretty close friends with A during this time period. I'll never be able to explain why or how this person came back into my life, but I like to think fate played a big part in it. I truly believe things happen the way they are supposed to in life, and what's meant to be will always find its way. I think I needed a friend during this time of my life—someone who would listen without judgment and be there for me as the friend I needed at that time—and that's what the universe handed me. We hung out here and there and eventually grew closer as months went by.

In March of 2019 I had been browsing through Instagram late one night when I stumbled across a post from my favorite actress, Lori Petty. I talked a little about this in a previous blog, but just to refresh your memory, she had directed a play the year prior in New York City, and I couldn't make it up in time to see it. This time, however, she was coming back for a special benefit reading of the same play in New York, benefiting a local shelter that advocated against sexual abuse in men, women, and children. It was a one-night-only thing, so I HAD to go. Because A and I had some super intense conversations on sexual abuse in the past, I decided to see if he would like to tag along. So at the end of March 2019, we traveled to New York City for the weekend.

We flew back to St. Louis on Sunday evening, and upon getting off our flight, we both received a text message from N. Mine read, "Wanna tell me who you were really in NY with?" The one to A said, "You really fucked up dude." It was OK for him to go hang out with the girl who ruined our marriage, but wasn't OK for me to take a friend with me to New York to see a play about sexual abuse. He had clearly gone off the deep end, and at this point I was scared. I didn't want to go home. I was terrified he was going to come after me, find my house, and hurt me. I remembered he was overseas in Japan at this moment, so I refrained from calling the police. This trip was his dream trip, one that I helped pay for. I didn't want to ruin that for him, so I told him we could talk when he returned. He replied, "You will be hearing from my attorney."

At that point, I knew our divorce wasn't so civil anymore. Prior to this, one day while packaging orders in the basement, we had talked about him keeping his stuff, and me keeping mine, and making this as civil as possible. In fact, I even asked him if we needed lawyers, and he said, "Probably not." Never trust a narcissist. So the very next day, I hired the best high-asset lawyer in town. Little did I know how bad this was truly about to get. I guess in my head, because we had talked about ending this civilly, I thought we wouldn't be spending a ton. Ten thousand dollars, max, was what my thoughts came up with. But, man, was I wrong. I said from the beginning, when he threatened a lawyer on me, that things were going to get bad. Why? Because I knew he wouldn't let this go until he won. I knew that being a narcissist, he would purposely probably drag this on just to rape my bank account because he couldn't place the blame on himself.

I served him divorce papers in April after they were drafted, and he first came back with a settlement saying he didn't want any alimony or maintenance, didn't want any of my belongings, the dog, nothing. The only thing he wanted was me to pay his attorney fees. I didn't necessarily agree with that, in fact I thought it was beyond ridiculous that he thought it was OK to even ask me to pay for those, considering he was the reason for this divorce in the first place, but I came back with a settlement proposal saying I would pay X amount of his lawyer fees, if and only if he signed the papers by August 15th. August 15th came and went, and nothing happened. Come September, he decided to change his mind. Now he wanted me to not only give him "substantial" reimbursement for losing his job, but he also thought alimony and maintenance should be required. Yes, folks, almost ten months in, and this man still had no job, even with an accounting degree from a four-year college. Laziness is what I call that, and it shouldn't be my responsibility to babysit and take care of an adult.

When I shut down my business in May, I did everything by the book. I filed for the LLC to be shut down, I paid off any outstanding debts the company had, I contacted employees (him) with an ample amount of time to find another job (five weeks), and I sold all products off at half price just to get them out the door and split the assets fifty-fifty, even though he only owned 30 percent of the company. I just wanted it done and over with, so I did it the easiest way possible. I couldn't run the two businesses anymore, not with the nerve damage I suffered, and not with running a thousand-person team on the direct sales side of things. It just wasn't doable anymore, so as a CEO of a small business, I did what I had to do, and I did it by the book. I did not leave him jobless; I did not leave him high and dry. But he seemed to convince his lawyer that I did.

After we said no to his request for alimony, maintenance, and whatever else, he decided that wasn't good enough. He came back saying he wanted more. After everything I left him—the house, his car, his money, all the furniture, my ten-thousand-dollar wedding ring, his wedding ring, new appliances—he had the audacity to ask for MORE. Now, not only did he want maintenance and alimony, he wanted "substantial" reimbursement for his job loss, PLUS 50 percent of my paychecks back-dated to the day I left him! I didn't want his things; I wanted my freedom. I left him with everything, and he still asked for more.

So, back to the original point of this story. After A and I got back from New York, he went off the deep end. I clearly was having an affair (when I wasn't), and he somehow got off scot-free on all of his previous women. What made this even worse is that after this all went down, he decided to reach out to my mom AGAIN. Little did he know, my mom knew everything. She knew about me leaving him, his abuse, his cheating past, his newly kindled relationship with his ex-girlfriend, the honeymoon fiasco, everything. But what he wrote to my mom was completely immature, and it completely crossed the line. Why he even thought reaching out to my mom was a good idea, I'll never know, but I can only assume it was because he knew he was fucked, and he wanted someone on his side.

"I'm still in Japan but I think you should know that Megan and I are officially getting a divorce. I waited for her, but I just found out that she's been sleeping with one of my friends for the last several months.

His name is A and he was a friend of mine for more than ten years. I apologize to you and your family as I wish things could've worked out. Tell her sisters that I'm sorry. I can't keep waiting when Megan has completely ripped my heart out. The irony is that Megan has been accusing me of precisely the thing that she's doing now. I never wanted it to get to this point but we are here now and it's all over. Sorry for wasting your and your family's time. This will be that last time you ever hear from me."

Unfortunately for him, I saw right through his words, and I let my mom know exactly what he was trying to do to her—manipulate her. He was a MASTER at manipulation. Manipulation is a huge part of narcissistic behavior. She, thankfully, saw right through it too. I called him out on this. I yelled at him the first time he reached out to my mom, about my supposed mental problems, and told him not to NEVER contact her again, because little did he know, my mom already knew the whole story, so he wasn't fooling anyone. But after he reached out to her a second time, I knew full well that leaving him WAS the right decision. His manipulation tactics even had my mind blown. He was truly grasping at straws at this point, and he was never going to stop. He had gotten so desperate at getting people on his side that he made himself look terrible in the process.

So months have passed of going back and forth between settlements, nothing getting solved, court date after court date, and here we are. To keep this story short, because I feel like I could write a book on the past twelve months alone dealing with his back-and-forth bullshit with the divorce, let's just say my lawyer and the judge have not been thrilled. He didn't show up to his first court date, and neither did his attorney. He missed meetings time after time with his attorney, and he dragged out legal matters dealing with taxes and other things for MONTHS. Truly, for such a smart human being, he really got fucking dumb. And here I am, one year and thirty thousand dollars in. The trial is set for March. Yes, trial. Five percent of divorces end in trial, and ours was one of them because he couldn't stand losing. Once the trial is over, I'm about to throw the biggest party on the planet in knowing I'm once and for all... FREE.

Intuition

February 7th, 2020

I feel like this blog has turned into a novel, and I do apologize as that was never my intention. I've always wanted to publish my blogs in blog form, but as stories have entered my memory, I just feel they need to be told. So I'm sure while reading through this blog you can pinpoint where everything seems to switch a bit, but please know it is with good intent, that I get my stories out there so people can find them, relate to them, and open their eyes a bit to real life scenarios that can cause harm to a person's life and well-being. With that said, here's another story!

I've always known I think on a much deeper level than most humans I know. In fact, I have been called out on this time after time by friends, family, coworkers, customers.... People say I feel differently from most, that I'm someone who will end up changing the world, someone who is an old soul with empathy for everything. I've known since a young age that I am an empath, but within the past five years or so of my life, I truly have gotten more in touch with that side of myself. N, however, didn't believe in this kind of thing. Anytime I had a "hunch" about something, where I knew my intuition was kicking in, he would tell me, "Your intuition means nothing. You're usually wrong, so would you stop?" I felt so challenged. How dare he belittle something that I found so strong? How dare he challenge my deep, inner thoughts? I suddenly questioned everything in my life. Was my entire life existence something I truly just made up in my head? Was this whole intuition/being an empath thing even real? He once again made me feel crazy.

I knew when cheating was taking place, I knew when he was talking to someone through texts, I knew when he was looking at pornography behind my back. I could feel all of this negative energy every day walking into our house. It's something that never went away. And nine times out of ten, when I had an intuition on something he was doing, I was right. But because that was challenging him, he couldn't have that. So he made me feel crazy by belittling me for this so-called power that I knew I had. And when I did catch him cheating on me and proving that my intuition was in fact right, he would yell and scream about how shitty a wife I was that I went through his phone and saw what I saw. But what is the real issue here? Me going through his phone, or him doing what he did, and me finding out? That question has yet to be answered. Remember, friends, he wasn't sorry for any of this when I was unaware it was happening, but suddenly when it all came to light, he was angry... which then led to him being sorry... which then led back to anger, and ended with lying some more. Don't you dare fall for the same bullshit I did.

Love, your friendly psychic,

Megan

Defending My Name

February 8th, 2020

I guess I've thought about this a lot. Defending my name. I've talked before in my blog on how sometimes picking your battles is the best decision. You don't want to let something take over your life so much that you make yourself look like an idiot trying to defend yourself. Look, I know my truth, and I ain't about to try to prove it to people. But he ruined my name. People I once was close to now thought of me as a terrible person. He tainted my reputation, which was something I really did work hard for. I had a huge social media following, and I prided myself on being real and raw, and now suddenly people were going to think the worst of me. He purposely tried to ruin my reputation just so he could have the final word and get people on his side even though he was to blame. But I knew better than to rebut him. I knew better than to make a scene, because I was going to hold my head high and show my power in silence. I was not going to reach out to his friends and family because I had nothing to prove to them. I wasn't about to start a war with a "he said, she said" game. I knew my truth, and I had nothing to prove to anyone but myself. These people could think what they wanted from the lies they were told, and it truly just shows not only what kind of person he was, but what kind of people they were during this.

If I could say anything about this, I would advise people not to be so blind to abuse just because he's your son or your friend. Don't ignore the red flags just because you were friends with him for longer than I had known him. Don't shove his actions to the side just because you marched on a drumline with him. Don't push his actions under the rug just because you think he's a good person. One of his friends actually told me once that with people in the music industry, you'll meet a lot of different personalities, and one of them might be "womanizers," and it's OK to just forget about their past and what they did to you and those other woman, and just move on, because that's just who they are. LIKE, WHAT? He was literally defending him and his actions, and I do NOT stand for that! As a woman who has been hurt in both mental and physical forms, I took a lot of offense to this.

After all is said and done, though, something that truly bothered me still lingers. The jokes about mental illnesses. I have always been open about my mental illnesses, but I never once would joke about them. After the abuse N put me through, forcing me to kill my child, the cheating, the gaslighting, the narcissism, the pain I'll always feel from him, the one thing that lingers is that he truly damaged my name and reputation with the stigma of a mental illness. Mental illnesses are not a joke, but mine was to him. He plastered it all around his friends and family to make it very clear to them that he was not the bad guy; I was. And frankly, that still stings a bit.

It's not about believing me or not believing me. It's not about whose side you chose to be on. It's about the facts. Not to make anyone hate a certain person, but to bring light to the subject of this normality, something no one seems to talk about, maybe because, like me, they were scared and embarrassed. And that right there is exactly why I am writing this book.

Hello, my name is Megan. And I will not let you tell anyone otherwise.

Selfies

February 9th, 2020

Random topic for a random day.

Selfies.

Why is it that when women (or men) post selfies, it's considered a bad thing? We somehow think it's OK to judge people because they post photos of themselves? I get that sometimes it can be annoying, but if someone feels good about themselves, why aren't they allowed to brag for a second?

I literally just read a comment about a selfie on my blog page that said, "I stay away from people like you. Look at those gauging marks on your arms (tattoos), and the look in your eyes. You people are bad news and I would never allow people like you in my life. Stop with the photos and get a life."

I get very into topics such as these—no idea why! But I think the psychological reason behind selfies probably stems from someone, at some point in their life, being bullied, being made fun of, picked on—and when they finally feel good about themselves and get the courage to show that to the world, who are we to judge? Apparently, there's even something out there called "selfitis" where selfies have become so much of a person's life that they start posting too many, and believe it or not, psychologists have actually studied this. I don't really believe in this. My personal viewpoint is, girl, if you feel good in that new outfit, you like that new makeup palette you just purchased, you finally fit into those size-eight jeans you've been working so hard at, or you just feel good for a date night, SHOW THAT OFF! I see absolutely NOTHING wrong with showing the world that you feel good about yourself!

In a world where society picks us apart, both men and women, we feel the need to be perfect every single day. Sadly, that's just not reality, though. No one is perfect, and no Snapchat filter will make you that way. But when you think to yourself, "Damn, I look good!" I think that's something to celebrate! Why? Because in a society where all people do is tear other people down, we feel good enough to show the world the middle finger!

So do me a favor.

Grab your phone! Take a selfie! I don't care what you look like, if you have makeup on or not, what you're wearing, or where you are. Take that selfie and post it! Show people that it's OK to be you! AND BE PROUD OF THAT! #theselfieproject

OK, I made that hashtag up. But for real. Do you. Be you. Who cares? End of rant.

Much love, from a person that probably takes too many selfies but really doesn't give a shit,

Megan

What Is Your Level Of "Have To"?

February 14th, 2020

Something I've always told my following and my direct sales team is this: when you are FORCED to succeed, you will. I don't think a lot of people understand where I'm coming from when I talk about this topic, but I truly believe when you are forced to do something, you'll do it.

In 2017 when I joined this company on a whim, I shouldn't have. I had –$462 to my name, no savings account, forty thousand dollars in debt, and twelve credit cards maxed out. I shouldn't have spent one hundred dollars to join a company like this, but I knew I needed something that could potentially bring in a little extra income for me, and this was the route I chose.

Now, before you all start freaking out and stop reading this—I know, I know, direct sales companies suck. Direct sales companies have a bad stigma. I'm not here to discuss opinions on that. I'm here to give you a little motivation that you can take and apply to your current life, your current job, anything that you are struggling with. So do me a favor and keep reading, OK?

As I said, when I joined this company, I shouldn't have. But I was tired of making minimum wage in a job that I was starting to hate, a job that bullied me and left my bills unpaid, and coming home crying every night after work. I was done. I needed something. ANYTHING! Something that could just give me a little extra money on the side to help with my bills. My goal was to make an extra two hundred dollars a month to pay my car payment. Within a month, I quit my job because not only was I making my car payment, I was making more money in one day than I was making in an entire week at my job. It was a no-brainer.

I quit my job and focused on this full time. I was FORCED to make this work, because I had to. I suddenly saw myself making five times the amount of money I was making at my old job, I was happy working from home, and I could focus on myself for a bit, which to me, is the American dream. Then suddenly I found myself earning trips I never thought I'd earn, making money I never in my life thought I'd see, and I found myself truly succeeding in something for once! (That's NEVER happened in my life!) Six months later, I am proud to say, I had every dime of debt paid off, including my car, and I was officially 100 percent debt free with a savings account! Why did this happen, though? Why did this happen for little ol' me? Because I woke up every single day, and I GOT SHIT DONE! I didn't half-ass it. I didn't wake up thinking success would just be handed to me and I'd be a millionaire overnight. I woke up every single day with the mindset of HAVING TO MAKE THIS WORK! Because that's the truth: I made it work because I HAD TO. I was forced to make a paycheck and pay my bills, so that's exactly what I did!

Fast-forward to a few years later, January 2019. I was gearing up for my company's annual convention in Nashville, Tennessee. Everyone there had their reason for being there. For some, it was simply wanting to learn more about the business. For others, it was because it was a fun way to meet their team and become the best version of themselves as team leaders. And some people were struggling, so they invested in themselves and attended this convention to become remotivated in their business. I, too, was struggling during this time, but my struggle was a bit different. Five days prior to this I had walked out of my ex-husband's house. I didn't know what I was going to do, I didn't have money to provide for myself, I lost touch with everything I once stood for, and I was overly confused and unmotivated. Not many people knew at the time what was going on, but those who did stood by me and made sure to help in any way they could. At convention this particular year, I was kicked off our leadership council. Something that I was so incredibly proud of was taken from me. And although I understood the reasoning, it stung—A LOT. I questioned whether I was in the right place in life; I questioned if this was my sign to quit. I went to bed that night ready to resign and find another path in life. But I woke up the next morning with an open mind, knowing you can't quit on a bad day, and that was my bad day.

On the way home that weekend, I was on the airplane heading back to St. Louis and started really examining myself. I told myself, "Megan, this isn't you, you're not a quitter, figure this shit out!" I started to go back to my "why." WHY I started this business. WHY I started with this company. WHY I needed a better job. WHY I needed to get out of debt. And I remembered that when I first started, I made myself a vision board in the notes on my phone. The day I signed up with this company I wrote down my goals, and we're talking like over a hundred goals! As nights went on doing these live Facebook shows, I referred back to this vision board after every one of them. I found myself checking off goal after goal. Everything from:

"Get 1 preorder." CHECK.

"Sell out of your kit." CHECK.

"Get 1 recruit." CHECK.

"Make $1,000 in one day." CHECK.

And the list went on and on.

At the very end of this goal sheet, I had written down my five-year plan. In my five-year plan I stated that I wanted to be one of the first five consultants to reach the very top rank. When you hit the top rank of Sapphire, you are handed a lump-sum, $10,000 check. I wanted that! That was in my five-year plan. After re-reading this on the airplane that day, I sat there and starred at this goal for a minute and told myself, "You can't do that." Want to know why I couldn't do that? Because at that very moment, I said, "No, you won't be one of the first five people to hit this in your first five years. You are going to be the FIRST to hit it. AND YOU ARE GOING TO DO IT THIS YEAR!" As I said that to myself, I lit a fire under my ass and was the most motivated I had been in a good while! I told myself I had twelve months to hit this, and I'd be damned if I didn't walk into convention next year being the first Sapphire consultant. You guys, what happened next should be in a damn Hallmark movie or something. I hit that very top rank just three months later and was handed that $10,000 check!

Now, why did this happen? BECAUSE I WAS FORCED TO SUCCEED. I had to make a paycheck because I was on my own! I had a house payment for the first time, I had bills I had to pay, and I no longer had my ex-husband's income to help me out. I had walked out of my marriage, taking only my pets and my clothes, I had no furniture to furnish my house because I left all that to my ex. I was desperately in need of something, and I was desperately needing to succeed. I received that $10,000 check from my company and was able to furnish my new house all on my own.

So, if you are reading this and asking yourself why you haven't been successful in whatever it is you are working toward, ask yourself what your level of "have to" is. My level of "have to" at first was to get out of my job and make something of myself, so that's what I did! My level of "have to" changed significantly when suddenly I was on my own having to provide for myself by myself. I was forced to succeed, and I made it happen. If you are doing mediocre work and half-assing what you are working toward, you aren't there yet. Figure out your level of "have to," and DO NOT STOP until you make it happen! I woke up every single day forcing myself to get shit done. And when I have a goal in mind, you best believe I'm not stopping until I hit it! I encourage every single one of you to dig deep and find that level of motivation, because when you do, and when you are truly FORCED to make something work, you always will.

Love, the top ranked consultant in the entire company (yes, I'm bragging!!),

Megan Besler

Bullying

February 20th, 2020

When it comes to being bullied as a child, I recently learned that not everyone has the same view of "bullying" as the next. That is 100 percent OK, but I wanted to shed some light on this, or at least offer my personal opinions. Obviously, these are only my personal beliefs on the matter, but I would like you to at least keep an open mind while reading this, even if your opinion may be different.

I've become more outspoken in the past few years about the bullying I suffered when I was younger. It has come as a shock to some of people in my past, including my friends and family. I didn't talk about it much while it was happening. In fact, I don't remember talking to ANYONE about it except for the school counselor at the time, and the only reason that even happened was because she got word that I mentioned thoughts of suicide because of how ugly I felt after being bullied.

Middle school was where it all started. Middle school was rough for me, as I'm sure it was for many people. In my school district, we spent kindergarten through sixth grade in an elementary school in my hometown. Seventh and eighth grades (middle school) brought three elementary schools together in another town. Ninth through twelfth grades were in the same town, with those three schools still combined. Going from one class that you grew to know over the course of six years, a class of about twenty people, to three schools combined to form a middle school class was a rough adjustment. A lot of different personalities came into play. Suddenly, the people you grew up with were now classified according to different social situations. You suddenly had your "popular kids," your "jocks," your "band geeks," your "nerds," when in the previous six years, all you knew were just classmates.

Now suddenly each of those classmates had roles. It was weird to me. Someone I had grown up with was suddenly different. I was different. Everyone was different. It was like throwing wild dogs together and seeing which ones got along with who, and based on that, you get cliques.

I felt very segregated in middle school because I saw all these groups and cliques and I understood why certain people went a certain way, but I could never identify just where I was supposed to go. I was definitely an awkward kid, but I had normal issues too, the same ones everyone going through puberty had to go through. Skin issues. Self-esteem issues. I was also dealing with my parents splitting up around that time, not really living "poor" exactly, but we definitely didn't have money. I went to school in pajamas most days because I didn't have "good" clothes like the rest of the school. I had acne like most kids my age, yet I was the one getting picked on. And because of having acne, I had oily skin, which meant I also had oily hair. My curly, frizzy, hot-mess hair was not fun in the nineties, when the "thing" was to have stick-straight, long hair! You can see where I'm going with this. To be honest, I never really had an issue with it, until a certain person started a rumor. That rumor changed my life in the worst way possible. I know the person who started the rumor, but they will go nameless for the sake of this blog. I truly don't believe in making a person feel bad, even though I wish I could tell this person the lifelong impact they had on me with just that ONE rumor they decided to spread about me.

I walked into school that morning. Went to my first and second period classes, reading and math, then walked to my third period class, science. As I was walking through the hall, I overheard somebody, who I thought was a good friend of mine, laughing. She was pointing at me and asking me when the last time I showered was because of how greasy my hair was. I shrugged it off, knowing my hair only looked greasy because I have crazy natural curls, and with textured hair comes natural oils. They of course didn't care to know that part though. Then as I walked into my science class, another person was staring at me from their seat and covering their mouth from laughing. They, too, had heard the rumor. And by lunch, my good friend came up to me asking me if I had heard what people were talking about. I remember saying no, even though I knew what she was going to say. She responded, "People are saying you don't shower because of your greasy hair and bad skin."

I went straight to the front office and asked if I could go home because I wasn't feeling well. They sat me in the nurse's office for almost the rest of the school day.

I was mortified. I didn't know how to wear makeup. No one had ever showed me. I didn't want to wear makeup because no one ever had the year before in sixth grade, so why the sudden change? I didn't have nice clothes to wear like everyone else, and of COURSE I showered every morning, but with naturally textured hair, you have OIL! But kids are cruel, and they picked on me until the day I graduated because of this. And even to this day, I feel I still get targeted for having bad skin.

Now, here's my question, and the point of this blog. Was that bullying? Or was that just getting picked on? Is there a difference? What it boils down to, in my opinion, is that regardless of what you want to call it, it's not OK. What we had here was a seventh-grade girl who was now being told she was ugly and disgusting. People were laughing at her for going through puberty, basically. People laughed at her, called her names, and belittled her for looking the way she did, when she physically couldn't help it. And this wasn't just a one-day thing. It lasted until I graduated and even after that. So is that considered bullying? Or is that just kids being kids? Either way you want to look at it, is it OK? If your child did this to someone, would you be OK with it? Or if YOU did it to someone, does it help you sleep better at night if you just tell yourself this person was only being picked on, not being bullied? To me, both go hand in hand. No matter what you think it was called, it made a child want to commit suicide at one point. It made her so self-conscious that even now, at thirty-two years old, she still cannot walk out of her house to get groceries without makeup on.

This same person who started these rumors went on to bully me more throughout my school years. In the locker room, after gym class, I refused to shower with the rest of the class because I was being targeted now for not having big boobs—or, well, boobs at all. I was being made fun of now for having a small chest. In fact, someone once told me I looked like a little boy because I never grew in like the rest of the girls. This may have been just getting "picked on," but it was the reason for getting a breast augmentation later in life because I had lived a life feeling ugly because of it. Then, because I never showered with the other girls after gym class, another rumor was spread (probably by the same person) that I didn't want people to see I had an eating disorder. I have always been a very tiny, petite girl; it just runs in my family. Suddenly now I was being targeted for being too skinny and accused of puking my guts out in between meals. It was NOT at all true. I'm actually pretty proud to say I've never had an eating disorder, but thanks to those good ol' high school years, everyone sure as shit thought I did. So now, as a thirty-two-year-old woman, I constantly feel the need to gain weight when I can't, thanks to those cruel "friends."

I'm not writing this for pity, and I'm not writing it for an apology. I'm writing this to make it VERY, VERY, CRYSTAL CLEAR that just because you may think you're aren't doing any harm to someone by simply picking on them here and there, you might actually be ruining their life. I don't care what ANYONE out there calls it—bullying, non-bullying, picking on someone, making fun of someone, whatever—what it is you are doing is NOT OK. And here I am, almost twenty years later, still dealing with the repercussions of YOUR actions. (Yes, I am addressing the bully directly here.) But don't you worry, I sleep very well at night knowing that I came out ahead on this deal and ended up the bigger person. And I say that because I read your post the other day. I read your post about never being a bully and not understanding why people are quick to judge a bully instead of the victim. It, to be honest, blew my mind. Because of YOU, I am the way I am. Because of YOU, I suffer from pretty bad body dysmorphia. Because of YOU, I lived the majority of my life thinking I'm ugly, trying so hard to fit in like the rest of you. I now understand, almost twenty years later, that I am beautiful in my own unique way, even if no one in high school realized that. Myself included. So whether in your mind you considered it bullying or normal kid actions, what you did wasn't OK. I just wish, for the sake of future generations, that people can read this with an open mind and think long and hard about what they say to someone, about someone, or rumors that they think would be "funny" to start. What can it actually do to a person?

Thank you for attending my TED Talk,
Megan

Abuse On Others

February 21st, 2020

A constant thought recently has been, "Am I the only person he treated badly?" And then I start questioning why. When I think long and hard on this topic, I find myself thinking about scenarios that always made me uncomfortable. Scenarios that didn't just include me being treated badly. Scenarios that I now view as toxic, but at the time, they just seemed normal.

Whenever I'd bring N to Iowa to visit my family, it always seemed he wanted to leave as soon as we got there. He knew that I didn't get to see my family as often as I'd like, and I always regretted not being able to see my sisters grow up. Part of seeing your siblings grow up is attending their school functions, their sporting events, their proms and dances. My sister always wanted me to watch her volleyball games and gymnastics meets, and the fact that she excelled in both of these sports made me want to watch them even more! I was never much into sports growing up, only softball. I loved softball, though, and seeing my family at my games brought me so much joy. That's something I will always treasure—seeing my grandma and grandpa at my softball games, seeing my mom go to every choir concert of mine, playing catch with my dad in the yard. It's really hard for me to admit that, for my volleyball stud of a sister, I've only watched ONE of her games, and that one game happened about six months ago while she was a senior in high school. Her last season. The ONE sport she has such passion for, the one that she does so well in—I've only gotten to watch her play ONCE. I can't get that time back. And she used to be super involved in gymnastics, but do you think I've ever seen one of her gymnastics meets either? Nope.

Once when we were in Iowa for a function I can't even remember, my sister happened to have a home volleyball meet that Monday. I begged and pleaded with N to stay one extra day because he didn't have to work that Monday, I believe due to a holiday. He didn't want to stay, though. He refused to even attempt to have an open mind about it; it was just an instant NO. I missed out on so many memories I could have had with my sisters because of this. It happened more times than I would like to admit. My own mother even pointed it out once and asked why he never wanted to stay and watch her games. I never had an answer for her. That particular day, it would have made more sense to stay an extra day and watch her game since he didn't have to work the next day, but the weather started getting bad and he wanted to rush home. Turns out that was just an excuse to get home faster.

Then, as I started thinking about every time this happened with N, it occurred to me that he did stuff like this with other people too. My mom once made us a huge Christmas meal, only for him to show up and say he wasn't hungry, even though he knew she was cooking for us. That was always heavy on me because as it was happening, I could tell my mom felt defeated, and I didn't know what to do or say to make that any better.

He also used to make fun of my friends—how they looked and what they wore. One of my closest friends posted a selfie, and he asked me, "Why does she always post photos like this? She looks terrible." Which, I mean, whatever, have your opinions on someone, but why say something like that out loud? Especially to me, someone who is so anti-bullying, and someone who stands up against sexism and advocates for women. In that very moment, I knew it was a losing a battle. Everything I stood for, he didn't, and that, to me, was very eye-opening. Suddenly I noticed him picking on people's photos, making fun of the gay community, being rude to my friends and family, being rude to his OWN family. But if I brought any of this up, I'd be considered crazy once again, and I tried to avoid every argument I could.

What I've learned in the past twelve months after leaving him is that narcissists flock to your strengths like a moth to a flame. They zero in on what makes you YOU, and they make it a mission to destroy that. If you aren't broken when you two meet, they sure as hell destroy you over time, and they certainly make you believe what they're saying to you is true. I can't say I wasn't broken when we met, as I definitely was, but not to the extreme that I am now. One of my biggest "strengths," if you want to call it that, was the closeness I had with my family. I've always had a VERY tight-knit family. We have our problems, and Lord knows we are overly dysfunctional, but, man, we have each other's back like you wouldn't believe, and I have always, ALWAYS been close to my family for that very reason. He saw that, and he needed that gone. So he did everything he could to make that happen. Suddenly it all makes sense, doesn't it? Keeping me away from something I was so close with. Whatever strength narcissists go for, they turn around and completely destroy it, and that's what he did. He was never close to his family, so I sure as hell couldn't be either.

I can never get those years back with my sisters. I can never get that time back that I craved with my grandparents, father, mother, or any other friends or family. That's the harsh reality of it. But, here we are.

Wanderlust

February 28th, 2020

Today marks the one-year anniversary of when I "officially" started on a new adventure in my life. I walked out of a toxic marriage only to be alone and overly confused. I knew that if I was going to go through with this, I actually had to do it and not look back. I knew that there was more to life than living unhappily and being mistreated.

I knew that somewhere in the past ten years I lost myself, and I only have myself to blame for that, but walking out on my ex-husband made me realize just how much of myself I was actually missing. I knew I had to regain some focus, realign my life, find my true self, and find that self-love for which I had longed for so, so long. The moment I walked out that door, I told myself I need to do WHATEVER it takes to find myself again, and it was right then and there that I remembered a solo trip I had taken to New York City a few years back. Traveling has always been a passion of mine, but traveling alone has been especially inspirational for me. So it was then that I realized this was how I was going to take the reins on 2019. The year 2019 was going to be a new beginning for me. I didn't care how much money was spent, where I went, or how I got there. I just knew that in order to find peace in my life, I needed to do this.

One year ago today was when this started. I decided I was going to go somewhere once a month for an entire year. I chose Vegas to start, to knock off one of my bucket list dreams to see Celine Dion in concert. People thought I was crazy; people told me I would spend too much money. And although, yes, it was very expensive, you cannot put a price in finding true happiness, and folks, I found that.

The year 2019 started off hard and then led to the happiest I've ever been in my entire life. It ended, once again, on some hard notes, but the promise to myself I made, I accomplished, and within that I found a true form of happiness, unlike anything I could have imagined—self-love and self-acceptance. So into the wild I went, losing my way but finding my soul.

I traveled to places I'd never been before, I met the most interesting people I've met in my life, I shared experiences with close friends and family, and I truly found what people considered "happiness." People told me the glow I had was like nothing they'd ever seen before with me. They told me I was smiling so much that I radiated positive energy wherever I went. I felt SO good about myself, and I just wanted to scream to the world that THIS IS EXACTLY HOW LIFE SHOULD BE! I had never felt that before. Especially not in recent years with an ex-husband who made me feel like the complete, polar opposite.

As months went by, going somewhere new at least once a month, I started realizing what I had been missing all these years, and suddenly it seemed so simple. I just needed out of that hellhole and away from being so controlled. Lions were not meant for cages, and this lion (Leo) needed to break free.

So here I am one year later, telling each and every one of you: TRAVEL. Money will always be there; experiences will not. Even if you can't do it once a month, do it once a year. It doesn't have to be a fancy, expensive trip. Go to a local hotel and spend the night. Find a bed and breakfast or go to a winery for the weekend. Get away when you can, and take that all in. Just do me one, simple favor: travel far enough away that you begin to meet yourself there.

Wanderlust,

Megan

Is It Over Yet?

March 1st, 2020

I think the running joke of this new decade is that January seemed to take ninety-seven years, and then February lasted about as long as my hiccups. But here we are in March already, and I'm just ready to move forward and get things done. I haven't written many deep blogs lately. I think I needed to take a break from them due to the emotions that seem to come out of me after I write one. I think a lot of obvious past trauma gets brought up with them, but more so than I imagined. Most of these past wounds of mine have been stitched together and forgotten about, but one wrong move, and they bust wide open, causing a massive amount of pain.

I hate being depressed. I'm not ashamed of it; I just hate it. As someone who is naturally a very happy-go-lucky, upbeat, witty girl, I don't like putting myself in a position where I feel so mad, so depressed, so unmotivated, and just so sad all the time. These blogs, although incredibly therapeutic, have often reopened past wounds, and it seems to have an effect on me, as if I'm reliving them all over again. So I apologize that I haven't written any "good" ones lately, but for those of you binge-reading this like a damn Netflix show, I'm sure it went unnoticed.

January, to me, seemed like a fresh start, but it was almost like I couldn't pinpoint where I needed to go to start whatever it was I was starting. February was like a transition month for me, and now that it's March, I feel ready to move forward. I have my divorce trial in eight days, and although I'm very much NOT looking forward to this, I feel in my heart that it's going to end up OK because even though I know I'm not right in a lot of things, this is truly something I feel very much RIGHT about, and I wholeheartedly know that I'm in the right place in this. So, in eight days, I will HOPEFULLY be free. Free from pain, free from being controlled, free from abuse, free from manipulation, and free to just be me again. It's really crazy to think it's been over a year and this is STILL going on, but here we are. The strong always survive, and I know I am a very strong individual, and this has made me even stronger.

So in preparation for next week, send me some good vibes, some prayers, and some funny memes to get me through! I love when you guys write messages to me on Facebook, comment on my YouTube channel videos, or reply to these emails. More often than not, it seems a "feel good" message arrives in my inbox on days when I need it most, and for that I appreciate you guys so, so much. The last year has been stressful, to say the least. The last few months have been not so good to me either. But the last few weeks have been me preparing for a big life move, and your good vibes are going to get me through this.

Thank you all, as always, for supporting me, believing in me, and just being here by my side to read and see me through this. I say it a lot, but I'll say it again—you guys help me just as much as I help you, if not more. Thank you for allowing me this platform to not only speak my truth but spread the word of my mission to help other individuals out there.

Godspeed,
Megan

Emotions Before Trial

March 4th, 2020

I have a lot of thoughts recently, and I'm having a hard time getting them out of my head and on paper. I'm overly angry lately, and I know it's because the trial is next week. My emotions are completely on edge, I cry at the drop of a dime, I've been having problems getting out what I really want to say, and my brain is racing nine hundred miles an hour and I have no idea how to shut it off.

I know things will all work out in the end. They have to, right? But, man, this is stressful. No one on this entire planet should have to deal with this. NO ONE! I wouldn't wish this on anyone. I know it makes a person stronger in the end, but that doesn't make it fair. I have put up with enough pain and suffering my entire life, especially the past ten years, only for it to end with this—more pain and suffering.

It's amazing to me the "hold" he still has on me even after over a year of being apart. I just don't understand how someone can be that way. How can someone sleep well at night knowing what they are doing to a person? I thought leaving him once and for all would make it all stop, but here we are over a year later, and although the marriage is clearly done, I'm still on his tight leash, and he knows it. He knows EXACTLY what he is doing. In fact, I've said from day one that this was all going to be part of his master plan. He put me through SO much in the almost ten years we were together, but I feel that's nothing compared to what he's dragged me through in the past twelve months, and I am just really tired of it and downright emotionally exhausted.

This relationship and marriage ruined me in a way that I can never fully explain, but this divorce has taken it to a whole different level. If I didn't lose all respect for him after what he did to me and put me through, I sure as hell lost it all in the last twelve months of the bull-shit he's dragging me through now, and he just won't stop. He doesn't know when to stop. And if he does, he is making it a point to NOT stop.

It's sad, really, when you look at the psychology behind why a person acts the way they do in situations like this. I imagine asking him, "What on earth did you go through to make you be this person?" And even after everything he did to me, I still would like to ask him that and get a real answer.

I hope and pray that he finds the help he needs. I hope and pray that he understands the severity of his actions. And I hope and pray that the next woman in his life doesn't suffer like I had to. I don't write these blogs to attack him; I write them so that people see the red flags that I missed and do something about it before it's too late. And in all honesty, I hope and pray that he does better, as a man, as a son, as a partner, and as a human, because this shit is not OK.

This past week has gotten the best of me. A lot of emotion has come out, and it's unfair to everyone who has had to deal with it lately. I am not ashamed of the emotion; I am just sorry that people have to deal with it when they shouldn't. I shouldn't even have to deal with this, yet here we are. As I said in my previous blog, I know I'm a strong woman for this, and this is a mere chapter in my story. But it doesn't mean it's not hard.

Kind regards,

Megan

225

My "Crazy"

March 9th, 2020

I've found myself asking "why hasn't he left yet?" more often than I'd like to admit. He doesn't know this, but it's a constant struggle I face, where I don't feel good enough for him, on top of all the bullshit he's had to deal with from the get-go coming into this relationship. Look, I know I'm a good person. Sometimes I'm too good to people. But I'm just going to be real here: no one who is starting a new relationship should have to deal with their partner's divorce, and I sure feel how unfair it is to make him have to deal with this with me. Yet here he is. And no one should have to deal with their partner's mental anguish when it comes to dealing with said divorce either. Yet here he is.

When I made the decision to once and for all go through with a divorce, November 2018, I didn't think it would be that hard, honestly. I know that sounds weird, but to me, nothing could be harder than the actual abusive, narcissistic relationship I'd been in, right? By comparison, this divorce should be a walk in the park. I knew what I wanted, I knew how to make that happen, and that's what I did. But here we are over a year later, and we are STILL dealing with these issues, and one particular person in this party doesn't want to cut the cord.

When you sign up for a new relationship, it's amazing at first. They call it "the honeymoon stage" for a reason, because everything just seems so perfect. No one gets into a relationship thinking, *This is going to suck, but I'm going to try anyway.* Or at least I wouldn't think they do! I'd assume in just about every scenario when new love arises, you fall in love with someone simply because they are who they are, and not necessarily the baggage they bring with them. Hell, half the time in relationships, the baggage isn't even mentioned until months down the road. My baggage, however, was mentioned up front. In fact, I told him about my baggage before we were even considered a couple. I think I even mentioned that it was overweight luggage at this point! Nonetheless, he stayed. And he continues to stay even after it seems to get worse and worse as the months go by. (My baggage, not our relationship.) So the question arises: why hasn't he left yet?

He truly is a godsend. A good man. No—a GREAT man. The most amazing human I've probably ever met. His kindness radiates, his positivity is so uplifting, and we have such intelligent conversations to where I just fall in love with him as a person all over again about a hundred times a week. I feel terrible that he has to deal with this stuff, because he shouldn't have to. But I'm so damn happy that I have him by my side to help me during these times. I thank him so often for everything, but part of me feels like I don't thank him enough. He was raised right, that's for damn sure. And it makes me so proud to call him my partner.

N's last words to me will forever haunt me, though. "Good luck with the next man in your life, giving him all your crazy. They, too, will have to deal with you, and I feel sorry for them." It haunts me to the core. Every time I say something wrong, spiral back into old habits, or think my past is coming back to haunt me. I stare at him and think, *This is my crazy. This is what N meant by that. I'm so sorry you have to deal with this.* I hate that after all this time I still let his words affect me, but it's damn hard not to! I try to motivate myself every day, telling myself those were just his abusive words, they didn't mean anything, he only said what he said because he knew it would get to you. But it sure is hard! I do feel bad that my partner has to deal with my crazy. I do feel bad they have to deal with all of this divorce bullshit alongside me. Am I thankful? OH MY GOD, YES! But it doesn't mean I wish this upon them. If we hadn't already had the "marriage talk," you can sure as hell bet the man would never get married after going through this hell with me, and he isn't even the one actually getting divorced!

This man is so much more than a boyfriend to me. He is my partner. He is the one who makes me glow, the one who brings a real smile to my face to the point that everyone notices it. If it weren't for him, I'm not so sure so where I'd be right now. He gives me new motivation every single day; he reminds me that my mistakes are only human, and that my past doesn't define me. He makes me want to be a better person and allows me to grow right alongside him. To only call him my boyfriend hardly does him justice. To finally understand what love is, is so incredible to me. After everything I've been through with this previous "life" of mine, this previous marriage, it all led to him. And for that, I will forever be grateful.

So thank you for dealing with my "crazy" even if it's not exactly what you signed up for. The fact that you can keep me sane through all this speaks volumes. In fact, you're the only thing I'm sure of right now in life. Thank you for sticking by me when times got hard recently. Thank you for making me smile when I feel there's no reason to. You are the reason I am truly happy today, and I thank you so, so much for bringing that light into my life. Till death do us part, right? (My ex-marriage jokes suck. Carry on.)

I Will Not Be Silenced

March 10th, 2020

As of about twelve hours ago, I am one step closer to being FREE. My trial date that was set for Monday was pushed back because we were given a new judge. At this point both attorneys had to go in front of the new judge to explain the case and get her caught up on everything. Both attorneys held a meeting with the judge yesterday, and to my surprise, N BACKED OFF EVERYTHING! EVERYTHING!!!!!!!!!! He no longer is trying to fight for half of what my business was worth, he no longer is fighting for alimony, no longer is fighting for hefty maintenance, no longer is asking for half my paychecks, no longer is keeping money that is owed to me. HE BACKED OFF OF ALL OF IT!!!! This is why my lawyer kicks ass and takes names. This is why I paid for the best of the best. I cannot and WILL NOT let him win this. This no longer is a case of she gets this, he wants this, split everything, blah blah blah. This is a case of what is right and what is wrong, and although I was preparing for trial for the judge to hear my story, and fight for basically the half a million dollars he wanted out of me, it looks to me like she saw through the bullshit of his, and once she made that very clear, they backed off of everything. Which proves my theory about him dragging this out on purpose. Well, newsflash, asshole, you want to put up a fight with me and play dirty, I'm a pro at playing dirtier.

Now, I am not totally in the clear yet, as we are drafting up final settlement documents now, but this is one step closer to being FREE. FREE from manipulation, FREE from abuse, FREE from being owned, FREE from being controlled. I, soon, will be FREE from him, and I cannot tell you how crazy this is to finally see the light at the end of the tunnel.

I know a lot of people reading this have said, "It's just a divorce. Many people have been there and got through it. Your story is no different than the next." But those people do not understand the severity of the toxicity I lived in. I truly feel that if I had stayed, my life would have been at risk. I've said it before, and I truly believe it, that if I had let things go much longer, it could have led to physical abuse, and that terrified me. But with that said, mental abuse is just as bad, and I will NOT be sorry for fighting for this. Not for me, and certainly not for anyone else out there who is suffering as well. I truly hope and pray that all of you reading this can make a promise to yourself that if you, or someone you know, is going through this and seeing those red flags, you will be that person who steps in for help! Do not let it get to the point I did. I hope and pray you all can find that peace in your life that I have, and I surely hope you don't have to go through what I did to get there.

Let it be known that this is the final step to freedom for me, and I am just so fucking happy right now that I put up a fight to make this worth it. Like I said before, this whole thing wasn't about money, it wasn't about a he said/she said game, it wasn't about who got to keep what or how assets were going to be split. It was about showing him what he did wrong and proving to him that I would not back down like he thought I would, based on my history of backing down at his commands. I will speak for those who have no words. And although I suffer from pretty severe PTSD because of him, I stood tall through all of this and came out the bigger person in the end, because even though he hurt me and beat me to the core for many, many years, I will not allow him to continue doing this. I WILL NOT BE SILENCED.

So here's to the men and women who feel they cannot speak up. Here's to those who have so much to say but no one will listen. Here's to those who have been hurt far too many times and need a way out. Here's to those who have similar stories and cannot find a way. Let me speak for you, because I will not allow you to be silenced either, my beautiful friends. There is an end. Let's get you there.

Chakra Opening

(An old blog I dug up)
March 16th, 2018

When I was in skincare school, my instructor at the time talked to me about the developmental stages of chakras and how about every seven years, you go through a major life change.

As someone who never truly knew what any of this meant until I started taking a holistic approach to skincare, I found this to be rather fascinating. I remember her telling me that around certain ages, you find something deep within you that greatly affects that time of your life. It was a major eye-opening conversation because as she was discussing this with me, I realized she was completely right as I examined my current life timeline, up until that point, and realized I was kind of going through exactly what she was talking about.

Well, this was 2011.

Seven years ago!

I know—ironic, right?

I think I recently hit another "milestone" in my life that's pretty significant, and it's rather interesting to see it play out.

Ages twenty-nine to thirty-five: This cycle relates to the throat chakra, which is in charge of our communication skills and our ability to express ourselves. It's in this stage of development that many people truly find their voice and are comfortable with who they are, thus allowing them to express themselves more freely and openly. Many people find their life's purpose during this time, or begin to refine it, because they've developed a greater ability to communicate what they want.

I doubt she will ever remember having that particular conversation, but thank you, K, for the eye-opening experience that I've had in the back of my head for the last seven years. I appreciate you! It's definitely allowed me to better understand life obstacles and allow myself to realize we continue to grow each and every year of our lives on such a deeper level than just physically.

Love, your fellow hippie,

Megan

Elective Surgery

March 15th, 2020

> "As human beings we all have insecurities that can affect our confidence and self-image. The ability to do something to feel better about ourselves, such as plastic surgery, is something I see as self-love."
> —*Dr. Antimarino*

Plastic and elective surgery have such a bad stigma, and I really don't like it. It's kind of the same for people with tattoos, people with fun hair colors, or people who like to wear extreme makeup every day. You'll always have those who just don't understand it and want to pick it apart, making their targets feel like crap. My thing is, it's not your body, so leave your opinion at home. If someone wants to enhance their features, who am I to say they can't? Hell, if it makes a person feel more comfortable with themselves, CONFIDENCE IS SEXY! I SAY DO IT!

I have had procedures done. I'm not ashamed of it. Some were because of deep-rooted self-esteem issues, some were just because I thought they were pretty, and others were because of health concerns. But all in all, why should it be anyone else's business what you choose to spend your money on? Now, disclaimer. I wouldn't recommend spending five hundred thousand dollars making yourself look more plastic than Barbie, but I would never judge you for it because at the end of the day, YOU are the one who has to be happy with yourself, and YOU are the only person who can make that happen.

Let's talk about my procedures. Not because I want people to see what I've done, but to show you guys that truly, it's OK to have things done and not feel bad about it, even though society may make you feel that way.

I've had plenty of elective procedures done, as well as procedures considered more along the lines of plastic or cosmetic surgery. Let's talk about the things we don't always think about when it comes to these topics.

- Laser facials

- Chemical peels

- Hair color

- Tattoos

- Nail care

- Makeup

- Microblading

All of these items listed above, I've had, and I'm sure plenty of you reading this have as well. I don't HAVE to do them, but they make me feel better about myself when I do, so I CHOOSE to have them done. I get chemical peels and laser facials to help with my acne scarring. I get facials a few times a year to help my overall health of my skin. I color my hair every ten to twelve weeks because I think it looks pretty! I get tattoos because I love the look of them. I get my nails done here and there because it's a good way to pamper myself. I get my eyebrows microbladed because they look one thousand times better when they are, and I love makeup because it makes me feel confident! All of these would be considered elective. I don't have to do them, but I like to because it makes me feel good.

Now let's move on to things society considers "plastic surgery."

- Breast augmentation

- Lip fillers

- Cosmetic dentistry

- Botox

Yes, I've had all of these, and no, I have never had a regret. I had my breast augmentation in 2013 after losing my child. I felt really bad about myself, and my breasts were something I wanted to change ever since being bullied about them at a young age. So I chose to finally do it. I went from a double-A cup to a 32-D cup. No one ever notices I've had this done, and I thoroughly enjoy that. Why? Because I didn't do the procedure to get noticed. I didn't do the procedure for anyone but myself. I just wanted to finally be able to fit into swimsuits without having a boyish figure. I wanted to be able to buy bras from a store instead of never finding my size. It made me finally feel like a woman, especially after the loss of my child, and I badly needed something to help make me feel normal again.

On to lip fillers and botox: honestly, I just really like the look of plump lips and no wrinkles! It's something I tend to find attractive, so I wanted to have that same look. As for cosmetic dentistry, I've had a very long road of recovery with this one. This was a health-related concern, at least until I was able to fix it. I grew up with very straight teeth, never needing braces. People always told me I was lucky for that. But I guess with that came a long line of other dental problems. I have what some people consider "soft teeth," where my enamel never truly formed, causing my teeth to be very thin and weak. Over time, they cracked from the inside out. Temporary bonding was put into place because it was not expensive, but that kept chipping off. Eventually I chose to go down the path of cosmetic dentistry to replace my teeth so this would no longer happen and stop the pain I'd been dealing with from my teeth cracking a few times a month. It's been a long road with over twelve surgeries, but here we are! Pretty teeth, healthy teeth.

Here's my point: cosmetic surgery isn't a "bad" thing. Is it considered a taboo topic, though? Very much so. But realistically, I just don't think it should be. Don't let anyone make you feel bad for what you want to do with your body—whether it's getting a tattoo or coloring your hair, taking care of your skin, or going through some weight loss. Get the boobs you want, get a tummy tuck after having five kids, give yourself a new nose, or take away those hooded eyes. DO NOT LET PEOPLE MAKE YOU FEEL BAD FOR THIS! THIS IS YOUR CHOICE, SO DO WHAT YOU WANT!

Something I need to say, though: please know that these things do not define you. You are beautiful because you are you. No amount of surgery will change who a person is deep down. If you are struggling with yourself and are trying to please somebody else, plastic surgery is NOT the answer. Do it because YOU want it, not because your husband wants it, not because you think it'll make you prettier in someone else's eyes. DO IT FOR YOU AND ONLY YOU. You are beautiful no matter what you decide to do to your hair, your skin, your body. But if you feel it will help with your confidence, GIRL, I WILL STAND BY YOUR SIDE.

Love,

Megan

COVID-19

March 21st, 2020

"You may say I'm a dreamer, but I'm not the only one. I
hope someday you'll join us, and the world will be as one."
—*John Lennon*

With the world on high alert during this pandemic, I feel so very
blessed to be able to work from home and provide for myself
and my family. With that said, I realize some people aren't so lucky, and
although my household is struggling right now due to layoffs, I find
comfort in knowing we are not alone.

Work-from-home businesses are probably going to boom this
year because of this, but if that isn't your thing or is not available for
you at this time, I want to try to help you make use of your time without
causing any more stress. Let's all make a pact to make the best out of
a bad situation.

1. Let's all take this time to take a breather. And I mean some
    DEEP breaths and a reset. We are all stressed right now. I know
    I have been stressed for the past year because of life. Let's
    make use of this time to reset, recoup, and start over. Wake
    up every morning and think of one thing you are thankful for.
    Pour your morning coffee, and just sit and listen to the birds
    outside for a bit. Watch your dog run around the yard and play.
    Color with your children. Do something to kind of eliminate
    the stress going on right now and take this time to really take
    in life. Remember why you are here, and use this as an oppor-
    tunity to destress and watch your kids grow.

2. Stay busy. I know it's easier said than done, but something I have always loved about traveling alone, whether it be to another state or country or just staying in a hotel by myself over the weekend, is the amount of "doing nothing" that ultimately resets my brain. When I say doing nothing, I mean taking a bath to relax, watching a movie you've been meaning to watch, taking up a new hobby, crocheting, knitting, painting, or something else relaxing. Find things to do that relax you but allow you to stay busy. Use that right side of your brain! Tap into the creativity! Because doing "nothing" sometimes is the best medicine for me. Stay in your PJs all day; we don't care! Do nothing, and your brain and your body will feel that reset and thank you SO much for it.

3. Keep your kids busy. We know this is VERY much easier said than done. I do not have children, but I will try to speak for those who do. This is a tough time! Kids don't understand the severity of what is happening here, but we have to try our best to keep them entertained. Find games they can play, find online tools to help them learn, bring out the coloring books, get creative! Something I saw someone doing was buying a big roll of white packaging paper, and having them draw their own yellow brick road. Something to keep their brain engaged while keeping them busy is probably key here. And if it's nice out, let them go outside! No one is saying they can't play in the yard right now. Let's all remember how we grew up. I, for one, played outside ALL day, every day during spring break, summer vacations, etc. Nowadays, kids gravitate toward electronics rather than fresh air. Teach them things outside, play in the dirt, teach them how to take apart things and get their hands dirty. This is a prime opportunity to help keep them busy while teaching them a few life lessons along the way.

4. If you are able to work from home, please do that. There are many, MANY individuals who do not have that luxury right now. I am treating this as a vacation for my boyfriend. His back injury has made it to where working is very hard for him, so

the fact that he gets to have some time off, to me, seems like a blessing, and that's what I'm treating it as! The fact that I can work from home and potentially pull in both incomes seems like a very hard task, but I know I've done it before, so I can do it again. I enjoy being a sugar mama every once in awhile! Haha! All jokes aside, it makes me feel incredibly good to know that I work for a business that can provide like this, and for that I am incredibly thankful.

5.   Stay positive. I know it's so hard right now, but as I said before, I find a lot of comfort in knowing I am not alone. Not only are my friends, family, and neighbors feeling this same stress I am and having the same things happening to them (job loss, income dropping, bills that need to be paid), but my entire city is, my entire state is, the country is, and the world. The fact that we aren't going through this alone is very comforting to me.

All in all, please take these issues very seriously. Please do not be one of those people who are not following the rules and has to go back inside for recess until you figure your shit out. Although the rules may seem dumb to you, there is a bigger picture here. If nothing serious ends up happening, awesome! But it's better to take precautions just in case, because these very precautions are what will save the country and the world a lot of headache later.

I may not have all the answers, obviously, but if there is anything I can do to try to ease your mind, please let me know. My boyfriend and I have done a live show already via Facebook, spreading some positivity out there, and although we are only two people with little impact in the grand scheme of things, this is exactly what it's going to take to eliminate some of that stress the world is seeing. Multiple people have messaged us saying they were terrified, but we provided a bit of comfort to ease their mind. Please do your part in spreading a positive message as well. Share this blog if you feel it's necessary. Share photos of your kids and family right now doing something fun. Anything POSITIVE is key here, and I will do everything in my power to help.

I love you guys. I love us as a country. I love us as humans for the world. Let's be the change we wish to see.

Love,

Megan

The Narcissism Lives On (No, this is not an April Fool's joke)

April 1st, 2020

Oh, how the narcissism lives on.

Yesterday I received a message from my lawyer. I thought this was done! Nope, not if N has anything to do with it. Remember, he can't lose! The email stated that he and his lawyer looked over the final settlement documents for the divorce and everything looked good, but suddenly N owes more in taxes than he thought he would from back in 2018, and because of his screw-up with the IRS, they seized his state tax refund. Lo and behold, he somehow thinks it's because of me, so I should have to pay it.

The amount of common sense that he's lacking recently really has me concerned. I mean, in the most comical way possible! Does he really think I'm that stupid? Yes, he does. However, no, I'm not. I read and re-read this email probably ten times trying to make sense of it myself, thinking maybe I'll give him the benefit of the doubt, and maybe somewhere down the line I missed something on my own taxes. He's saying it's business related, so I owe it. But the document he provided from the IRS clearly states "INDIVIDUAL TAXES." Now, although I don't claim to be smart with ANYTHING dealing with taxes, I do know the difference between a letter that says "individual taxes" and one that may say "business taxes." So, common sense here had me questioning his sanity, but I figured I'd look into it anyway JUST IN CASE I happened to miss something.

I logged in to my old sales ID/tax login with the state of Missouri. It shows that all balances from back when I closed the business have been paid in full. OK, so I owe nothing there. I looked into my individual taxes from 2018 and 2019 as well. I went both the federal route and the state route, and everything shows a $0.00 balance. I checked N's state taxes, and sure enough, his says he owes money. So, let's think long and hard on this, shall we? Because I'm all about talking FACTS here.

Individual taxes means an INDIVIDUAL.

Business taxes means a BUSINESS.

Nowhere on this paper does it say ANYTHING about a business. It specifically says INDIVIDUAL TAXES with HIS social security number.

The manipulation will never stop, will it? I'm beginning to gather that! He will draw this out until the MINUTE before the deadline from the judge just because he knows he can. It's like he somehow thinks he still has control over this stupid girl who doesn't know any better. NEWSFLASH, ASSHOLE: I'M NOT AS DUMB AS YOU THINK I AM. SO PLEASE GET IT THROUGH YOUR FUCKING BRAIN! OK, sorry—had to let that out.

What a joke, truly. At this point, both attorneys are having a hard time figuring him out, the judge doesn't want anything to do with his narcissism, and I sure as heck need him to back the hell off, because at this point, he's truly only making himself look worse than before, which honestly, I didn't even know was possible.

Here's the thing about a narcissist. They can't lose. And when they do, they fight back. They retaliate. They grasp at any and all straws they can so they can pretend to play the victim until they get what they want. Only problem is, I've gotten very smart when it comes to this. He can play dirty all he wants, but I can play dirtier. The difference is that I've chosen NOT to play dirty, and that says a lot. I could have gone after everything from him, but I chose not to. I chose to be the bigger person here. Why? Because I'm not an asshole, and not a single thing in this world would bring me down far enough to stoop to his level. I'll continue to sleep well at night, which is far more than he can say. Good luck N. I wish you well in life. You're on a great path.

Sorry for the terrible writing, I'm clearly just pissed.

Megan

I Am Strong, But I Am Tired

April 4th, 2020

I had a rough night last night. Everything seemed to annoy me. Everything made me want to cry. I just wanted to sleep all day. I had no motivation. And I felt like every single person was out to get me. My depression was back. And in full force.

Now, my depression never truly leaves, but I have moments where it is significantly worse than others. Last night was one of those nights, and it was rough. I cried a lot and I felt a lot of mental pain. And honestly, I felt a huge spiral of depression come on in almost an instant. I felt like every nerve in my body was tingly, causing me a lot of twitching and anxiousness. I felt like every emotion was on high. I wanted to lash out, but I didn't understand why. I felt the need to be angry but sad at the exact same time. I didn't want to get out of bed. I didn't want anyone to see or talk to me. I wanted to shut my phone off and sleep for five days. I felt like I needed empathy. I felt like I needed comforting, but no one was there to do it. I felt alone, even though I knew I wasn't. I felt hated, even though I knew that wasn't the truth. I felt useless, even though I've been working my ass off for the past few months. Last night was hard. Last night was very hard.

When you have a history of mental health, you always wonder if you'll ever be fully cured. I think, like most mental health issues, depression isn't something that just goes away over time. I think it comes and goes much like seasons. Some months you'll be good, and other months you'll be spiraling back down. Mine seems to go in spurts. Every few weeks I have a little bit of it come back into my life. Last night, though, was very different. I began questioning a lot in life, questioning if I did the right thing, if I'm on the right path, if I continue to do good in this world. Depression and anxiety typically go hand in hand, and last night was no different.

I tell you this because I'm no longer ashamed of my mental health, although I've been told for so many years that it's a terrible thing. I'm not ashamed to talk about it, because I want to end the stigma once and for all. But I do want to show the world that this shit is so very real, and it can creep up on a person with a history of it, so, so fast. It honestly was a bit scary. I remember having pretty dark moments in my life with my depression, but this came on very, very fast, and it went downhill very, very fast.

I woke up this morning in a much better place, thankfully. But I'm truly exhausted. The amount of anxiety that I dealt with, on top of the depression, was like an emotional roller-coaster for my senses and my emotions, causing me to wake up this morning very tired and exhausted. Almost like a physical exhaustion caused from all of the emotions my body felt in just a few hours.

I think I need more days to myself. I think I need to start traveling again. I think I'm working so hard that I'm beginning to lose sight of what makes me ME, and I don't like that. So if there seems to be a big gap between this blog and the next, I promise I'm OK. I just need some time.

Happy Birthday, Shelli

April 11th, 2020

Happy birthday to the most beautiful soul I've ever met.

I've been struggling really hard over this lately. I know you wouldn't want us sad, but the pain is unbearable most days. This pain is something none of us ever thought we'd have to endure.

You should be here. That's all there is to it. My life changed on November 6th 2019. So did everyone else's lives who knew you. You touched SO many people, I don't even know if you knew the capacity of it.

You were my hero in so many ways, for so many years. And my selfishness needs you here right now to help me cope with the loss of my best friend.

I miss you so much. SO, SO MUCH.

But please know, we are all celebrating your big 4-0 here today! You are so loved, Shelli. So, so loved.

I know you're dancing up a storm right now. You loved to dance! And I sure loved to dance with you!! Please keep dancing, we feel it!

Pressure Makes Diamonds

April 13th, 2020

The pressure of life has really dragged me down lately, probably harder than it has in a very long time. It has come in like a tidal wave and hasn't wanted to leave. I feel terrible, being quarantined to a house with another human who has to deal with my "moodiness," because I'm really not one of those women who have mood swings, like, ever. I feel like I'm incredibly annoying, not fun to be around, and just downright mean. But, oh, dear COVID, I will look at the positives to help me with this, like I always do. What you HAVE done for me is a little nicer to say out loud.

I've been able to focus back on my flaws. I know, that seems weird. I really don't like to focus on these much. I try to always stay positive and live life to the fullest, and when doing so, that doesn't really leave room to work on my flaws. We all have flaws, right? Don't go telling yourself you're perfect because I have some news for you: YOU'RE NOT. I have never claimed to be perfect, but I do strive for perfection, and I do work on myself on a daily basis. However, sometimes we forget who we are deep down, and during times like this, when we are forced to be in our own thoughts day after day after day after day (since, Lord knows, we have nothing better to do during this crazy time), we have the chance to really, REALLY dig deep within ourselves and try to figure out why we are the way we are.

With COVID and this whole crazy quarantine happening, I've been pretty forced into my own thoughts lately. I've been taking a lot of hot baths with lavender petals to relax my body and my mind. I've been coloring a lot lately, trying to pull some creativity out of my brain. I've been taking the dogs for a walk any time the weather is nice. We even took a weekend to go to the family lake house to decompress for a few days, or at least get away from these walls we've been staring at now for a month. But I've really had a LOT of thoughts rolling through my head during this quarantine, and I'm having some struggles with getting them out on paper.

I've really been questioning lately why I act the way I do. Why I feel the way I feel. Why I talk the way I talk. Why I work the way I work. Why I love the way I love. Why I hustle the way I hustle. And why I'm "crazy" like my ex liked to make very known. I think I've come to the conclusion that checks most of those boxes off, but that's another blog for another day. Point being, I am someone who has a history of depression and active thinking. Although I'm a hermit and stay inside all day, every day, even before this whole quarantine shit went down (I've been training my whole life for this!), I've found being forced to stay inside hard. And as a result of being forced to stay inside and be bored for days on end, my brain cannot and will not stop turning its gears. It's like it's on overdrive lately, and I cannot get it slow down.

For those of you who also deal with similar issues, let's reach out to each other and make sure we're all OK, OK? Did you take your medicine today? Did you do your daily meditation? Did you clean your house recently? Did you get a good sleep? Have you showered in the past few days? Life's hard under pressure, and we're all feeling that pressure recently. We're all stressed to the max because of money, jobs being lost, kids that need to be fed, spouses out of work, the virus spreading, and so on. Life's put a LOT of pressure on us lately. But what comes from pressure? DIAMONDS. Rare, beautiful diamonds. And you, my friends, are those diamonds. No pressure, no diamonds. Simple.

So, pick up a new hobby. Read a new book. Learn that musical instrument you've always wanted to learn. Paint your house like you've said you'd do for the past two years. Finish the extra room you've always wanted to finish. Do something to keep your brain stimulated, because times are tough right now. And I know just how hard it is to be stuck with these crazy racing thoughts that you can't seem to get rid of. Let's all have some fun with this and show the world some positivity.

"Here's to the crazy ones, the misfits, the rebels, the troublemakers, the round pegs in the square holes, the ones

who see things differently. They're not fond of rules.... You can quote them, disagree with them, glorify or vilify them. About the only thing you can't do is ignore them, because they change things. They push the human race forward. And while some may see them as the crazy ones, we see genius. Because the people who are crazy enough to think that they can change the world, are the ones who do."
—*attributed to Steve Jobs*

I love you guys. Stay safe out there. And for fuck's sake, stay inside.

Megan

This Is What Anxiety Looks Like

April 16th, 2020

I posted a photo today of my hands. My nails to be specific. It's something I've been embarrassed about since I was young, but here it is for the world to see. Some people call it Dermatillomania, I call it anxiety.

This is what anxiety looks like.

This is what depression looks like.

This is me.

Anxiety isn't all about being nervous in front of people, crying uncontrollably, not being able to relax, or racing thoughts that never seem to go away. It's about picking your nails until they're raw, then picking the skin around them until they bleed... over and over and over. Not feeling the "pain" involved, and not caring about the looks you get when you hand over money at the grocery store or write something in front of someone who can clearly see the scars you're left with.

It's about driving home from work just to sit in your car for twenty minutes because you're not ready to go inside and face your everyday life.

It's about getting a phone call and not being able to answer it. You really can't explain why.

It's about someone ringing your doorbell but not being able to open the door, even just to sign for a package.

It's about being on edge, every second of every day, thinking the worst of the worst is going to happen, and playing out scenarios in your head to the point where you begin to think they're real.

It's about asking your significant other several times a day if they love you, because your need for reassurance is incredibly annoying but very, very real.

It's procrastinating cleaning your house, not because you're lazy but because you're overwhelmed and cannot focus on the task at hand because there is too much to do.

It's taking two or three hot baths a day because you just need to relax your body and your mind.

It's having to worry about something every day because you don't know how to stop your mind from wandering.

It's trying so hard to understand the difference between rational thoughts and emotional thoughts, and having a very hard time differentiating the two.

It's not being able to control your body's response to things because of PTSD from something in your past.

It's not being able to understand, yourself, what exactly is going on, but you know it's there.

It's feelings of abandonment, resentment, guilt, anger, and sadness all in one.

Anxiety isn't just being nervous in crowds. Oh, no. It's taking day-to-day living and making every scenario so intense that your body and mind become so exhausted that you need to sleep just to recover. Some days are more manageable than others, and some knock you down like a ton of bricks. It's incredibly embarrassing and hard for me to share this, but this is real, and this is the truth. I have a lot of followers ask me to write blogs on anxiety all the time, so here it is.

Anxiety has crept back into my life lately, as well as my depression. It's very real and has become very intense for me lately. Every time I look down at my hands, I become disgusted. It's a vivid reminder that some days I'm just not as strong as I think I am. But I hold my head high and wake up knowing today is a new day. And every day for me is a work in progress.

This is me.

Hi, I'm Crazy

April 22nd, 2020

I don't know if it's because I have been feeling a lot of "mental health" issues lately or if I'm really just trying to zone in and focus on WHY I have such mental health issues in the first place, but one thing has become very clear to me in the past few months. I suffer with something I've never told anyone or talked openly about. I'm not quite ready to open that box yet to the world, but bringing it up to my partner was a huge step for me.

It probably sounds stupid, but for a long time, I told myself that when I am able to open up to someone about everything in my life that haunts me, including this topic, that specific person will be my soul mate. I know I've said it before, but I know A is my soul mate, and this kind of just proved that theory to me. The other night we were sitting on my porch, drinking wine, wrapped up in blankets talking about life, and out of nowhere, I blurted it out. I've felt this conversation brewing for the past few months, but it's been on my mind for over a year, and I just want to say, the fact that he didn't instantly say what I assumed he would say really caught me off guard. I think it's because I'm used to judgment. I'm used to being picked on for being the way I am. I'm used to a narcissist having the upper hand with me and controlling how I feel. Im use to being called crazy. I was fully prepared and ready for him to say, "Yes, I know you have that, it's obvious because of the way you act," but he didn't. He asked questions. He wanted MY thoughts on it before ever giving his opinion. And that honestly was the last thing I expected. I told myself if I can open up to someone about this, it'll either make them run away fast or stick around for the party!. (Yes, I'm

251

making a joking reference to my mental health craziness. I'm allowed. It's a party, what can I say!) Well, he didn't run!

I pride myself on being very open with the world in hopes that it spreads awareness about these topics and ends the stigma about mental health issues. But this is something I just haven't quite been brave enough to talk about. I'm sure it'll eventually come out, but for now being able to say I've talked about it with the one and only person who I find important enough to discuss it with was a huge leap for me. And for that, I'm proud of myself.

I need to not be ashamed of how I act, how I feel, who I am, and why I am the way I am. I need to just own it, because ultimately, mental health issues or not, this is me. So, it's a work in progress. I encourage everyone to become open about such issues. Even if it's just coming to me to talk about them to. It's incredibly uplifting, empowering, and brave, and it just proves that you aren't alone.

From one crazy to another, I love you guys.

Megan

The Wedding Ring

April 28th, 2020

I have been looking at wedding rings lately. I know I know, I'm never getting remarried, but the thought of a pretty ring is fun, I suppose. I've always had a weird fascination with wedding rings and how to make them look unique, so when I start looking online at them, I end up falling down a rabbit hole, and fourteen hours later, I've designed twenty seven rings for no reason whatsoever. In looking at rings recently, I've had some memories pop up in my head. I find myself pulling up rings on my phone that I love and asking my boyfriend what he thinks of them. My brain seems to be trained in thinking I need his opinion on something that only I would wear. Doesn't make a lot of sense, does it? Let me further explain.

Seven years ago when I proposed to my ex-husband, I got his ring well before we ever had mine picked out. I knew what I wanted but clearly needed his first to do the proposal with. I know I've mentioned already how we had to hide our engagement for an incredibly long time. And by "we had to," I mean he forced us to, for whatever reason. So my ring didn't come along for like a year or so. I had looked at countless rings online and even won a thousand-dollar gift card from a local jeweler to use toward an engagement ring. That didn't encourage him, though. To him, rings were too expensive and not a necessity to get married with. Finally, only after a huge fight broke out, did we decide to go look at rings, more than a year later.

Look, I get it, diamonds aren't cheap. And I'm not one to want no fifty-thousand-dollar ring. But at the time I did want something nice. Something that I could show off and love. I had this idea in mind. I wanted a solitaire princess cut, white gold, one-carat stone, with a cute, quirky band, set in rose gold. He didn't like that idea. He said the band wouldn't match, and neither would the rose gold. I told him that was the look I was going for. I liked the "uniqueness" of textured, stackable bands, and I wanted the two-toned look of white gold/rose gold for something different. He told me it would look stupid and that nobody in their right mind does that with their rings. Of course he had to have a say in what I wore. Something he didn't have to wear, but I did, and of course, since he claimed to have some kind of ownership over me, he couldn't have his fiancé out there having a mismatched ring, now could he?

So after a year and a half of being engaged and not telling anyone, we finally went to the jewelry store. We sat in the jeweler's office picking out stones for about an hour after I had found a setting I liked.. There was an incredible deal on a one-carat princess cut stone that fit just perfectly in the setting I had picked out. He said it was too much money, although it was only about two thousand dollars more than the one he liked. That probably seems expensive, but we were only paying about four thousand dollars for the entire ring, plus we had the thousand-dollar gift card, so to me, it didn't seem like that much in the grand scheme of things. The one he had chosen, although beautiful, was just not quite the right shape. It was a princess cut stone, but elongated, looking more like a rectangle instead of a perfect square, and my OCD just wasn't loving it. But he didn't budge. The jeweler had stated that if we ever wanted to upgrade, they offered a program where no matter the cost of the upgrade, you could bring in your old stone and put the exact price toward a new one. So I figured it was OK. Eventually, maybe, I could change it out if he allowed. We ended up buying the ring with his choice of stone that day, with the thousand-dollar gift card and him paying the overage.

A week later, the ring was sized to my finger, and I was able to pick it up. I wore it for about a week or two and just really had issues with the center stone not being shaped right, so I brought it back in and asked what could be done. Even if I had to pay a little more to get a square stone, I was willing to do that. I just didn't want him to know what I was doing, because he surely would say no and throw a fit. Turns out, the original one-carat stone I fell in love with was still there. I ended up paying the two-thousand-dollar overage out of pocket for it and had them set it in my ring. N never noticed, nor did I ever tell him.

Eventually we went back in closer to the wedding date to pick out my wedding band. I wanted something small and quirky to go alongside the engagement ring, and I thought it would be cool if, for our one-year anniversary, I got another stackable band to go with it. I have an unhealthy obsession with stackable bands, don't judge me. N didn't like that idea because that costs more money and was a stupid materialistic "want," not a "need." We went in to choose the wedding band, and I found the cheapest and smallest one possible, because I knew he wouldn't spend much. I was able to find a beautiful rose gold one for eight hundred dollars. He gave me the OK to get it but didn't love the idea of it being rose gold yet. Once I got it sized and back in, I picked it up and put it on with my ring to see how it would look. I thought maybe if he saw it with the ring, he would see how pretty the colors of the metals were together. Nope, he still didn't like it.

At this point, I tried to figure out my options, because if he really didn't like the ring, we'd have to get another band to his liking. Why I cared so much about what he thought about the ring, I have no idea. It's not like he was the one wearing it his whole life, yet I knew I had to make him happy before myself, so I called the jeweler to see what could be done. They stated I couldn't return the ring since it was resized to my finger, but they could dip it in rhodium to give it the white gold look. So we did that. However, it always had a very slight pink tint to it, which bothered my OCD like MAD! But N never cared. The ring matched now, and as far as he was concerned, it was good.

So a year later, on our one-year anniversary, I told him I wanted an anniversary band. Just a plain diamond band, that's it. He actually didn't mind the idea of an anniversary band, surprisingly, but at this point in life we were making two hundred thousand dollars a year and could afford it. I told him how I wanted to stack the bands with the ring and give it that quirky look I was going for. He thought it was the stupidest thing ever. To the point where the jeweler even soldered it all together completely wrong, because I'm pretty sure that's what he told them to do. I picked it up and didn't say a word in front of N, for fear he would have something to say about it in public, and I didn't want that. A week later I returned to the jeweler and said I wanted it soldered together differently, and I wanted to get a new wedding band since the one I had was terribly pink at this point. My original plan was to get the same one, just in white gold, and not mention it to N because he'd never notice. They ended up not having the exact same one, but one a little larger that was very similar, so I opted to get that one instead. I forked out the eighteen hundred dollars, and never told N what I had done, because I knew he would have something terrible to say about it.

At last, I had my perfect ring. It truly was beautiful. A one-carat princess cut, perfectly square diamond, extremely shiny, on a solitaire ring, all white gold, with diamonds along the band. Incredibly petite, just perfect for my tiny hands. Alongside it was the new wedding band, and on top of that was a beautiful new anniversary band. Truthfully a VERY beautiful ring. I was very happy with it and finally loved my wedding ring! Even though, there for awhile, I hated it. It finally was what I wanted, and not what HE wanted.

Looking at rings now, I find myself getting my boyfriend's approval. Why? Because of stories like this. Because my brain is so trained to make someone else happy before myself, I have a hard time picking something out that I will be wearing for the rest of my life. It baffles me that I once again would let someone have that much control over me. It blows my mind that I let someone dictate what I could and would wear, and how I would be wearing it. And it pisses me off to think I allowed myself to live like that for so long.

Stories like this are so small in the grand scheme of things, but they have a purpose. All of these stories just show the true control he had over me, and he knew it. All of these stories show that HE owned me, and I never could have a true identity. And, to be honest, it's just so sad to me. As someone who struggled with my identity for so many years, how could I allow someone to have that much control over who I was?! It's truly like a prison. I felt like I lived in captivity. And I am just so freakin' thankful that I no longer live like that.

(Side note: I never did get my wedding ring back. He admitted to taking it and hiding it from me before I left. So there's that.)

Let's Talk About Sex

April 29th, 2020

Let's talk about sex. Why? Because it's important.

This is the chapter that my grandparents can just skip right over. Like, please!

Sex should be something beautiful, whether you do it for procreation or to share the love and the bond you have with your partner. I'm a firm believer in sex when it comes to someone you are romantically involved with. I have always been the type of girl, though, who does not have sex with just anyone. I've even had people act surprised when I tell them my "number." I'm someone who cannot and will not have sex with someone unless we are dating, and to further that, I cannot and will not have sex with someone unless there is a true emotional connection. Why I'm telling you all this will be understood in a few.

Now, disclaimer, what you do with your sex life is up to you. I never judge anyone. To be honest, even if you have sex to pay your bills, I give you props. I truly do not, and never will, care what anyone does with their body. Never, EVER, EVER will I judge someone for that. I want to make that very clear before I move further with this blog.

I was sexually assaulted when I was young, which is probably why I will not ever have a one-night stand or give my body to just anyone. It sounds prudish, I'm sure, but whatever. I just do not find myself physically attracted to anyone unless I'm emotionally attracted to them. Therefore, sex, to me, isn't even an option. I don't like the idea of sex with just anyone, and I sure will not subject my body to just anyone, without that emotional tie.

Now, I'm sure you're asking yourself, "Well, how did you and your husband manage this?" The simple answer is, we didn't. At least not toward the end. The beginning was all about sex. For someone who was as addicted to sex and porn as he was, I had to make him happy somehow, so I thought it was my due diligence to do what made him happy. Eventually, though, this stopped. I got to a point where everything he did to me, including how he treated me, just wasn't attractive anymore, and I began to find myself very much not attracted to him physically. And what was hard for me was how bad he would make me feel for that, even though the reason I was like that in the first place was because of what HE did to me.

He always made me feel terrible for it. He would plant a guilt trip on me saying he felt like an old pervert who had to touch himself because his wife wouldn't. His addiction to pornography was very, very real and very, very scary, but he would never admit that.

When we were on vacation once, I woke up one morning to him trying to initiate sex. I wanted it, but not with him. And I remember feeling so terrible for that. I remember feeling how unfair that was to him as a man. But also, how unfair it was to me as the other party involved. I remember I just started crying my eyes out as he touched me, as if I couldn't make him stop. It felt like I was being sexually assaulted all over again every time he grabbed my breasts or put his hand under my shirt and pants. I couldn't hold back the tears. I remember saying, "If you're gonna do it, just do it," and he then held back, saying something along the lines of, "A wife shouldn't be saying that to her husband," and all I could think was that he was right. I ran to the bathroom crying, feeling terrible that I couldn't satisfy him, but also feeling terrible because we had just gotten married a few months prior, and seriously, it's not healthy for a wife to not want to have sex with her husband. He told me later that day that I wasn't normal for feeling the way I did about sex, and it was very apparent. We all have our off days—days when we are just lazy, not in the mood, having that time of the month, or tired. But this wasn't one of those off days. We didn't even have sex on our wedding night. In all honesty, it had been almost a year since we had sex, and I just couldn't get myself to do it because I knew that emotional tie was no longer there. And I truly think that's when I knew something was very, very wrong.

When he wanted sex, he got it. Even if it wasn't with me, which is really sad for me to admit. He was very addicted to sex when we first started dating, and I'm sure that led to the countless women he slept with during that time period. There were at least six women I found during this time who he was stringing along, myself included. Then there was the pornography. He watched this religiously. I would hear him in the bathroom every morning before work watching it. I would hear him after work watching it. I would hear him get out of bed to watch it. He watched it while I was on the floor screaming in pain while going through the abortion. He watched it while he thought I was asleep next to him. It was terrible. I asked him to get help multiple times, but as we know, you can't tell a narcissist what to do, so he never got help for it.

One time about a week after the abortion, he woke me up to initiate sex. I was feeling so down about myself and felt so terrible that he had to deal with me that I gave in because I thought it would make him happy. Now that I think back on this particular instance, I question why I even allowed sex to happen in the first place, that close to the procedure. Really stupid on my part, I know. But he wanted it, so he got it. I wasn't going to NOT give in and have him find it somewhere else, because that would have ruined me. So, to me, it was better to give in and just make him happy, even if it was not recommended after such a procedure when your body is healing. We started sex like normal, and about five minutes in, he looked down and said, "Um... you're bleeding... everywhere." He got up with the most disgusted look on his face, grabbed a towel, wiped himself off, threw me the towel, and said, "Clean this up." I remember covering my face in embarrassment as I cried so many tears. This was not only so embarrassing for me, but literally this was the aftermath of my child being killed by him, and it was almost like reliving it when I was trying so damn hard to forget. He got dressed and left the house after that. And to this day, I have the most irrational fear of having sex and starting a period at the same time because of the embarrassment that he left me with.

Sex should never be forced. Sex should be a privilege you give to someone who has such a deep emotional connection with you that you can share that bond and make it stronger. Sex should never be one sided, EVER. I know I may sound old-school with this, but it's truly my belief. I definitely know I grew up with a lot of morals, and I really do pride myself on that. I don't believe in the whole "don't have sex before you're married" thing. That's stupid and unrealistic. But what I do believe in is sex with someone who you feel connected to. And the last almost ten years of my life, besides my current boyfriend, I've only been with my ex-husband, and sadly that connection was lost very, very early, and it wasn't fun. Sex was never fun. I couldn't open up, I couldn't become vulnerable, I couldn't have fun, I couldn't talk about what I liked or didn't like. I was there for his pleasure, and his pleasure only. So moving to a new relationship after that has most definitely been hard. It's most definitely been a work in progress, because suddenly I'm in a relationship where there's two people involved, instead of two people where one has control over the other.

It's another big characteristic of a true narcissist. They typically are addicted to sex. Their desire for sex is never quenched. They have an unbelievable appetite that must be fed. They are known for cheating and having affairs, for taking risks, and for living a life filled with lies and deceit. Obviously, some of you reading this will be able to relate to what I'm saying, and some may be able to relate but not live with a narcissist. I'm not saying every narc does this, but clearly the history and behavior of my previous relationship holds true. It's yet another big red flag that truly went ignored. I beg you all who are reading this, do not let this happen to you.

I'm Sorry I Can't Hang Out. I'm Busy Doing Absolutely Nothing.

May 1st, 2020

Something I have often thought about is how people view me when my anxiety kicks in, and recently it occurred to me that I never explain my anxiety to people, so I'm 90 percent sure people think I'm ditching them in an effort to purposely NOT hang out with them, call them, or see them. One big part of my anxiety is interacting with people. It's not that I'm nervous in front of crowds, or nervous at all for that matter. I just simply have this uncontrollable and indescribable feeling of anxiousness roll over me.

It's happened a lot actually, and I'm sure some of you can attest to this if you deal with similar anxiety. You get a text from a friend you haven't seen in awhile, you make a lunch date to hang out, but when the day comes, you suddenly don't want to go. It's not because you're too good for them, hate them, or simply don't want to see them; you just have anxiety start to take over and realize that it's not a good idea to go see that person. In fact, most of the time you WANT to see that person. You WANT to be normal and have normal friend dates. You WANT to catch up with someone you haven't seen in a long time and talk about life and whatnot. But alas, you can't. You can't because you have anxiety.

I cannot even begin to count the times that I have canceled on a friend or canceled an appointment at the last minute due to my anxiety. I'm actually pretty damn sure my dentist office knows me as the "last-minute canceling client" because I've done this so often. It happens with friends, family, dentist appointments, doctor appointments, scheduling handymen to fix something in my house, when I schedule a package delivery, and on and on. So I PROMISE you, this is a weekly occurrence in my life, and it's my anxiety to blame.

I guess my point in writing this blog is to remember that we're not alone. I know that some of you deal with similar anxiety tendencies, and I find comfort in knowing I'm not alone.

So if you're reading this, whether you are an old friend, a new friend, or one of my physicians, mail carriers, or otherwise, just know that when I've canceled in the past, it's not because I wanted to. It's truly because I had to. Anxiety plays a huge roll in my life, whether I want it to or not, and fact is, this is just one part of it. But as always, I'm working on things!

Love,

Megan

How I've Changed Since Her Death

May 6th, 2020

I've been dreading this blog for awhile now, but I know I have a lot to say.

Six months ago, time stopped for a brief moment. I don't know how to explain the feeling of loss, but the stop of time seems accurate. The moment I found out she was gone, time immediately froze, and everything changed right along with it.

I find myself still having spirals of emotions. I find myself crying for her one day, then celebrating her life the next. I find myself angry at the world more often than not, even though I know in life, death is inevitable. It's going to happen to everyone, but the way it happened to her I just find so unfair. I find my depression the worst it's been in over a decade, and yet, some days, I find so much happiness at the same time. I don't know that I can pinpoint exactly how I've changed these past six months, but it's very apparent that life halted for a brief moment, and then changed for myself and for my entire family.

To say I've moved past her death is a lie. I haven't. I will never claim to have moved on from this. It's something people will tell you that time will heal, but I really don't believe in that statement. I think time only allows us to find coping mechanisms, but the reality is, the pain will never truly go away. At least not for me. Maybe for some, but everyone obviously grieves differently. Some things that have changed in the past six months are not good changes. Others are more eye-opening than actual changes. But some are terrible thoughts, while others are the most incredible.

I have found myself in a deep, dark place lately. Some days are better than others. But since her death, the depression has come back in full swing, and as much as I try to combat it, I just cannot seem to get ahead. Realistically, I know that's normal. Suffering a loss such as this, where someone literally gets stripped from your life in a matter of one split second, it's normal to have those feelings of sadness, anger, and guilt, all rolled into one. I think I'd be considered crazy if I didn't feel the way I do. But I hate those feelings. I hate waking up sad on a daily basis. I hate having to fake wanting to take a bath at night, just to go to the bathroom and cry alone so I don't bother anyone. I hate having to hold back tears because I should be strong for everyone else involved. I hate selfishly needing her back into my life because there's so much I'd like to share with her. I hate crying myself to sleep some nights remembering my mom calling me with such sadness in her tone, crying the words "she died" to me. It's like a terrible nightmare that just won't end. I hate putting my boyfriend through such scenarios, waking up with a depressed girlfriend every day, and coming home to someone who's constantly in a bad mood because she had someone taken out of her life who deserved to be here more than she does. I hate thinking I will never have another family wedding with her where we can drink and dance the night away, I'll never hear her contagious laugh again even though I play it in my head over and over. I hate that her kids and husband are suffering, along with her family and friends. I hate it. That's the only phrase I know is accurate in this situation—I. HATE. IT. It's like a part of my heart, my brain, my body, was just cut out and taken, never to be returned. I'm no psychologist by any means, and I sure as hell know I don't have all the answers. I will never give you a step-by-step outline on how to grieve or move past something. I think it's very apparent in these blogs that I really have no idea what on earth I'm talking about half the time, but the purpose of this is to show the real, raw, and true story, right?

There are days when I can't get out of bed. Days when I have to force myself to take a shower because I know that's what you're supposed to do. There are days when I can't even get off the couch because I'm just so emotionally drained and emotionally gone. I hate to admit my sadness most days, and I hate to show I'm struggling, because, bottom line, she wouldn't want that. And I know that. But it doesn't, for one second, take the pain away. And, man, let's not forget the fact that I've aged ten years over this. No joke! I have wrinkles I've never had before, skin issues I've never dealt with, and grey hairs that just keep sprouting up.

In respect to Shelli though, because I know this is what SHE would have done had this been something that happened to her, I have really become in tune with my spiritual side, even more so than I had been already, and I guess I have her to thank for that. Little did I know, we were more alike than I ever thought we were, and I hate that it took this happening for me to see that. So how have I changed since her death? Besides the depression, the sadness, the tears, the anger, and the constant pain? I try to always find the silver lining. Is there a silver lining to death? I don't know. But the fact is she is gone and not coming back. So how I look at this is either to stay sad my entire life or find ways to cope, as I stated before.

I have really gotten in touch with my spiritual side. I've always been very spiritual with animal symbolism, signs from someone who has left this world, energy, and things like that. I reached out to a psychic medium after her passing—HER psychic medium to be exact. That helped me a lot. I see signs from her everywhere. I promise you they don't go unnoticed, Shelli! It gives me a moment of comfort, even for just that split second, and that is something I'm very grateful for. I have also slowed down. A lot. With work, with life, with business, with everything. I have really taken the time to slow down and appreciate everything. I sit outside a lot and listen to the sounds of the wind, the birds, the cars, the people. My grandpa once told me to sit and be quiet, and just listen to the birds outside, because one day you won't be able to do that. I've found beauty in things I normally would pass up and ignore. I've tapped into the creative part of my brain again, even just to de-stress. It helps. And I suppose it is very therapeutic in a sense. I've gotten closer with my family. I've leaned on them for support and have offered myself to help those also struggling with her death. I've learned that it's OK to grieve, it's OK to cry, it's OK to be mad, and it's OK to be sad. No one can tell you how to grieve, and no one can tell you how you are approaching it is wrong. I've realized her kids are stronger than anyone is giving them credit for, and I for one just wish I could have an ounce of that willpower. But her kids have her blood. It's obvious they are grieving how she would have done.

I didn't realize how many things I needed to say to her or talk to her about or fill her in on. I'm constantly having things pop in my head and thinking to myself, "Damn, this would have good to tell Shelli!" but I can't. I find myself looking at photos of her and instantly crying. Everyone has shared the video of her and me from my cousin's wedding dancing to Whitney Houston's "I Wanna Dance with Somebody," and I have yet to be able to listen to that song again. It's far too painful. I see so many signs from her, and just for a split second, time stops, and I'm able to take a deep breath and know she's there. But, man, life has sure changed. It's almost as if this is a completely different life I'm living, and it's one she's not a part of. It's this constant feeling that something is missing, but I can never get it back. It's that hole, or that void, that people talk about trying to fill that can never be refilled. Life moves on, but don't for one second think it's easy.

I think about things we all won't be able to experience with her. Things she would have loved so very much. Her daughter's prom, her daughter's track meets, the crazy Halloween costumes her son would always come up with. I think about having a child of my own someday and not being able to share that moment with her. I think about her never being able to meet A, and how painful that is for me to say because she was the first and only person who knew about him for a long time. It's so painful for me to think about that I'm actually really struggling with writing this right now, because it just still doesn't feel real.

I guess six months is still very fresh. Although I don't really know if there is a time limit on grieving. Death changes everything; time changes nothing. I will forever miss the sound of your voice, and the contagious laugh that we all knew and loved. I'll forever miss your wittiness and your humor. I'll forever miss your blessed heart of gold and the amount of kindness and love you put into this world. I miss your hugs, and I miss your advice. I miss you.

Growth Is Uncomfortable

May 9th, 2020

I don't know if it's because I wrote the blog I did the other day or if it's just a sudden life-altering moment I'm having, but the last few days I've let a lot go, and it's been very freeing. I let go of some pain I was festering with my cousin's passing. I let go of some anger and resentment I've been holding onto regarding past relationships. I've been digging incredibly deeply, trying to find out just who I am, and having had some very intense conversations with my boyfriend about a lot of this, it's really opened my eyes. Honestly, I think I'm finally at the point where it's almost the end of this book, which means another chapter of my life is closing. And that is VERY surreal to think about. This pain might finally be gone.

Last week, I had a minor epiphany. And by "minor", I actually mean "MAJOR". A moment that brought me to some intense realizations. I decided I am ready to change. I do not want to be sad anymore, I do not want to hold on to anymore anger, and I do not want to wake up miserable any longer. I want to take control of my personality quirks, my depression, and my intense anxiety. I decided I don't want to ruin what good I DO have in this life. And that's when it occurred to me. I realized just how easy it is to delete it all. The power we have at our fingertips in this day and age to literally, at the click of a button, delete a life we've shared. And just like that—I deleted 4,298 photos and videos from my phone and my social media accounts.

I knew I'd probably feel weird about it the next day, scrounging for photos that I once shared as memories. Photos that I can't really replace if I absolutely needed to. My life the last twenty years was on that phone and in those accounts. I sure as hell don't have printed copies of any, because who does that anymore? But oddly enough, I woke up the next morning having slept one of the best night's sleeps I've had in very long time.

Deleting those files deleted the anger. Deleting those files deleted the sadness. Deleting those files deleted a past I was holding onto that no longer needed to be remembered.

WHOA, GUYS. HOLD ON. PAUSE.

I don't believe I ever told you guys about the feather story, but one literally just landed on me as I am typing this blog... At my cousins funeral a feather kept showing up, and to this day, feathers seem to follow me everywhere. One literally just landed on me! THAT IS A SIGN!!

After a five-minute crying break just now, I can resume.

Whoa guys, that... was nuts. She's here, I'm telling you.

Alright, back to my blog.

Deleting those files deleted the anger. Deleting those files deleted the sadness. Deleting those files deleted a past I was holding onto that no longer needed to be remembered. Every time I'd tell a story of my past and pull up a photo to show of it, I was instantly brought back to a moment in time where something bad happened. The brain does the craziest things doesn't it? Associating sometimes very happy pictures with something very bad?

EXAMPLE 1: I still have wedding photos saved of me. Why? I'm not married anymore, and I sure as hell don't like remembering that day.

EXAMPLE 2: Pictures I took of the Packers game I went to in 2013. These photos were the night of my birthday, August 14th, 2013. Three days prior to this, I had had my abortion.

EXAMPLE 3: Vacation photos. Because even though Barbados was beautiful, I don't need to be reminded of a very fake honeymoon.

I honestly thought that maybe if I deleted such photos and albums, then it would be some kind of metaphor for them to be deleted out of my life. But I think it truly, actually worked.

So here's to a new start. AGAIN. Here's to Megan at almost thirty-two years old, deciding she once again is still a badass who knows how to fall so far, and somehow always climb out. And here's to all of you who are right there, riding this journey out with me.

Carrying on bravely,

Megan

CHEERS!

May 10th, 2020

Long story short, I survived. And I did so with my integrity. I can sleep well at night knowing I fought long and hard, in the right way—fighting to let YOU know that YOU can no longer win over me. No, sir. The final win was mine. No longer will you have control over me. No longer will you continue the abuse. No longer will you continue to manipulate me and everyone around us. No longer will I cry over you because of the PTSD I suffer from, where every little thing reminds me of the pain you've put me through. No longer, no longer. This is the moment we've all been waiting for. I am finally free. Like a butterfly stuck in a cocoon for far too long!

I feel like my cousin really came to visit this weekend. I've never felt more empowered than this week. Thank you, Shelli. Your presence was most definitely noticed. I thank you for helping me through the most troubling times of my life, just like you always did, and you came the day after I decided to take control of my life again. You continue to show me just how much of a badass female I am, and no matter what, I always come out on top. You've told me since I was very young just how important I am and how strong I've always been. Seeing signs of your presence this week helped me so much. I know you're out there looking out for me as always, and although it is painful for me to still know you can't physically be here to celebrate this with me, I know you're enjoying that glass of wine on the other side, blaring some Whitney Houston right now with me, ready to dance—because WE WON.

I have never been so happy to see an email arrive. An email stating I AM OFFICIALLY DIVORCED. I honestly never thought this day would come. The feelings of having those heavy chains on me has followed me for over a year now. I left my ex-husband's house in December of 2018, and here we are, May of 2020. When I left his house, I felt such an empowering feeling, but I felt like a tight leash was still on me. I felt weighted down with heavy chains that wouldn't allow me to run free. I left with only freedom on my side and somehow managed to fucking make shit happen. I know I deal with a lot of my own demons that like to follow me around, a lot of depression, a lot of anxiety and self-esteem issues, but sometimes I think I even shock my own demons when I dig deep down and pull the "Megan" out that we all know and love. This week has been one of those weeks.

Ironically, two days after writing a very hard blog for me and letting go of a lot of anger, resentment, and bullshit... this email arrived. Yes, folks, manifest that shit. I know it sounds stupid and crazy, but it's real life. Manifest what you want, and put a plan into action. You will NEVER fail if you do it! I swear to you. Do it, and do it with passion. Don't hold back on whatever it is that you want, ladies and gents, because I promise you, when you want something badly enough, life will give you what you've always dreamed of. And for me, that was a life without pain.

Look, I know some of you reading this will say this is bullshit. I know some of you will get to the end of this book and say, well, this is a joke, none of this helped me. Listen, Linda, I didn't say I was a professional. What I did say is I wanted something that someone could read that WASN'T a step-by-step, "how to recover" book. I wanted something raw. I wanted something real. I wanted something where someone could read what REALLY happened to a person, and hopefully help someone along the way. I hope it opened up some of your eyes to the reality of life, struggles, relationships, and abuse. And I hope and pray that if anyone is dealing with anything similar to what I've dealt with, this will at least allow you to open your eyes and question whether you're being treated right or not.

I just want to say how fucking proud I am of myself. How fucking proud I am of all of you who have got this far. Life isn't a trip—no, ma'am. A trip is just a trip. I'm on a journey. And all of you who have gotten this far reading this are on this journey right along with me. We're all waiting for something in life, something to happen to help us overcome whatever it is we need to overcome. We're all waiting for that "magical moment," and this was mine. This book. I never realized I was the revolution I was waiting for.

So CHEERS! (Quarantine style!) Ironically, the last glass of champagne I had to celebrate something was on my one-year wedding anniversary in New York City. It seems crazy to think that now I'm throwing up some CHEERS because I've finally left that asshole who held me down for so long, and I'm FINALLY FREE! So CHEERS to all of us fucked-up people. CHEERS to those of us who have been hurt, battered, and abused. CHEERS to those who got out faster than I did, who helped me out along the way. And CHEERS to those who haven't quite gotten there yet but are truly on the right path. CHEERS to new beginnings. CHEERS to old amends. CHEERS to YOU, and CHEERS to ME. We're all on this journey together, and I forever will be there to help along the way.

CHEERS,

Megan

"This is our Nashville"

May 11th, 2020

In good old COVID fashion, there's nothing like celebrating while quarantined with three bottles of champagne and some old-school music!

The other night, after getting the news of my divorce finally being final, A and I popped open some champagne and listened to music all night long. What could have been an amazing night out we celebrated inside, while under quarantine, and I wouldn't have changed it for the world.

We listened to my entire bipolar playlist, from Broadway, to Marilyn Manson, to Backstreet Boys, Cher, 80s music, and even some Shania Twain. Cher's "If I Could Turn Back Time" came on, and it seemed rather fitting and got me in a fun mood. I told A how badly I wanted to do karaoke at a bar right now and get white girl wasted! But I realized quickly how bad that would suck, because I can't handle the next morning's hangover! This is when you know you're getting old! He said, "We should go to Nashville and do this!," which sounded like SUCH a good idea! In fact, I started tearing up because no one's ever wanted to do stuff like that with me! But we both realized we are far too old. I said, "Remember when we were like twenty-two and used to be able to do this?!" So instead I blared Shania Twain, took a drink of champagne, and said, "This is our Nashville."

I wouldn't want to be stuck inside with anyone else during this time. This quarantine craziness has brought the two of us so much closer, if that was even possible. Personally, I enjoy being stuck inside right now. He keeps me smiling and reminds me every morning that I wake up to such an amazing life with him a part of it.

Happy quarantine,

Megan

A Letter To Him

May 14th, 2020

"So many people from my past know this version of me that doesn't exist anymore. That's called growth. And let me tell you something: if you knew the whole story, you'd be proud of me. Because what people don't know is, I pick up the pieces differently."
—*Megan Besler*

You fell for me and made me fall in love with you. You couldn't handle a good person in your life giving you the world, so you chose to throw it all away the only way you knew how. Abuse. You took a life from someone and will forever have to live with that guilt. You are the reason for so much heartache in my life and so much defeat. You broke me down to the point where I didn't think I could get back up. But little did you know: I pick up the pieces differently. I built myself back up and turned everything you did to me into stepping-stones to such a bigger and better life. Yes, you, sir, will no longer abuse me. You will no longer have control over me. You will no longer own me.

I did not simply unlove you overnight. No, I unloved bits and pieces of you over time. As I moved into a new home, with new walls, my thoughts started to emerge, and writing began to take place. As I found myself writing more and more, I found myself opening up more and more, and saying these stories out loud really made me realize how fucked up this whole relationship had been. I have since grown a new skin that you could never touch. A new heart that you could never break. And a new soul that you could never corrupt. This is how I unloved you. Because I had to.

275

The past year has been incredibly disheartening. If I had any respect left for you, it's all thrown out the window. You are no man in my eyes; in fact, you're barely human. But you know what? I understand. I understand you are angry at me for leaving you. I understand you are hurt. I understand you lost someone and are grieving. But what I will never understand is your vindictiveness. The narcissism that will never go away. The reins you had over me even after I had left, and the fact that you KNEW how manipulative you were being until the day it was finally over. You always won, and you probably will continue to always win, because that's who you are. You are someone who cannot lose. But you WILL lose this fight. You DID lose this fight. I finally won, and I will always take a stand for that and scream at the top of my lungs that you no longer own me!

Now, it wasn't all bad. In fact, I will always remember some of the good times we had. The crazy story of how we first met and fell in love with each other, the days you'd kiss my forehead before work every morning, the endless baseball games we went to together, and the crazy amount of hot dogs I ate! The times we spent with your family—man, I loved your family so much. I will miss them the most. And last, the amount of love you had for Bo I will forever cherish! I know she misses you. And trust me when I say I hate that she had to be taken from you. It pains me a lot to know she doesn't see her dad, but I promise you with all my life, she is in such great hands. She plays in the backyard all day and still loves her frisbee the most. She has now become my emotional support dog, so truly, thank you for allowing me to talk you into getting her when you didn't want to, because she's helped me so much. Please know you were a part of my life that allowed me to grow into who I am today. To be honest, I ought to thank you. You legitimately are the reason I am able to help so many men and women. You are the reason I have so much love for myself these days. But honestly, thank you for making me fall to such a deep, dark place, where the only thing I could do was realize how bad a life I lived. Thank you for allowing me to see that I deserved better. Thank you for allowing me to see I AM BETTER. If you had been the man I had always wanted, I wouldn't be the woman who I am today.

Yes, I grew smaller as your ego grew larger, and the day I left, you knew I was about to spread my wings. You tried so hard to not allow that to happen, but you did not succeed. One final loss can go down in your books, because you didn't win this time. If you even remotely think you've won, you didn't. I won my freedom. And never will you ever win over me again. EVER.

So before you run my name through the mud even more than you already have, be sure to mention how good I was to you. Be sure to mention how I fought for you time and time again. Be sure to mention how I truly wanted to help you with your demons and get you the help you needed when no one else gave a shit. Be sure to mention how good of a person I was to you, and despite everything you did to me, I still loved you with everything I had. And please, be sure to tell people the truth. Because you know what? People know the truth. People see through the lies and your deceit. You don't fool anyone anymore.

So here is me letting you go. Finally. After fifteen years, I am letting you go. I am putting you in my past, locking that vault up, and never again crying tears of sadness and pain. I am forgiving AND forgetting. The right path is never the easiest, and you wasted such good years of my life. Years I will never be able to get back. But thank you for being the person who allowed me to see life through a different set of eyes. If it weren't for you, I wouldn't have dropped so far, only to get back up and fight one last time. I wouldn't have ever found such a love for myself, because you sure as hell never gave me that. If it weren't for you, I wouldn't have realized what it's like to have a true man in my life, someone who loves me for who I am, and gives me the love I deserve. Thank you for allowing me to see the pain of abuse. Thank you for allowing me to see the pain of loss. Thank you for allowing me to grow up faster than I anticipated. And thank you—oh, God, thank you—for being such a terrible person to me. Because if it weren't for you treating me like you did, I wouldn't be writing this book helping others with their stories.

I am choosing now to move forward. I am forgiving AND forgetting you, and everything you ever were to me. I truly believe there are good people in this world, and I truly believe that someday you will make someone very happy. It just wasn't me, and that's OK. I truly hope you find the help you need, and I truly hope and pray that you never do this again to anybody. From this moment forward, I have deleted every ounce of memory that I had of you. All your photos, videos, and texts are gone and deleted, never to ever be brought back up. You are now only a memory a few of us can share, and something that I will keep hidden from here on out. I am not ashamed any longer of what I went through with you; I have just finally chosen to move on and move forward.

> "Someone I loved once gave me a box full of darkness. It took me many years to understand that this too, was a gift." —*Mary Oliver*

The Final Chapter

May 15th, 2020

Yes, this is the final chapter not only of this book but of a part of my life that will be closing. I truly never thought this day would come. Where do I even come up with the words for closure? I'm not so sure I can.

This journey you all have been on with me is unlike anything else I've experienced. People from all over the world have read my blogs every week, watched my live videos via Facebook, binge-watched my YouTube channel, and reached out to me with their struggles. I knew I was out to do big things; I just wasn't sure of the magnitude.

It's truly astonishing to me. It's almost as if I, myself, am reading a book and watching myself grow, only this time, the book is about me, and you all are reading and growing along the way. I don't think any amount of words I can say can begin to give you the true THANK YOU that you all deserve. Thank you for giving me this platform and always allowing me to speak my beliefs. Thank you for always letting me vent out my frustrations, and thank you for being the therapy I truly needed to change my life. I guess in closing, I just want to say a few things. And I need you all to listen very closely.

I don't care if you are in a relationship or marriage for a month, a year, or a decade. If you, or someone you know, is being treated badly, SAY SOMETHING. DO SOMETHING. Do not ignore the red flags. Get out somehow, some way. You deserve better. You ARE better. Your kids deserve better. Find your worth and make shit happen.

If you are at a point in your life where you are unhappy, even if it doesn't deal with a relationship, take the same advice. Make shit happen, and do not stop until it does. Decide what you want, and what it's going to take to get you there. Hey, look, it's not going to be easy. If it were easy, everyone would do it. You, my friend, are going to be one of the strong ones! You are going to be one of the brave ones! One of the few who made it through to the final round. Yes, friends, you are on your way to winning. Wake up tomorrow morning, make your coffee, and go listen to the birds. Decide: Is this the life you want to live? Is this the person you want to love? Is this the best you can be? Is this who you think you are? Now take a deep breath and decide where to go next. It's not going to be easy; it's going to be really fucking hard. I will never deny that or sugarcoat it. There's going to be so many tears, I can't lie to you, and no one really knows if it'll take a week, a month, a year, or a decade to get your life back on track, but what I will tell you is this. If you decide you are worth more than what you're giving yourself credit for, nothing will ever stop you as long as you keep pushing forward.

So, in closing:

Dear brave one, put on your game face, sweet cheeks. You are now completely unstoppable to whatever comes your way. Find that worth and never let it go. Hold on tight, and love yourself more than you've ever loved anyone. You're on a journey, and this is all part of your story.

I love you all so very much. I have so many emotions and goosebumps writing the final words of this book. A book that may not ever truly amount to anything, but if it helps just ONE person, I will forever be grateful. My story is just my story. Your story is unique and probably very different. But one thing is for certain: we can both be strong, and I will always be strong for you. One day you will tell your story, and everything you've been through will become someone else's survival guide. This is why I do what I do. You only live once, but if you do it right, once is enough.

Cheers friends. It's finally over.